The Peoples of the British Isles:
A New History
From Prehistoric Times to 1688

Books in the Wadsworth British History Series

The Peoples of the British Isles: A New History
From Prehistoric Times to 1688
Stanford E. Lehmberg, University of Minnesota

The Peoples of the British Isles: A New History
From 1688 to 1870
Thomas William Heyck, Northwestern University

The Peoples of the British Isles: A New History
From 1870 to the Present
Thomas William Heyck, Northwestern University

The Peoples of

the British Isles:

A New History

From Prehistoric Times to 1688

VOLUME 1

STANFORD E. LEHMBERG

University of Minnesota

Wadsworth Publishing Company
Belmont, California
A Division of Wadsworth, Inc.

History Editor: Peggy Adams
Editorial Assistant: Tammy Goldfeld
Production Editor: Angela Mann
Designer: Andrew Ogus
Print Buyer: Barbara Britton
Art Editor: Kelly Murphy
Copy Editor: Melissa Andrews
Technical Illustrator: Maryland Cartographics
Cover: Laurie Anderson
Compositor: Weimer
Printer: Fairfield

1 2 3 4 5 6 7 8 9 10—96 95 94 93 92

Library of Congress Cataloging in Publication Data

Lehmberg, Stanford E.
    The peoples of the British Isles: a new history/Stanford E. Lehmberg.
        p. cm.
    Vols. 2-3 by Thomas William Heyck.
    Includes bibliographical references and index.
    Contents: v. 1. From prehistoric times to 1688—v. 2. From 1688 to 1870—v. 3. From 1870 to the present.
    ISBN 0-534-15078-0 (v. 1: acid-free paper).—ISBN 0-534-15079-9 (v. 2: acid-free paper).—ISBN 0-534-15080-2 (v. 3: acid-free paper).
    1. Great Britain—History.   2. Ethnology—Great Britain.   3. Ireland—History. 4. Ethnology—Ireland.   I. Heyck, Thomas William.   II. Title.
DA30.L44 1992
941—dc20   91-18180

Contents

Preface

There have always been compelling reasons why Americans should study English history. It is full of famous incidents and fascinating people. It helps us appreciate one of the world's great literatures, written in a language that we readily comprehend. Perhaps most important, it is in a special sense our own early history: the cultural and political institutions that were being molded in England during the centuries before the American Revolution would eventually form the basis of the Constitution of the United States and its legal and political systems. In religion and the arts, too, a strong English base underlies American developments. Without understanding English history we can hardly understand our own.

In the last several decades, however, many of those who teach English history have come to believe that their subject has been conceived too narrowly. As modes of historical research shifted their focus, it became evident that traditional histories of England dealt too exclusively with past politics. Social history needed to be added if we were to understand the lives of ordinary people, since high politics is necessarily the work of small numbers of people, generally men enjoying special privileges. In the continuing evolution of historical study, social history itself has come to center on new topics—population studies, family history, and the role of women, for instance—that need to be woven into the story of England. Older textbooks do not deal adequately with such matters.

Recently, some of us have become uneasy with the geographical narrowness of courses in English history. England shares a single island with Wales and Scotland and is a near neighbor of Ireland. The close link between the history of England and that of these outlying areas has always been appreciated, but too often they have been part of the narrative only when England was involved in wars or diplomatic encounters with them. Ireland, Scotland, and Wales have interesting histories that need to be appreciated on their own terms, not merely as they influence the development of another realm. Especially in the United States, where many citizens can trace Irish, Scottish, or Welsh elements in their own ancestry and where the search for our "roots" has become increasingly important, the history of the smaller units of the British Isles needs to be set alongside the history of England.

This, then, is a history of the men and women who lived in all parts of the British Isles, not just England. It begins in prehistoric times and continues through 1688, the year of the Glorious Revolution. It may be read in conjunction with two similar volumes written by T. W. Heyck, which deal with the period from 1688 to the present.

Professor Heyck and I are not the first to argue for the study of British rather than English history. J. G. A. Pocock pleaded for it in an article published in 1975, and Richard S. Tompson has written an interpretive political history of the British Isles, aptly titled *The Atlantic Archipelago* (1986). Hugh Kearney's book, *The British Isles: A History of Four Nations* (1989), also uses this approach, but without the detailed narrative needed in a textbook. Professor Heyck and I believe that our books provide the first texts for British history courses written specifically to meet the needs and reflect the interests of American undergraduate students.

Despite these newer, broader approaches, the inner core of this volume remains a history of England. This is appropriate, since England was the largest of the four realms considered here and since it came to dominate all of them. It is also necessary, since less scholarly work has been done on the history of Scotland, Ireland, and Wales. Political history, too, remains the basis for the organizing narrative, since many of the changes in society occurred in response to political developments like the Anglo-Saxon invasions or the Norman Conquest and can best be understood in connection with them. Books that are not firmly anchored in events and personalities run the risk of becoming abstract or amorphous, and many students have told me that they find them boring.

I have not emphasized historical documents, since many instructors will wish to use a volume of documents in conjunction with the textbook, nor have I devoted a great deal of space to consideration of rival interpretations of major events, since studies of historical problems are often used as supplementary reading. I have made a special effort to include women's history whenever possible, but there is still less than I would like. Early sources for the study of women's role in society are inadequate, and many interesting topics still remain unexplored. Intellectual, religious, and artistic history— subjects that I myself find especially interesting—have a place here, but I have denied myself the pleasure of writing about them at length because of the constraints of space and balance. A brief bibliography, suggesting books for further reading, is appended to each chapter. I have included a few historical novels that are especially successful in evoking the feel of the past. No book appears more than once in these lists; in cases where a single volume relates to more than one chapter it has been cited at the point where its usefulness begins. Throughout, I have been mindful of the experience of teaching British history to thousands of students for more than three decades. I have attempted to explain terms that have puzzled them, and I have tried to emphasize those topics that they have found most engaging. I hope that readers will come to share my continuing enthusiasm for the subject.

Finally, I would like to thank the reviewers Timothy Harris, Brown University; Michael J. Moore, Appalachian State University; Retha M. Warnicke, Arizona State University; Henry G. Weisser, Colorado State University; and Diane Willen, Georgia State University, for their helpful comments.

Stanford E. Lehmberg
Minneapolis, Minnesota

List of Maps

List of Illustrations

The physical features of the British Isles

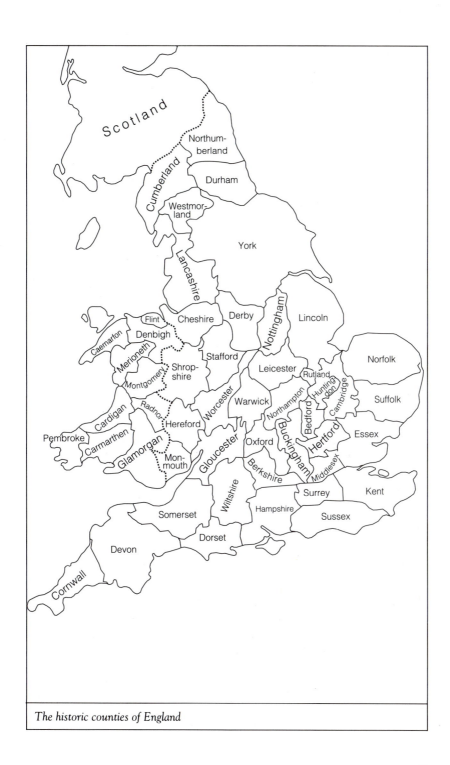

The historic counties of England

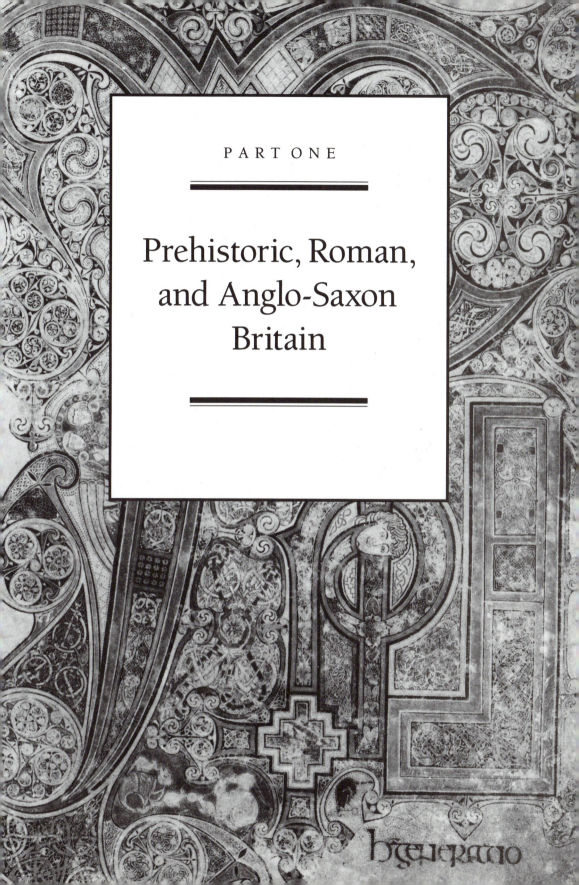

PART ONE

Prehistoric, Roman,
and Anglo-Saxon
Britain

CHAPTER ONE

═══════════

The Land and Peoples
of Early Britain

Geography of the British Isles

Because the development of any country is determined in part by its physical setting, a history of the British Isles must begin with a short description of the geography of England, Wales, Scotland, and Ireland.

Students are often surprised at the small size of these areas. England proper contains only about 50,000 square miles. Wales, much smaller, adds only another 7,500. Thus the land ruled by the kings of England before 1603 was smaller than most American states. (Minnesota, for example, has an area of about 84,000 square miles.) Scotland has a land mass of about 30,000 square miles, Ireland about 27,000.

Because Britain has been such an important world power, actively involved in colonization and international trade, its location is also surprising. England is not central to the great continents of Europe, Asia, or North America. It lies farther north than any part of the United States except Alaska and any great capital except Moscow. London is at about the same latitude as Newfoundland, not as New York, which is more central. Britain's temperate climate is determined by the nearly constant temperature of its surrounding waters and by the warmth carried to its shores by the Gulf Stream.

Each part of the British Isles has its own physical characteristics. England can be divided into two halves by drawing an imaginary line diagonally from the mouth of the River Exe, near Exeter in the Southwest, to the mouth of the River Tees in the Northeast. Most of the fertile soil in the country lies in the lowland zone to the southeast of this line. The land is flat or gently rolling, with low hills and long navigable rivers, the most important of which, the Thames, determined the location of the great city of London. As long as English society was primarily agrarian, before the Industrial Revolution of the eighteenth century, the bulk of the population lived in this area.

Northwest of the Exe-Tees line is a highland zone where the land is rocky and mountainous, more suitable for pasture than for intensive cultivation. Rivers are short and generally not navigable for great distances; some have rocky shoals or waterfalls. The famous Lake District, nestled in the Cumbrian mountains, boasts England's most spectacular scenery. Until recent times, communication between the east and west coasts was made difficult by the Pennine chain of mountains, which bisects northern England. Wales shares this infertile land. Its terrain includes lush valleys as well as the craggy Cambrian mountains.

That Scotland developed its own civilization and government, separate from England, is largely explained by the band of barren moorland that forms the border between the two countries. Farther north the Scottish Lowlands include fertile soil, rolling wooded hills, sparkling streams, and a chain of lakes, one of them reputedly the home of the Loch Ness monster. The bulk of the Scottish population has long lived here, in the cities of Edinburgh and Glasgow. Still farther north are the Highlands, the traditional home of the clans with their kilts and bagpipes. It has always been difficult for even a small number of people to eke out a living from such inhospitable surroundings, beautiful though they are.

Ireland's saucer shape includes areas of bog and marsh as well as woodland and some very fertile tillable soil. Mountains are concentrated near the coast; the central lowlands dominate the island. The Shannon is the longest river in the British Isles, flowing down the western coast of Ireland for more than 200 miles, but it is not the heart of a great river system, and it has not been of much economic value. Rainfall is heavier than in England. Frost and snow are almost unknown in the interior of the island. The capital, Dublin, lies on the east coast facing Britain. Separated from the larger island by the Irish

Channel, on an average about 50 miles wide, Ireland has developed its own unique civilization, frequently dominated by Britain but never integrated racially or culturally.

Prehistoric Britain

Historic times begin with the availability of written records. Peoples who do not read and write, no matter how advanced their civilization may be in other ways, live in the prehistoric era. Because literacy is the criterion, the end of prehistory came at different times in different parts of the world. The ancient Egyptians, Greeks, and Romans produced written documents long before the beginning of the Christian era, while prehistoric cultures lasted until recent times among Native Americans and in several Third World areas. The Romans produced the earliest written records describing Britain at about the time of their first invasion in 55 B.C., so prehistoric times are usually said to end in that year.

It may seem paradoxical to talk of the history of prehistoric peoples, yet thanks to the science of archaeology a good deal is known about prehistoric life in the British Isles. Archaeologists usually divide the long spans of time they cover into periods on the basis of the material used for implements and weapons. Thus they speak of the Stone Age, the Bronze Age, and the Iron Age. Different dates for these eras apply in different parts of the world.

Archaeologists work by digging. Human beings, fortunately from this point of view, are notoriously messy, and merely sifting through our trash reveals much about our way of life. If a trench is dug in an area that has been continuously inhabited since prehistoric times, the top layers consist of objects deposited in recent years. Lower down the digger may find medieval artifacts, and still lower the remains of prehistoric settlements. Objects from different sites can be classified on the basis of burial customs and the artistic style used in ornamenting pottery, and they can now be dated scientifically by the use of carbon 14. A radioactive form of carbon, this has a known half-life, and any object that was once living, such as a bone or woolen textile, can be given an approximate date by measuring the remaining radioactivity. Increasing use of carbon 14 tests, together with techniques involving analysis of tree rings and pollens, has led to a revolution in archaeological dating during the last decade or two. Many developments are now thought to be earlier than was previously believed.

Antonine
Wall
Hadrian's
Wall
Great
North
Road
York
Lincoln
Great West Road
Wheathampstead
Verulamium
Cirencester
Avebury
Bath
Stonehenge
Winchester
London
Colchester
Pevensey
Chichester
Exeter
♦ Saxon Shore Fort

Prehistoric and Roman Britain

The earliest known part of a human skeleton found in the British Isles is the so-called Swanscombe skull, excavated in southeast England in 1935. It is probably the head of a woman. It cannot be dated by carbon 14, which is not effective for articles more than about seventy thousand years old, but archaeologists believe that it comes from a period about 200,000 B.C. Some coarsely worked hand axes found nearby may be even older, perhaps as early as 300,000 B.C. During the late nineteenth century, it was believed that an apelike skull unearthed at Piltdown was the earliest example of human life in Britain and that it supported Darwin's theory of evolution. We now know that this was an elaborate hoax: in fact it is a human skull of no great antiquity joined to the jawbone of an ape. The earliest human remains so far found in Scotland and Ireland are dated much later, about 17,000 and 10,000 B.C. respectively.

The Stone Age, in which implements were fashioned of stone rather than metal, lasted from about 200,000 B.C. to about 2000 B.C. This long period can be divided into the Paleolithic, or old stone age; the Mesolithic, or middle stone age; and the Neolithic, or new stone era. At the beginning of Paleolithic times, the climate in Britain was mild, so men and women could live without clothes or shelter. Then the glaciers descended, and the inhabitants responded by making simple clothing from animal hides and by seeking shelter in caves. They also learned the use of fire, probably discovered accidentally when sparks fell from pieces of flint onto piles of dry leaves.

Recent research suggests that the Neolithic age began about 4000 B.C., considerably earlier than previous writers believed. During this period a milder climate returned, but the advances taught by necessity remained. A culture group called the Windmill Hill people crossed the Channel (perhaps then no more than a wide river) from northern Europe about 3000 B.C., bringing with them a way of life that included settled agriculture, the keeping of such domestic animals as sheep and dogs, the use of well-shaped flint arrowheads, and the making of pottery ornamented with spiral or thumbprint designs. The skeletons of their dead were buried intact (this is called inhumation, as opposed to cremation, the burning of remains), usually in groups rather than individually. Long mounds or "barrows," strikingly similar to the burial mounds of Native Americans, were erected over these burials. Today, especially when viewed or photographed from the air, they help identify sites where the Windmill Hill culture was established. The culture spread to Yorkshire, in northern England, and to Ireland.

A later Neolithic group, the Beaker Folk, migrated from northern Europe, probably between 2500 and 2000 B.C. Their name derives from the characteristic shape of their pots, which resemble the beakers used in chemistry laboratories. Such pottery has been found at sites throughout England, Ireland, and southern Scotland. The Beaker Folk usually buried their dead singly, in round barrows. The earliest known textile from the British Isles was found in one of these. Beaker sites have also yielded bronze drinking cups and jewelry, but these articles were probably acquired by trading with more advanced peoples on the Continent. A few settlers in England may have learned how to work in metal by this time, but the Beaker Folk do not seem to have known how to produce metal articles themselves.

The Bronze and Iron Ages

During the Bronze Age (now dated about 2000 to 1000 B.C.), the art of working bronze came to the British Isles. Bronze, an alloy of copper and tin, has a low melting point and thus is easier to handle than iron. It is also more attractive for decorative objects, but because it does not take a hard cutting edge it is less useful for knives and weapons like swords or axes. The most important Bronze Age group, usually called the Wessex Culture, came from the Continent to southwest England but soon spread throughout the British Isles. These invaders brought with them their skill in producing bronze articles. Some of the existing inhabitants may also have acquired the ability to work metal. Archaeologists used to attribute each technological leap to a fresh wave of immigrants from the mainland of Europe, but new work suggests that some advances were a natural, native growth. The dead of the Wessex Culture were cremated, with an urn being inverted over the remains; burials might be single, in mounds, or grouped, in urnfields. Objects from as far away as Egypt and Greece have been found in these burial sites, proof that the Wessex people were involved in international trade.

The art of working iron came to Britain about 1000 B.C. Bronze continued to be used for ornamental objects, with gold and silver also available in small quantities, but iron superseded bronze for utilitarian purposes. Large-scale settled farming was now practiced, with corrals, threshing floors, and storehouses or barns, and additional forested land was cleared for agricultural use. Recently, an interesting attempt has been made to recreate an Iron Age farm at a site in southern England (Butser, in the county of Hampshire). Here ancient breeds of sheep, pigs, and cattle (similar to the extinct Celtic Shorthorn) are raised, and a range of cereal crops, notably several varieties of wheat and barley, are grown. The environmental archaeologists involved in this experiment use only implements and farming techniques that would have been available in prehistoric times.

Stonehenge

The most imposing monument remaining from prehistoric Britain is undoubtedly Stonehenge. This great stone circle—actually it is several concentric circles of stones—was erected on Salisbury Plain, near the middle of the south coast of England. Work on the site may have begun as early as 2500 B.C. The initial construction of the great circle can be attributed to the Beaker Folk, with modifications and additions by later peoples between 1900 and 1400 B.C. About 300 feet in diameter, it includes a set of enormous uprights weighing as much as 50 tons each, quarried near the site, and sixty smaller bluestones, hewn from the mountains of Wales and transported, probably mainly by water, for 135 miles.

Scholars remain undecided about the reasons why this great monument was created. The alignment of stones suggests that it had something to do with sun worship, though notions of white-robed Druids dancing by moonlight or exacting human sacrifice may be dismissed as romantic inventions unsupported by hard evidence. One recent theory, advanced by the physicist Gerald Hawkins, holds that Stonehenge was actually an observatory, used to predict the movement of stars as well as eclipses of the sun and moon. Such a structure would have been of great value to an agricultural people, since it would enable them to mark the changing seasons accurately, and it would have conferred seemingly supernatural powers on the religious leaders who knew how to interpret its alignments.

There are other henge monuments in the British Isles, including a large henge of irregular stones at Avebury, not far from Stonehenge, and a similar circle at Castlerigg, in the Lake District. The small islands off the Scottish coast are particularly rich in these structures. The best surviving examples are the Ring of Brodgar on Orkney, where a ditch surrounds a ring that originally contained sixty-six stones, and the Callanish Standing Stones on Lewis. It is thought that these are earlier than Stonehenge and that the tradition of erecting such monuments may have spread southward from Scotland to England. There are comparable structures in Ireland and on the Continent, especially in Scandinavia. Whatever their original purpose, they

Stonehenge (aerial view), a prehistoric monument located on Salisbury Plain, near the middle of the south coast of England.
Reproduced by permission of English Heritage.

The Castlerigg Stone Circle, a henge monument in the Lake District of northwestern England.
Reproduced by permission of English Heritage.

bear testimony to the high state of political and religious organization of the people who built them.

Prehistoric remains in Ireland also include more than a thousand mega-lithic tombs, in which great stone slabs were erected for the burial of important persons, or perhaps for ceremonial purposes. Some of these include finely carved ornaments, and some were carefully aligned to catch the rays of the sun at the time of the winter solstice (December 21). Remarkable stone cairns, where several members of a family or kinship group were buried, also exist in Scotland; one of these is over 200 feet long.

Because Stonehenge is now visited by hordes of tourists, it is hard to recapture any sense of mystery or awe, and visitors are struck primarily by the magnitude of the engineering feat. More remote burial sites, however, can retain an almost magical quality. A sensitive viewer cannot but ponder what beliefs and myths prompted the building of the megalithic tombs and what rituals, songs, and dances took place at them. We will never know, for the Neolithic peoples left no record other than the evidence of place.

The Celts

The last prehistoric invaders of Britain were the Celts, members of a large culture group that came to encompass most of northern Europe. The terms *Celt* and *Celtic* have been used by different writers in so many different ways that it is difficult to give any simple account of them. A Celtic culture apparently developed first in central Europe, along the Danube River. It spread into what would now be France, Spain, and the Netherlands, and eventually to the British Isles. It is hard to say what prompted these migrations of Celts. The pressure of increasing populations used to be given as an explanation, but this no longer seems satisfying. It may be that the energetic, aggressive personality of the Celts themselves is the underlying factor. Roman writers describe them as warlike or even "war-mad" and tell us that Celtic women were equal to the men in stature and courage. In physical appearance most Celts were tall, with blue eyes and red or blond hair.

The Beaker Folk and members of the Wessex or urnfield culture may have been Celts. The earliest Celtic group known to us from documentary evidence—indeed, the earliest people in Britain for whom any written evidence exists—are the Belgae, who are described in Julius Caesar's famous account of his Gallic wars. Writing a few years before the time of Christ, Caesar says that northern France was inhabited by a Celtic tribe called the Belgae (the word lies behind the name of the modern nation Belgium) and that relatives of these people had crossed the Channel and made settlements in England.

Although the Celts were illiterate, they are said to have been eloquent in speaking and to have enjoyed storytelling. Linguistically the Celts of the British Isles can be divided into two groups, distinguished by the use of a "p" sound in one and a "q" in the other. The first of these tongues is called

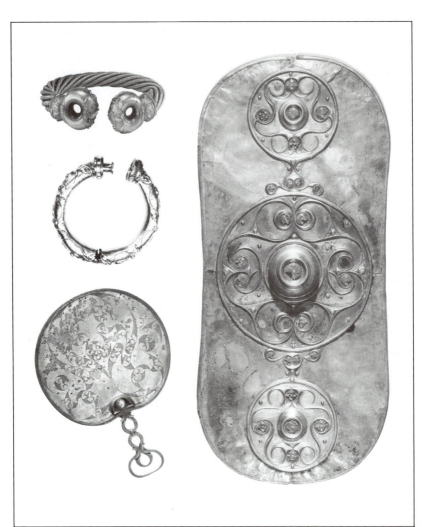

The Battersea Shield (right). This shield was made during the Iron Age. It was found in the River Thames near London.
Reproduced by permission of the British Museum.

The Snettisham Torc (top left). This is perhaps the finest example of Iron Age gold jewelry made in England.
Reproduced by permission of the British Museum.

The Broighter Torc (center left). This was found in an Iron Age hoard at Broighter, County Derry, Ireland. Note the typically Celtic swirling ornament and the sophisticated clasp.
Reproduced by permission of the National Museum of Ireland.

The Desborough Mirror (bottom left). This bronze mirror was found at Desborough in Northamptonshire. The flame-shaped curving lines are characteristic of Celtic art.
Reproduced by permission of the British Museum.

The Broighter Boat. The exact significance of this gold boat, from the Broighter hoard, is not known.
Reproduced by permission of the National Museum of Ireland.

"Brythonic." It came to dominate in England and Wales, and it forms the basis for modern Welsh and Cornish. The words *Britain* and *British* are derived from it. The "Q Celts" spoke the Goidelic language, now represented by Irish, Gaelic, and Manx (the dialect of the Isle of Man).

Under Celtic custom, land was held by kinship groups rather than by individuals. The Celts lived mainly on farms, some of which were large and well organized, and in small villages. Their artwork was superb: the Celts in Britain fashioned beautiful, highly sophisticated pieces of jewelry, the finest surviving examples of which are the Desborough Mirror and Snettisham Torc, made in England, and the gold Broighter Torc or collar, part of a hoard unearthed in northern Ireland. The Broighter hoard also included a small gold boat with oars. This is the earliest representation of a ship in British art, but no one knows just why it was made. The bronze shield found at Battersea, near London, is another famous example of Iron Age work. The Celts used gold and bronze coins (some of the late prehistoric coins from England are of excellent quality) as well as iron bars as a form of currency. They were sufficiently advanced economically to conduct trade with the Mediterranean countries as well as with France.

The last prehistoric inhabitants in Scotland, probably related to the Celts, were the Picts and the Scots. The Picts dominated most of the area, both Highlands and Lowlands, with their chief settlements along the southeast coast. Their name, given to them by the Romans, means "painted men," a reference to the use of tattoos or blue body coloring. It has been argued that the Picts spoke a language that can be classified as "p" Celtic, but proof is difficult, since not a scrap of their writing has survived. The group called the Scots originally lived in Ireland, not Scotland. A number of these men and women migrated to the Southwest of Scotland, probably in late prehistoric times, and eventually gave their name to the entire area. Some writers have held that the Picts were matrilineal: that is, their kinship groups were organized through women, and inheritance was through the female line. Although others deny this, they do acknowledge the importance of women in Pictish society.

The Rise of Roman Britain

Roman contact with the Celts in the British Isles began with the invasion by Julius Caesar in 55 B.C. Already a great military leader, Caesar had conquered France several years earlier (he describes his campaigns in his book) and was ready to turn his attention to England.

Caesar was attracted to Britain for several reasons. He had heard rumors (unfortunately incorrect) that the British Isles were rich in gold and other treasures. He probably believed that he could not hold northern France securely without having control of the land across the Channel, since the Belgae might use England as a springboard for attack. Perhaps most important, he thought that the conquest of a distant, dangerous area like Britain would enhance his personal reputation and advance his ambition to rule the entire Roman world.

In August, 55 B.C., Caesar sailed to England with about ten thousand men. Unused to the wind and weather in the English Channel, he anchored his ships near a rocky coastline, where some were smashed and others severely damaged in a storm. He was forced to direct his attention to the rebuilding of his fleet and was not able to explore England fully. But he returned the next year, coming earlier with more men. Once again some of his transport vessels were ruined in a storm—he should have known that there was a safe harbor nearby—but he was now able to penetrate into the area north of the Thames. Here he confronted Cassivellaunus, the ruler of the Belgae, whose capital, Wheathampstead, was near the present city of St. Albans. Forced to return to France to suppress a native uprising, Caesar made Cassivellaunus a client king who agreed to acknowledge the supremacy of the Romans and to pay them an annual tribute.

Caesar may have intended to return to England but never did so. His later career and his assassination by his friend Brutus are among the best-known episodes in ancient history. England paid the tribute for only a few years and then reverted to its prehistoric independent condition for nearly a century. Then, in A.D. 43, the Emperor Claudius decided to undertake a second conquest of the British Isles. He believed that Caesar had always intended this, and he found the Empire peaceful, with surplus troops available. His timing was perhaps determined by the fact that the king of the Belgae, Cunobelinus, had just died, leaving the natives without an established leader. Claudius sent a larger force than Caesar had gathered, perhaps as many as forty thousand men. His generals finally found a safe harbor, and they met little resistance as they marched inland. During a brief visit (he was only in England for sixteen days), Claudius organized southeast England as a province under direct Roman rule and accepted the submission of native tribes in other areas. Returning to Rome, he erected a triumphal arch to celebrate his victory.

The progress of the Roman conquest was interrupted in A.D. 61 by the revolt of Boudicca, queen of a Celtic tribe called the Iceni, who lived in eastern England with their capital at Colchester. A Roman writer described Boudicca as being "huge of frame, terrifying of aspect, and with a harsh voice; a great mass of bright red hair fell to her knees; she wore a great twisted golden torc, and a tunic of many colors, over which was a thick mantle, fastened by a brooch." Angered by the Roman governor's attempt to assume direct control of her territory and infuriated by the Roman soldiers' mistreatment of her daughters, she waited until the Roman legions were occupied in Wales, then gathered an enormous force of natives (perhaps more than 200,000) to ravage Roman settlements. Her troops burned three great Roman cities (London, Colchester, and Verulamium) and are said by a Roman writer to have killed as many as seventy thousand Roman citizens and their friends. It would be hard to exaggerate the horror of these events. Ultimately subdued by the Roman legions, Boudicca probably poisoned herself. She is often regarded as an early British heroine—her statue now stands on Westminster Bridge in London, near the houses of Parliament—but in fact her revolt brought nothing but death and devastation to her people, as well as to her enemies.

During the years after Boudicca's revolt, the Romans continued the military conquest of Britain. By A.D. 78 they had completed the subjugation of Wales. Making their way into what is now Scotland in A.D. 84, they defeated the Picts in a battle fought at Mons Graupius, an unidentified site probably

Hadrian's Wall, showing one of the adjoining forts. The Romans built the wall between A.D. 122 and A.D. 128 during their military conquest of Britain. The wall is 73 miles long. Reproduced by permission of English Heritage.

near Aberdeen. But the Picts remained unfriendly and warlike. To protect their northern frontier, the Romans undertook the construction of a great wall stretching from the mouth of the River Tyne, on the east coast, to Solway Firth, on the west. Known as Hadrian's Wall in honor of the emperor who ordered it built, the wall is a superb piece of military engineering, 73 miles long, finished with dressed stone, and well supplied with forts and sentry posts. Hadrian's Wall was built between 122 and 128; much of it still stands in good condition.

Tempted by the fertile lands in the Scottish midland plain, the Romans in 142 constructed a second frontier farther north, the Antonine Wall running from the Firth of Forth to the Firth of Clyde, near the present cities of Edinburgh and Glasgow. Much shorter and simpler than Hadrian's Wall, the

Antonine Wall was soon abandoned, as the Romans gave up hope of controlling Scotland and concentrated on maintaining control of England. They never attempted to invade Ireland.

The Decline of Roman Rule

For ethnic and social reasons Roman rule of Britain was always shaky. A two-tier social structure was based on ethnic divisions. The prehistoric Celtic natives were not driven out of their homelands; they remained as workers, tilling the soil, paying taxes, and providing servants. Roman soldiers and civil officials formed a relatively small governing class. In the later centuries of Roman rule some natives adopted Roman ways, learned Latin, and gained acceptance in Roman society. But the basic situation did not change. Naturally, Roman rule did not please the Celts, who had been used to managing their own affairs. As long as the Romans maintained their garrisons at full strength they were able to retain control, but any show of weakness was likely to produce a revolt or uprising. One writer has likened the situation to the condition that prevailed during the period of British rule in India.

The first such uprising occurred in 197, when the Roman governor of Britain, Clodius Albinus, drained troops from England in his abortive attempt to become emperor. The Picts stormed Hadrian's Wall, but it was quickly rebuilt and Roman rule was reestablished. Nearly a century later, in 296, another Roman leader named Carausius declared himself to be the emperor of Britain, independent of Rome itself. He was murdered by his own minister of defense, but not before an onslaught of Celts and Picts disrupted the government. At about this time the south and east coasts of England began to be subject to raids by the Saxons, who lived in northern Europe. The Emperor Diocletian commanded the construction of the Saxon Shore Forts to defend Roman Britain from this threat.

By the late fourth century the entire Roman Empire was in decline; the government lost control of one area after another and was eventually unable to hold Rome itself. Roman forces were gradually withdrawn from Britain to meet more pressing needs elsewhere. In 367 Britain was attacked simultaneously by Celts from Ireland, Picts from Scotland, and Saxons from the Continent. Many of the inhabitants of England also turned against their rulers. Shortly after this, Hadrian's Wall was breached and not rebuilt. The end came, undramatically and without any actual fighting, about 410. In that year the pathetically weak Emperor Honorius sent letters to the residents

The Saxon Shore Fort at Pevensey, Sussex. The fort was constructed to defend Roman Britain from raids by the Saxons. Reproduced by permission of English Heritage.

in Britain and some other outlying parts of the Empire, saying that they would have to be responsible for their own defense, since Rome could no longer guarantee their safety. Honorius may not have meant to abandon Britain forever, but in fact Roman officials never returned.

Life in Roman Britain

Recent estimates of the population of Roman Britain are surprising. It used to be assumed that about two million people lived in England during the height of Roman rule, about the same number as in the early Norman period or in the reign of Henry VIII. But new research suggests a population somewhere between four and six million, a figure that would not be reached again until the seventeenth or eighteenth century.

The people, both the Roman newcomers and the descendants of the prehistoric Celts, were ruled by governors sent out from Rome—for most of the period we know their names and dates—and by financial officials called procurators. Large standing armies were maintained. Officers were Romans, or at least men who had learned Latin and adopted Roman ways, but many natives were drafted into military service. As soldiers they attained Roman citizenship, which conferred certain legal privileges. In the later years of Roman rule they were allowed to marry, and living quarters were provided for their families. Slavery was common in the Roman Empire, and some wealthy inhabitants of Roman Britain had personal slaves.

Although agriculture remained basic to economic life in Roman Britain, urbanization produced important social changes. Indeed, urbanization was probably essential if the large population was to be accommodated and employed. Unlike the Celts, the Romans were great city builders. Hundreds of Roman cities and towns can be identified, often simply by the derivation of their modern names, and excavation has revealed Roman remains in many of them. The Romans are responsible for the establishment of London, built on a marshy bank of the Thames, which had been avoided by the natives because of the difficulty of building there. Originally a commercial center, London had become the capital of southern England by about 200 and was already the largest city on the island. Its population probably reached at least thirty thousand. York was established as the Roman capital in the North; recent excavations there have yielded Roman as well as Viking remains. The Romans also built a spa at Bath in the Southwest. They reconstructed the native capital at Wheathampstead and changed its name to Verulamium. (This was the only city in Britain that the Romans called a *municipium*.) They established a host of towns that were originally military camps (in Latin, *castra*) and whose present-day names betray their origin. Among these are Chester, Colchester, Winchester, Chichester, Cirencester, and Exeter. The Romans built a few cities, called *coloniae*, specifically for the resettlement of retired army personnel. Lincoln is the best known of these.

Roman cities were regularly laid out with streets on a grid pattern and were walled for defense. Public buildings, temples, theaters, baths, and facilities for games and circuses were erected at their centers. They generally had an engineered water supply, with fountains and sewers—it is thought that some inhabitants may have suffered from lead poisoning because of the lead piping used for water distribution. Local government was provided by urban councils, which elected two senior and two junior magistrates to manage urban affairs and preside in local courts.

To connect their cities the Roman armies built a great network of roads, almost all radiating from London. The Great North Road ran to York and on to Hadrian's Wall; the Great West Road led to Chester. The alignments of these remain today as the highways designated the A1 and A3. Many other Roman roads survive. They can often be recognized because they run for long distances in a straight line. Medieval roads tended to twist and turn, following the boundaries of fields; only the Romans and the twentieth-century freeway engineers assumed the power to cut direct paths through the countryside.

Some wealthy Romans, and perhaps some natives who were able to adopt their way of life, lived in villas scattered around the countryside, surrounded by farmland. These villas may be compared to the plantation houses erected in the American South before the Civil War. More than six hundred villas have been located, and a number of them have been excavated. The larger ones were often luxurious, with mosaic pavements, central heating, and walled gardens. One of the best-known villas, at Fishbourne near Chichester on the south coast, was of considerable size and elegance; most likely it was the residence of a high-ranking Roman official. Another, at Woodchester, had more than sixty rooms. The Mildenhall Treasure, a hoard of silver platters, bowls, and goblets that is now displayed in the British Museum, also gives an idea of the sophistication of life in Roman Britain. Unearthed in the twentieth century, it was probably buried by a villa owner not long after 410, in the hope of preserving it from a barbarian attack. Because the treasure was not recovered, we presume that the owner was killed. Some of those who lived in villas also had town houses in London or other cities, since they were involved in business or governmental affairs that could not be managed easily from the countryside.

The history of religion in Roman Britain is important but obscure. Both the Celts and the Romans originally adhered to a variety of pagan cults, including the worship of the sun and of specially sacred sites as well as mythic gods and goddesses. Some Roman emperors were worshiped as well, and they were occasionally identified with the sun. Christianity gradually gained acceptance in Rome and then in outlying parts of the Empire like England. A full account of its early development will be deferred to Chapter 2, but here we may note the first English martyr (St. Alban, executed near Verulamium, most likely about 208 rather than the traditional date 304) and the first English heresy (Pelagianism, a belief in free will and the ability of individual men and women to work out their own salvation). Both pagan temples and Christian churches have been excavated, and in some cases there is evidence to suggest conversion from pagan to Christian use.

The Roman villas and cities alike fell into decay shortly after 410. A Romanized way of life may have lingered on in some places, but the Celtic natives who remained after the Romans left did not share their enthusiasm

Roman mosaic. This mosaic floor, from a villa at Hinton St. Mary in the county of Dorset, includes the earliest known portrait of Christ from the British Isles. It has been dated to the first half of the fourth century. Reproduced by permission of the British Museum.

for urban life. They were generally not literate and not interested in Roman civilization; they seem to have had no central government. Roman coins do not appear to have been used after 420 or 430. The fact that the Roman theater at Verulamium was used as a rubbish dump in the fifth century is a telling symbol of the difference between the two cultures.

In the end the Romans made few permanent contributions to British civilization. Their governmental system, famous for maintaining peace and order, disappeared, as did the Latin language. Roads, walls, and towns decayed, although they could be reconstructed later in the Middle Ages. Celtic artwork, always finer and more imaginative than that of the Roman invaders, continued, uninfluenced by the rational style of the Romans. The chief legacy of the Roman period was the Christian religion, which had been accepted by a number of the natives and which survived among the Celts after the Romans departed.

Suggested Reading

Birley, Anthony, *Life in Roman Britain* (New York: Putnam, 1964).

Birley, Anthony, *The People of Roman Britain* (Berkeley: University of California Press, 1979).

Bottigheimer, Karl S., *Ireland and the Irish: A Short History* (New York: Columbia University Press, 1982).

Bradley, Richard, *The Prehistoric Settlement of Britain* (London: Routledge & Kegan Paul, 1978).

Chadwick, Nora, *The Celts* (New York: Viking Penguin, 1971).

Crossley-Holland, Kevin, and Andrew Rafferty, *The Stones Remain: Megalithic Sites of Britain* (London: Century Hutchinson, 1989).

Cunliffe, Barry, *Fishbourne: A Roman Palace and Its Garden* (Baltimore: Johns Hopkins University Press, 1971).

Darvill, Timothy, *Prehistoric Britain* (New Haven: Yale University Press, 1987).

Dickinson, William Croft, *Scotland from the Earliest Times to 1603* (Edinburgh: Thomas Nelson, 1961).

Frere, Sheppard, *Britannia*, 3rd ed. (London: Routledge & Kegan Paul, 1987).

Fry, Plantagenet Somerset, *Roman Britain* (Totowa, N.J.: Barnes & Noble, 1984).

Hawkins, Gerald, *Stonehenge Decoded* (Garden City, N.Y.: Doubleday, 1965).

Herity, Michael, and George Eogan, *Ireland in Prehistory* (London: Routledge & Kegan Paul, 1977).

Jenner, Michael, *Scotland Through the Ages* (New York: Viking Penguin, 1989).

O'Brien, Máire, and Conor Cruise O'Brien, *A Concise History of Ireland* (London: Thames and Hudson, 1972).

O'Kelly, Michael J., *Early Ireland: An Introduction to Irish Prehistory* (Cambridge: Cambridge University Press, 1989).

Powell, T.E.G., *The Celts* (London: Thames and Hudson, 1958).

Renfrew, Colin, *British Prehistory: A New Outline* (Park Ridge, N.J.: Noyes Press, 1974).

Rutherford, Edward, *Sarum* (New York: Ivy Books, 1987) (a historical novel).

Salway, Peter, *Roman Britain* (Oxford: Clarendon Press, 1981).

Tompson, Richard S., *The Atlantic Archipelago: A Political History of the British Isles* (Lewiston, N.Y.: Edward Mellen Press, 1986).

Toynbee, Jocelyn, *Art in Roman Britain* (London: Phaidon, 1962).

The Anglo-Saxon Era,
410–1066

Anglo-Saxon Invasions
and the Heptarchy

The Anglo-Saxons were a Germanic people whose original home was northern Europe. Following early writers, historians sometimes separate them into three groups: the Angles and the Saxons, both of whom lived in North Germany, and the Jutes, who occupied Jutland, the modern Denmark. However, these tribes seem to have intermingled and intermarried prior to their invasions of Britain; the distinctions among them should not be exaggerated.

These peoples, great seafarers and warriors, had begun raiding the coasts of England as early as 300, looting cities and pillaging villas. The Saxon Shore Forts were constructed to protect Roman Britain against them. As long as these forts were fully manned, England enjoyed reasonable security, but with the decay of Roman rule the Anglo-Saxons returned. Indeed some may have been invited to come: a native British leader, Vortigern, is alleged to have imported Saxon mercenaries to defend Britain against the Picts and

Scots, and Saxon brothers named Hengist and Horsa are said to have established the kingdom of Kent, probably shortly before 450. When the Saxons found the country attractive and resistance minimal, they undertook invasions reaching far inland. Eventually they migrated to England in large numbers, establishing settlements throughout the country during the half century between about 450 and 500.

Our knowledge of this period is imprecise: if there is a "dark age" in British history, this is it. Both the Celts and the Anglo-Saxons were basically illiterate peoples who did not generate documentary sources. Our information comes partly from archaeological remains and partly from later writings, mainly a work called *The Ruin of Britain*, composed by a British monk named Gilas about 540, and the much finer but chronologically more remote *Ecclesiastical History of the English People* by the Venerable Bede, another monk who was the most learned man of the Anglo-Saxon era. Bede, who spent his life in the monasteries of Jarrow and Monkwearmouth, lived from 673 to 735 and wrote biblical commentaries and scientific treatises as well as his famous history. He was the leading figure in an intellectual awakening sometimes referred to as the Northumbrian Renaissance. The so-called *Anglo-Saxon Chronicle*, actually a number of different chronicles maintained in Anglo-Saxon monasteries, is also valuable, but it is much less reliable for the fifth and sixth centuries than it is for later times.

The legend of King Arthur has its roots in the period when Roman rule was breaking up and Germanic invasions were beginning. Although many characters in the Arthurian romance—Lancelot, Guinevere, Merlin, and the Knights of the Round Table—are fictional creations of the Middle Ages, Arthur himself was probably a genuine historical figure, a British native who had adopted Roman ways and who led his people in an attempt to fight off the Anglo-Saxons. In a battle at Mons Badonicus, or Mount Badon, an uncertain site in southwest England, he did defeat the invaders about the year 500. Some archaeologists believe that his capital has been found and excavated, at South Cadbury in the modern county of Somerset.

But Arthur's campaign, if indeed it was truly a historical event, proved to be no more than a temporary setback for the Anglo-Saxons. By the early sixth century they had gained control of virtually all of England. Their conquest was fundamentally different from that of the Romans: no more advanced than the Celts, the Anglo-Saxons did not wish to coexist with them. Instead they wanted the land themselves. Thus the Celts were pushed farther and farther to the west as the Anglo-Saxons gained control of eastern England. Finally the Celtic natives were driven into Wales and Cornwall, the peninsula at the southwestern tip of the country. (Their situation was in some ways similar to that of Native Americans, who centuries later were forced by American pioneers to move west and settle on infertile reservations.) The ethnic divisions brought about by the Anglo-Saxon conquest persist today; the Welsh and Cornish, like the Irish, remain basically Celtic peoples, cherishing their own traditions and languages and displaying physical features different from those of Anglo-Saxon descendants.

England was not ruled as a unified country during the earlier centuries of the Anglo-Saxon period. Separate groups settled in separate parts of the country, establishing their own governmental systems and recognizing their own rulers. At one time as many as twelve such kingdoms existed, but only seven lasted. These are referred to as the Heptarchy. It is customary to say that three areas were settled by the Saxons: Essex, home of the East Saxons; Sussex, the South Saxon kingdom; and Wessex, the West Saxon realm. The Angles controlled most of the east coast, the Midlands, and northern England, including some territory that now lies in Scotland; their kingdoms were East Anglia, Mercia, and Northumbria. The Jutes (superseding Hengist and Horsa) settled the kingdom of Kent, at the southeastern corner of the island. Inheritance laws and farming patterns that were unlike those in the rest of England existed in Kent throughout the Middle Ages, probably reflecting customs of the Jutes that predate the conquest.

Although these seven kingdoms coexisted for centuries, one of them was generally dominant, and its ruler came to be known as the "bretwalda," or paramount king in England. Conveniently for historians, the supremacy shifted more or less regularly each century. During the sixth century Kent dominated, with Ethelbert as its most important bretwalda. Northumbria, led by Oswald and Oswy, was paramount in the 600s. The introduction of Christianity, to be discussed below, looms large in the history of these bretwaldas. Mercia, under a powerful king named Offa, dominated in the 700s. Offa is remembered chiefly for his role in the construction of Offa's Dyke, a great earthwork running for nearly 150 miles to provide a defensible frontier separating Mercia from Wales, where the Celts remained hostile. This was the most demanding earthwork constructed in medieval Europe, although there was a similar smaller one at the southern base of Denmark. Around 800 the rulers of Wessex established themselves as bretwaldas, and about 830 Egbert began describing himself as king of all England. The House of Wessex then became firmly established, and England became unified under its leadership. The present British royal family can trace its ancestry back to Egbert and his heirs.

Christianity in
Anglo-Saxon England

Several legends attempt to explain the coming of the Christian faith to the British Isles. According to one such account, Joseph of Arimathea, the wealthy Jew who gave his own tomb for Christ's burial, later undertook a missionary voyage to England, converting many souls and founding a great monastery at Glastonbury in southwest England. He is said to have brought with him the staff of St. Joseph, which took root when placed in the ground and produced the Glastonbury Thorn, a rose that miraculously flowers each year at Christmas. Another legend, unsupported by historical evidence, suggests that St. Paul visited England during one of his missionary voyages.

It is much more likely that Christianity came to Britain in a less spectacular way. Soon after the Resurrection the Christian faith was accepted by some members of the Roman army, perhaps because it promised them life after death during a period when death was all too common among the soldiers. After several centuries in which Christians were persecuted in Rome, Christianity was granted toleration by the Emperor Constantine in 313. By the end of the fourth century it had become the official religion of the Roman Empire. Many Celtic natives, as well as Roman soldiers and government officials, adopted Christianity during the later centuries of Roman rule in Britain. Pagan temples were converted for use in Christian worship, and new churches were built. British bishops were active in the early fourth century—three of them attended a council of church leaders on the Continent in 314—and a surviving set of vessels used for celebrating communion seems to date from about the same period. Recent studies suggest that the survival of Christianity after the decline of Roman government was more pervasive than was formerly believed. It is said that Germanus, a bishop from the Continent who came to Britain to combat the Pelagian heretics, actually led the Britons in warfare against the heathen Picts and Saxons, teaching his men to shout "Alleluia!" as a battle cry. This incident occurred about 430.

Because the Anglo-Saxon settlers remained pagan, Christianity survived in 450 or 500 only among the Celts in Wales. Despite biblical commands to convert others to their faith, the Celts had little interest in preaching to the Anglo-Saxons: it was bad enough to have to share England with them, and the thought of sharing eternal life in heaven must have been appalling.

St. Mary's Abbey, Iona. This is a later building on the site of St. Columba's monastery.
Reproduced by permission of the Royal Commission on the Ancient and Historical Monuments of Scotland.

Celtic Christianity did spread, however, first to Ireland and then to Scotland and northern England.

Famous missionary saints are associated with this movement of the faith. St. Patrick, who died in 461, is traditionally credited with the conversion of Ireland. His story, which is reasonably well documented, is an interesting one. He was born into a wealthy Romanized family, probably in or near Wales. His grandfather had been a priest and his father was a deacon. (Clergy were not then prohibited from marrying, and it was not unusual for landowners to take holy orders.) Patrick led an idle life until he was kidnapped, at the age of sixteen, and taken to Ireland to work as a cowherd. Eventually he escaped and made his way back to Britain. By this time he had determined to become a Christian missionary: he wrote that he had heard the voice of Christ, commanding him to convert the Irish, and also received entreaties from the Irish themselves. He studied on the Continent, was consecrated a bishop, and learned about the organization of the Christian church as an international body with the pope as its recognized head. Patrick received papal support for his mission to Ireland, in which he is said to have performed miracles and converted many to his beliefs. In fact there were probably a number of Christians in Ireland before his coming, and some other leaders, including a bishop named Palladius, should be given a share of the credit

St. Martin's Cross, Iona. Stone crosses of this
sort were erected at locations scattered throughout
the British Isles.
Reproduced by permission of the Royal
Commission on the Ancient and Historical
Monuments of Scotland.

that the legends accord to Patrick alone. The most advanced forms of Roman
Christianity, introduced by Patrick, did not survive very long under the
isolated conditions in Ireland, and the Irish church soon became quite similar
to the Celtic church that lived on in Wales.

In 563, St. Columba, an Irish aristocrat who had become a missionary
abbot, established a monastery at Iona, just off the southwest coast of Scotland. This was in the area inhabited by the group of "Scots" who had migrated from Ireland. From the island site at Iona, Columba was able to
undertake missionary journeys while still retiring to his protected cell at times
when he wished privacy for prayer and meditation. He may have found
scattered Christian communities already in existence, as a result of the earlier

The Carew Cross. An example of a Celtic cross from
Wales.
National Monuments Record for Wales Collection,
Royal Commission on Ancient and Historical
Monuments in Wales.

missionary work of a British bishop, Ninian, about 400. St. Mary's Abbey, erected at Iona centuries after Columba's death, memorializes his work.

Christianity flowed from Scotland to northern England in 634, when Oswald, the ruler of Northumbria, asked the monks of Iona to send a missionary to his kingdom. They dispatched St. Aidan, who again chose an island site, called Lindisfarne, or the Holy Isle. This was conveniently connected to the Northumbrian coast for a few hours each day, during low tide. By the middle of the seventh century, then, the beliefs of the Celtic church had been accepted in northern England as well as in Wales, Ireland, and southern Scotland. Celtic crosses, recognizable because of the circle incorporated in the cross itself, were erected throughout the area where the Celtic church flourished. Two fine examples are St. Martin's Cross at Iona and the Carew Cross in Wales.

St. Augustine

Meanwhile the Christian religion had been brought to the southeast of England from a different source. Pope Gregory the Great supposedly became interested in England after seeing handsome Anglo-Saxon youths in a Roman slave market. Exclaiming that they should be angels, not Angles, he decided to send a missionary force to Britain, and in 597 St. Augustine, formerly the head of an Italian monastery, landed on the coast of Kent. Making his way to the capital at Canterbury, Augustine found that his preaching was well received by the bretwalda, perhaps because the queen, Bertha, was already a Christian. King Ethelbert and hundreds of other men and women of Kent were baptized and accepted the Christian faith. Augustine found the remains of a Christian church dating from the years of Roman rule and undertook to build a cathedral at that location, the site still occupied by Canterbury Cathedral. He is regarded as being the first archbishop of Canterbury, and his successors remain the spiritual leaders of the Church of England and Anglican communion throughout the world.

The form of Christianity that Augustine instituted was considerably more advanced than the one that survived among the Celts. Some differences, like the method of calculating the date of Easter and the style of tonsure or shaved head for members of the clergy, were relatively superficial. Other Roman practices, such as the use of the Latin language rather than native tongues in worship and the organization of the church into dioceses led by bishops, receiving direction from archbishops and ultimately from the pope, were of fundamental importance. As the Celtic and Roman forms spread into the English Midlands they came into contact and, inevitably, conflict.

Oswy, king of Northumbria at a time when it dominated the Heptarchy, undertook to resolve these differences. In 664 he invited leaders of both churches to a conference or council held at the great nunnery of Whitby, not far from Lindisfarne. Oswy had hoped for an agreed compromise, but when this proved impossible he decided to make a settlement himself. According to the Venerable Bede, who himself lived in Northumbria and wrote his history of the English church only a few decades later, Oswy chose the Roman form because of assurances that the pope could guarantee his salvation. This argument was based on the biblical passage in which Christ gave the keys of the kingdom of heaven to St. Peter and on the belief that the popes were Peter's successors. Actually the king's decision may have stemmed from more sophisticated reasoning, probably including the fact that trade and intellectual intercourse with the Continent would be promoted by close connections

St. Augustine's Chair, Canterbury Cathedral.
Although tradition associates this Purbeck marble
chair with Augustine, it actually dates from the
thirteenth century. Archbishops of Canterbury sit in it
at the time of their consecration.
Reproduced by the kind permission of the Dean and
Chapter of Canterbury Cathedral.

with the church in Europe. Oswy may also have believed that the centralized organization of the Roman church, with authority flowing down from the top, would assist him in his attempt to gain control of a united England, an effort in which he was not permanently successful.

During the years following the Council of Whitby, England was divided into a group of dioceses, each placed under the supervision of a bishop. Theodore of Tarsus, who was sent from Italy to follow Augustine as archbishop of Canterbury, was chiefly responsible for the establishment of this new organizational structure. The inspiration of Celtic Christianity remained strong, however, especially in the monasteries, which served as houses of spirituality and learning. Parts of Scotland accepted diocesan organization shortly after the Council of Whitby, but a full system of episcopal government was not in place there until 1192, and the archbishopric of St. Andrew's was not established until 1472. The situation in Wales is obscure. Dioceses do not seem to have been fully organized until the years following 1066, but there may have been a bishop of St. David's several centuries earlier. The Irish church was not organized on territorial lines until the twelfth century.

The First Danish Invasions:
King Alfred and the Danelaw

Just as Anglo-Saxon England was gaining unity in church and state it was beset by a new wave of raids and invasions. In English history the invaders are usually referred to as the Danes, although their homes lay in Scandinavia generally, not merely in Denmark. In other contexts the same people are known as the Norse, Northmen, or Normans, who conquered Sicily and part of France; as the Vikings, who sailed to North America; and as the Varangians, who established trade with Russia and Constantinople. Their physical appearance was similar to that of the Anglo-Saxons, but they were probably larger and more likely to have blond hair and blue eyes. They were more interested in exploration, trade, and urban life, and they were fiercer warriors.

The Danes started raiding the east coast of England about 787. They sacked the great monasteries at Jarrow and Lindisfarne, in Northumbria; they attacked Lincoln; and they looted the city of London. Just before 800 they ravaged Iona. In 850 a group of Danish raiders spent the winter in England, near Canterbury. The so-called Great Army came in 865. Marching through much of the land, it devastated Northumbria and Mercia, and in 870 it turned its attention to Wessex.

Here the Danes met the Anglo-Saxon king, Alfred. The grandson of Egbert, he was only twenty-two when he succeeded to the throne in 871. He was inexperienced in military affairs, and he realized that the Anglo-Saxon troops under his command were not strong enough to defeat the Danes. He bought time by agreeing to pay the Danes a tribute called the Danegeld. During the years of truce that he secured in this way, he set about reforming

Anglo-Saxon military institutions. The army, called the fyrd, was essentially a militia composed of all able-bodied men. It had suffered badly from the defection of its members, who were reluctant to leave their families for long periods and who often went home to supervise the harvest or other farming operations. Alfred solved this problem by dividing the fyrd into halves, each to serve part of the year in the army and remain at home part of the year. (A third group, the clergy, was exempted from military service but was commanded to pray for victory.) Alfred also established a new aristocratic class of thegns: these men were given land and prestige but were made responsible for leading the Anglo-Saxon warriors in battle.

With these reforms in place, Alfred was finally able to defeat a Danish army in the Battle of Edington, fought in 878. The Danes then agreed to a negotiated settlement in which they were allowed to settle in what was called the Danelaw. Within this area, which included much of east and central England—East Anglia and parts of Mercia and Northumbria—the Danes were allowed to use their own legal codes and manage their own government.

During the later, more peaceful years of his reign, Alfred was able to concentrate on political and intellectual matters, which interested him more than warfare. In order to secure more efficient rule of his realm, Alfred divided England into shires or counties. He provided a unified legal system for England by collecting the legal principles or "dooms" of the several parts of the Heptarchy and replacing them with a single code, often called the Dooms of Alfred. He attempted to establish Anglo-Saxon as a single written language, capable of literary use, by ordering monasteries to keep the *Anglo-Saxon Chronicle* in the vernacular; by arranging for the transcription of epic poems like *Beowulf*, which had previously been passed down only by word of mouth; and by personally translating Bede's history and some other religious works from Latin into Anglo-Saxon. He also established a court school, with learned teachers brought from the Continent to educate members of the royal family and sons of thegns.

The surviving accounts of Alfred's reign agree in describing him as a man of high intellect, purpose, and commitment; he was one of England's greatest kings. He died in 899.

Alfred's successors, especially his great-grandson Edgar the Peaceful (959–975), were able to oversee the recovery of the Danelaw. This was possible because the Danes had intermarried with the Anglo-Saxons and had gradually accepted their language and laws. Edgar's archbishop of Canterbury and chief advisor, St. Dunstan, was also influential in restoring England's great monasteries, which had suffered badly from the Danish attacks. Dunstan introduced the Cluniac Benedictine rule, which established a set way of life for monks and nuns. Under his direction Glastonbury, the greatest abbey in Wessex, became a recognized center of learning and spirituality.

The Second Danish Invasions: Ethelred and Canute

This era of peace and unity was disrupted about 980 by a second group of Scandinavian invasions, now led by Olaf Tryggvason, king of Norway, and Swein Forkbeard, king of Denmark. In 982 the Danes sacked and burned London; in 1012 they attacked Canterbury and murdered Archbishop Alphege.

It was unfortunate for the Anglo-Saxons that the ruler now destined to confront the Danes was Ethelred, the incompetent younger son of Edgar the Peaceful. He is usually called Ethelred the Redeless; the descriptive title does not mean that he was unready, although he was, but rather that he was ill-advised or devoid of good counsel (the Anglo-Saxon word *rede* means counsel or advice).

Ethelred met the Danes' demand for a new payment of the Danegeld, but he failed to use the resulting truce to strengthen his own forces. Instead, he fled to Normandy, where he was welcome because he had recently married, as his second wife, Emma, the duke of Normandy's daughter. Eventually he returned to England but failed to meet the Danes in battle before his death in 1016. His son, Edmund Ironside, followed him but died later the same year.

Although the throne normally passed by heredity from father to son within the House of Wessex, each new king was in theory elected by the witan, a group of Anglo-Saxon leaders and advisors. The election was normally a formality, but in 1016 it assumed serious proportions. With no adult descendants of the Wessex line available, the witan turned to the Danish conquerors and named Canute (or Cnut), the son of Swein Forkbeard, as their king. Canute ruled England from 1016 to 1035.

Although he was a Dane, Canute governed peacefully according to Anglo-Saxon customs. He retained the witan as an advisory council. He appointed Anglo-Saxons as well as Danes to the chief offices. He took the oath of an Anglo-Saxon king, and he abided by Anglo-Saxon laws. His sole innovation was the division of England into four earldoms, an arrangement that he believed would give him assistance in maintaining control in outlying areas. An able warrior, he won victories over the Norwegians and the Scots.

Canute married twice. His first wife, an Anglo-Saxon heiress named Elfgifu, bore his elder son, Harold Harefoot, who followed him on the throne. After the death of Elfgifu, Canute married Emma, the widow of Ethelred the Redeless; by her he had a second son, Harthecanute. Both sons proved incompetent and dissolute. Harold Harefoot was probably murdered by Emma, or at her command, so that Harthecanute could have the throne, but Harthecanute died of drunken convulsions in 1042.

Edward the Confessor (1042–1066)

Once again the witan met to choose a new monarch. Their decision brought back a descendant of the old House of Wessex, Edward the Confessor.

Edward was the son of Ethelred the Redeless and Emma. His formative years were spent in Normandy. French, not Anglo-Saxon, was his native language, and French manners and customs came naturally to him. He scarcely knew his father and did not see much of his mother once she married Canute. Edward was brought up by churchmen and became so pious that he acquired the nickname "the Confessor" because he regularly confessed his sins.

It was probably with some reluctance that Edward accepted the English throne, since he had little interest in ruling. Once in England he proved to be more alien than Canute: Edward gave high offices to his Norman friends, thus angering Anglo-Saxon leaders in both church and state. His chief enemies were Godwin, earl of Wessex, and Godwin's sons Harold (earl of Mercia) and Tostig (earl of Northumbria). For a time Godwin was forced into exile for his opposition to Edward's rule. Anglo-Saxon leaders in the church were antagonized when Edward tried to appoint a Norman friend to the archbishopric of Canterbury. Eventually the witan forced the king to accept an Anglo-Saxon named Stigand as archbishop, but the pope never recognized Stigand, and relations between the king and the church remained acrimonious. In an attempt to win over the Anglo-Saxons, Edward agreed to marry Godwin's daughter Edith (or Eadgyth), but he did not love her and the marriage produced no heirs.

Edward's reign was generally difficult and unsettled. His chief legacy, and the project dearest to his heart, was the establishment of Westminster Abbey.

Built in a marsh adjoining the Thames, near the royal palace west of the city of London, the Abbey was nearly complete when Edward last visited it just before Christmas 1065. He died January 5, 1066.

The Events of 1066

Because Edward had no children, the witan was once again forced to choose among rival candidates who had minimal connections with the old royal family. Two claimants to the throne were Godwin's sons, Harold and Tostig. They could assert that their sister (Edith) had been queen, so they were brothers-in-law of the old king, but this did not actually give them royal blood. Harold sought to inherit the entire kingdom of England, while Tostig would have been satisfied if it had been divided into halves, Harold ruling the south and Tostig the north.

A third claimant to the English throne was William, duke of Normandy, the large duchy in northern France just across the Channel from the British coast. William was able to put forth a hereditary claim of sorts, for he was descended from the same duke of Normandy as Emma, the former wife of both Ethelred and Canute. But no English blood flowed in his veins, and his own birth was clouded by the fact that he was an illegitimate son of his father, Duke Robert. William also asserted that he had been promised the English throne by both Edward the Confessor and Harold. This was probably true, but circumstances make the promises of doubtful value. Edward always favored Normans, but he had no right to give away the throne; Harold had sworn an oath not to challenge William, but only under duress, while he was being held prisoner at the Norman court after being shipwrecked on the French coast. In reality the chief factor in William's favor was simply his own ambition and powerful personality.

The witan predictably favored an Anglo-Saxon over a Norman and an older son over a younger one: it declared Harold to be king of England. His rule was challenged almost immediately. Tostig proceeded to form an alliance with the king of Norway, Harold Hardrada, who also believed that he had a claim to the English throne as a result of an earlier treaty. Tostig and Hardrada were able to field a large army in northern England, but King Harold defeated them in the Battle of Stamford Bridge, fought on September 25, 1066. Tostig and Hardrada were both slain on the battlefield.

Only three days later, on September 28, Duke William landed on the south coast with a large force of Norman warriors. Harold heard of the invasion and marched his army south as speedily as possible, hardly pausing to sleep or eat. William, following a high-minded code of chivalry, waited for the rival force to appear so that a decisive pitched battle could take place.

This combat, the Battle of Hastings, began about 9 A.M. on October 14. Harold's troops formed a shield-wall that held firm throughout a succession of attacks by mounted Norman knights. It began to fail when the Normans feigned retreat, thus causing the English to break ranks and pursue them. Finally, in a characteristically novel and daring ploy, William ordered his archers to shoot arrows high into the air over the Anglo-Saxon line. Bewildered by this unexpected threat from above, the Anglo-Saxon warriors gazed upward and abandoned their formation. Eventually the battle turned into a disorganized melee, every man for himself. A number of Anglo-Saxons were killed by arrows that fell into their eyes—eyes were vulnerable because they were virtually the only part of the body not protected by armor. Harold himself disappeared during the later stages of the combat, but when the fighting was over his body was found on the battlefield, an arrow in his right eye; his disfigured remains were recognized by his wife, Edith Swanneck. Before he left Hastings, William swore that he would build a monastery (called Battle Abbey) on the site of his victory, in memory of the dead on both sides and in expiation of the sin of spilling blood.

Harold's death in the Battle of Hastings left William without rivals for the English throne. The witan acquiesced in his election, and on Christmas Day 1066 he was crowned king in Westminster Abbey. His accession ended the Anglo-Saxon period in English history and ushered in Norman rule.

Anglo-Saxon Society

Some older writers waxed ecstatic about the "democratic" virtues of Anglo-Saxon society, formed in the "Teutonic forests" they inhabited before migrating to England. The loss of these democratic institutions was blamed on the fact that the English were forced to assume the "Norman yoke" after 1066. In fact, little is known about the social organization of the early Anglo-Saxons, and such evidence as we do have argues that Anglo-Saxon society was strongly aristocratic. The tradition of a powerful monarchy seems to have existed among the Angles, Saxons, and Jutes even before their invasions of England, and the Anglo-Saxon kings, like their Norman successors, seem always to have been assisted by followers of high social status, wealth, and prestige.

The British Isles in Anglo-Saxon times

The royal dynasties of the Anglo-Saxons traced their ancestry back to Germanic gods, generally to Woden (or Wotan). They regarded the monarchy as being hereditary within their families, but they did not follow the principle of primogeniture, according to which the oldest son of the king was automatically his successor. Instead, it appears that rulers could designate their heirs, naming a younger son if he appeared more able. The elective principle was also present to some extent: the witan or royal council of wise men did elect the king, but only from the range of men qualified by birth. (It is probably this procedure that misled some devotees of democratic institutions.) Coronation ceremonies were important events. From the late eighth century on, these were religious in character, with clergymen officiating and consecrating the king to the service of God.

The king's household held an important place in government and society. Although no buildings or even excavated sites survive, there are literary references to royal palaces in a number of cities, the most important of which was Winchester, the capital of Wessex and principal home of the Anglo-Saxon rulers after Alfred. The Bayeux Tapestry (to be described later) depicts Edward the Confessor seated on the throne in a great stone hall, probably part of his palace at London, near the site of the present houses of Parliament.

Retainers and noblemen often visited the king's court, and a number of priests were permanently resident there. Because the royal chaplains were learned, literate men, they often handled correspondence and record keeping as well as religious services.

Local government was highly developed before 1066. The division into shires provided manageable administrative units; the shire boundaries generally remained unchanged until an administrative reform of the 1970s. Each shire had its county town or seat of administration. County government was placed in the hands of a prestigious aristocrat called the ealdorman or eorl (the title "earl," a later rank of nobility, derives from this source), and the shire-reeve or sheriff, an administrative officer appointed by the king who presided at shire courts and helped settle disputes about the ownership of land. (Sheriffs and counties, of course, remain today as agents of local government in both Britain and America.) Shires were often divided into smaller units called hundreds, wapentakes, or (in the North) ridings. The kingdom of Northumbria seems to have been unique in lacking subdivision into counties or smaller areas.

Trials in the Anglo-Saxon legal system used compurgation and ordeal as a means of determining innocence or guilt. Compurgation involved the calling of "oath-helpers" who would swear to the good character and truthfulness of a defendant, thus clearing his name. Under ordeal an accused person would be subjected to a physical trial. The most common forms were ordeal by hot iron, in which molten metal was poured into a defendant's hand (if it healed without infection he was pronounced innocent), and ordeal by water, in which the defendant was thrown into a river or lake (if he floated he was innocent, since it was believed that God would not allow the water to receive the body of a guilty person—the proof of innocence was perhaps not much consolation if the accused person drowned!).

The legal system also provided an excellent measure of ranks in Anglo-Saxon society, for every person had a value or price, called a "wergeld." Thus, if an aristocrat were killed, his murderers would be liable for the payment of a large sum of money to his relatives, while the compensation for the death of lower-ranking persons was much less. Ordinary working men were called "ceorls" or "churls." (The word then had no derogatory connotation, as does the modern adjective *churlish.*) Most of the ceorls were involved in farming, but a few were craftsmen, for instance blacksmiths or makers of jewelry. The ceorls were free men in the sense that they were not slaves; they possessed certain legal privileges and the right to live where they wished, although they might be subordinate to more important men or lords. Below the ceorls was a class of serfs, men who were personally free (again not slaves, because they could not be bought and sold) but bound to remain on the soil where they were born and work for a higher-ranking landlord. The only peasants who were entirely free, in the sense of being completely independent, not subordinate to some person of higher status, seem to have been the "sokemen" in the Danelaw.

Women

We know a good deal more about women in Anglo-Saxon England than we do about those who lived in Roman Britain. It has been argued that Anglo-Saxon women were more nearly the equals of their husbands and brothers than were women who lived just before or after, since society under both the Romans and the Normans was more military in organization and thus more completely dominated by men. To some extent the Christian church also emancipated women from a patriarchal spirit.

During the Anglo-Saxon period, loyalties may have been shifting from kinship groups to those based on marriage and friendship. Literary evidence points to the existence of "companionate" marriages or close loving families and shows that there could be equal delight at the birth of daughters and sons. Women, and even unborn children, could have a wergeld in the Anglo-Saxon legal system; women had property rights and could inherit land or hold it jointly with their husbands. A number of Anglo-Saxon place names are based on the personal names of women. These include Audley (from Aldgyp), Balterley (from Bettu), and Eddington (from Eadgifu).

One of the most interesting Anglo-Saxon women was Ethelfleda, the daughter of King Alfred. About 880 she was married to the ealdorman of Mercia. She appears to have held powers equal to his. During his lingering illness she assumed control of his government, and she personally governed Mercia for seven years after his death, with the title "Lady of the Mercians." In alliance with her brother, who succeeded Alfred in Wessex, she fought the Welsh and the Vikings, and she is credited with building several fortresses. A Latin poem was written in her honor; it emphasizes the contrast between her feminine nature and her manly achievements. Two other literate and influential women were Queen Emma, the wife of Ethelred the Redeless and Canute, and Queen Edith, or Eadgyth, the wife of Edward the Confessor.

A number of women assumed roles of leadership in the church. Although they could not be ordained as priests or bishops, women could become nuns. Nunneries were important institutions in Anglo-Saxon England. King Alfred's wife, Ealhswith, founded the "Nunnaminster" adjoining the cathedral at Winchester, and St. Etheldreda, a member of the royal family of Northumbria, was the founder and abbess of the great religious house at Ely, in East Anglia. Etheldreda's story is fascinating. Two marriages to important political leaders were arranged for her, but her call to a religious life was so strong that she renounced them and found her true vocation as head of the double monastery at Ely, housing both monks and nuns. Similarly, St. Hilda (or more properly, St. Hild) is credited with founding the abbey at Whitby, a few years before King Oswy's council was held there in 664, and ruling it with great wisdom. Her spirituality and learning were praised by Bede. Double monasteries like Ely were common in the Anglo-Saxon church before St. Dunstan's reforms abolished them, and in several cases women like Hilda and Etheldreda provided leadership for them.

Economic Conditions

Throughout the Anglo-Saxon period, England continued to be primarily agricultural. Even in the Southeast, large areas of forest remained; the trees were not yet felled to provide land for cultivation, and the forests were valuable sources of timber and wild game. Where the soil was tilled, mainly in the Midlands, wheat was the principal crop, though barley and rye came to be grown in the later part of the period. The open-field system, generally thought of as being typical of agricultural organization after 1066, had probably developed before the Norman invasion. (The open-field system is described in Chapter 3.) Windmills were unknown, but water power already supplemented human labor for grinding grain into flour. Much of eastern England, in Cambridgeshire and Lincolnshire, was a marshy area called the fens. Here the land might actually be under water part of each year, and the so-called Isle of Ely, now merely a district surrounding the cathedral city, was actually an island of dry land surrounded by fens. Draining schemes had been undertaken by the Romans but were evidently beyond the expertise of the Anglo-Saxons, and these areas were sparsely populated during their time.

Not an urban people, the Anglo-Saxons lived almost entirely on farms or in small villages. Roman cities became depopulated and decayed, except for a few like London, Winchester, and Canterbury, which were important as ports, commercial centers, or administrative and religious capitals. Indeed, the total population of England in Anglo-Saxon times declined to about two million, probably less than half of its peak under the Romans. Foreign trade, however, seems to have prospered. Known imports included glass from France (used for goblets and church windows but too expensive for ordinary houses) and swords from Germany. Most of the kings had their own mints; many gold coins and silver pennies survive, and their excavation helps historians establish trade routes and centers of commerce. A single national coinage had been established as early as 830, but it did not gain permanent acceptance. The Vikings issued their own coins, many of them minted at York. A new national coinage was reintroduced successfully about 975.

Scotland and Ireland

The political history of both Ireland and Scotland in the early Middle Ages is poorly documented and confusing. The general pattern that emerges—one of increasing unification—is in some ways strikingly similar to that in England.

At the beginning of the Anglo-Saxon period there were three ethnic groups in Scotland. The largest of these, the Picts, dominated the North and the east coast. The so-called "Scots," who had migrated from Ireland, were settled in the Southwest, and a group of Celts formerly resident in England had pushed their way north of the modern boundary, the River Tweed. Seven provinces existed as virtually independent territories in Scotland at about the same time as the Heptarchy in England, although a paramount or "high" king was sometimes recognized. Unity was achieved in the ninth century by Kenneth MacAlpine, a Scot who succeeded in taking over the monarchy of the Picts and blending the two royal houses. He reigned from 843 to 858.

Kenneth MacAlpine's descendants ruled Scotland for centuries thereafter, but it is difficult to keep track of the succession because mature younger brothers of a dead king were generally preferred to his own minor sons. Thus there was in effect an alternation between two branches of the Scottish royal family, and much hostility: six kings were actually killed by their successors and four more died as a result of feuds. The most famous rulers—famous because their story, duly romanticized, was popularized by Shakespeare—were Duncan (1034–1040), Macbeth (1040–1057), and Duncan's son Malcolm (1141–1165). Macbeth murdered Duncan, and Malcolm, in turn, assassinated Macbeth. Primogeniture as an accepted principle of succession was not established until the twelfth or thirteenth century. Despite these problems Scotland emerged as a single realm with something like its modern boundaries. Its leaders succeeded in gaining control of that part of Northumbria that lay north of the River Tweed, and they conducted several invasions of the English borderlands. They also prevented the Vikings from gaining permanent control of territory on the mainland, although the Norse settled some outlying islands.

Society in Scotland was organized into social classes similar to those in England. Below the king were the aristocratic earls and thanes, followed by freemen or small landowners and carls, similar to the English ceorls. As in England, varying monetary values were placed on their lives. The Scottish "cro" was the equivalent of the Anglo-Saxon "wergeld." Scotland was even more dependent on the soil than was England; the chief crops in arable lowland regions were oats, barley, peas, and beans, and grazing predominated in the infertile Highlands.

Ireland, too, was divided into a number of independent territories in early medieval times. As many as seven kingdoms sometimes existed, but these were later reduced to four, roughly corresponding to geographical quarters of the island. They were Munster (southwest), Connacht (northwest), Leinster (southeast), and Ulster (northeast). A high king or over-king sometimes dominated; the O'Neills formed the leading dynasty. Unification was not achieved until about 1002, when the famous Brian Boru proclaimed himself as king of all Ireland, and even his success was temporary.

By this time Ireland had suffered severely from the Viking invasions. Beginning about 795 as raids, these soon turned into settlements; the Norse founded cities, including Dublin, Wexford, and Waterford, and dominated life in them for several centuries. These immigrants were eventually assimilated into Irish society, but a second wave of Danish attacks hit the country about 915, and hostility continued for a century. In 1014 Brian Boru defeated the Vikings during a great battle at Clontarf, near Dublin. He himself was killed, but his victory was significant, since the Vikings were never again strong enough to seek fresh conquests. The population of Ireland always remained small—it was probably less than half a million in 1066—and the economy was always based on farming, fishing, hunting, and pasturing pigs and cattle.

Intellectual and Artistic Life in the British Isles

Despite the unsettled conditions and devastation caused by the Danish invasions, the peoples of the British Isles succeeded in maintaining an interest in education and art throughout the Anglo-Saxon period. Monasteries and cathedrals formed natural centers of learning in England, and important libraries of manuscripts were collected at such places as Jarrow, Monkwearmouth, and Durham, all in Northumbria, and at Canterbury. Armagh, St. Patrick's ecclesiastical foundation in Ireland, performed a similar function.

Each monastery maintained a school, where novices were instructed, and a scriptorium or writing room, in which books were copied and often illuminated with beautiful initial letters or portraits of the four evangelists. The Lindisfarne Gospels, written in Northumbria about 700, are the finest example of such work produced in England, and the Book of Kells, now displayed in Dublin, shows the Irish capable of equally exquisite calligraphy and art. The Lichfield Gospels, produced in Mercia, may originally have been of comparable quality but have not been well preserved. Some similar manuscripts that survive in European libraries almost certainly originated in England. Portraits in Anglo-Saxon and Celtic art are flat and formal, their features abstracted in order to produce maximum impact rather than a realistic reproduction of nature, and decorations are curvilinear, based on flowing curves and fantastic intertwining lines rather than the rational right angles that the Romans favored.

The churchmen were also the historians of this period. Saints' lives were a popular literary form. One of Bede's works is a biography of St. Cuthbert, a seventh-century abbot of Lindisfarne, which served as a model of its kind. Lives of St. Patrick and St. Columba were written in Ireland. Biographies of

The Lindisfarne Gospels, written in Northumbria about 700. These represent the finest work produced by the English monasteries. Top: shown here is a portrait of St. Matthew. Bottom left: this is an ornamental page in the form of a cross. The interlacing curved lines are characteristic of Anglo-Saxon art and may represent a continuation of Celtic style. Bottom right: this table shows where parallel passages can be found in the four Gospels. Note the architectural setting and the symbols of the four evangelists at the top of the columns.
Reproduced by permission of the British Library.

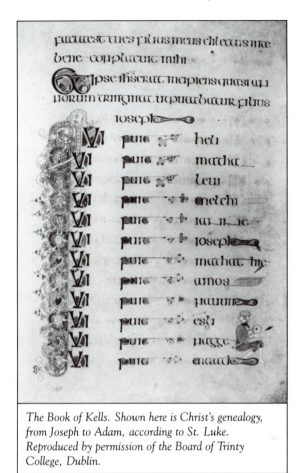

The Book of Kells. Shown here is Christ's genealogy,
from Joseph to Adam, according to St. Luke.
Reproduced by permission of the Board of Trinty
College, Dublin.

secular leaders, especially Alfred and Brian Boru, also survive, as do musical
manuscripts containing the notation of the chants used in the services of
the church.

The Anglo-Saxons built large numbers of churches, but relatively few
survive. Because they were not as grand as the churches erected by the
Normans and their successors, most of them were torn down after 1066 and
replaced by newer, larger structures. But Anglo-Saxon churches could be
imposing in their own way. They are characterized by thick, heavy walls with
very small windows. The carved heads of both humans and animals were
sometimes used as ornament. No cathedral includes significant Anglo-Saxon

Anglo-Saxon church tower, Earl's Barton,
Northamptonshire. This is among the best of the
surviving parish churches of the Anglo-Saxon
period.
Reproduced by permission of the Royal
Commission on the Historical Monuments of
England.

work. Among the best of the surviving parish churches are those at Deer-
hurst, a village near Gloucester, and Brixworth and Earl's Barton, both near
the modern town of Northampton. St. Benet's Church in Cambridge,
completed shortly before the Conquest, is another excellent example,
displaying the bell tower with arched openings, which characterizes such
late Saxon work.

    Two special examples of Anglo-Saxon art deserve fuller description. The
earlier is the Sutton Hoo Ship Burial, excavated in 1938 and now displayed
in the British Museum. This is probably to be associated with the burial of
Redwald, a king of East Anglia who died in 625. A great wooden ship, about

Tower of St. Benet's Church, Cambridge. This is another example of a surviving Anglo-Saxon parish church. The bell tower with arched openings characterizes late Saxon work. Reproduced by permission of the Royal Commission on the Historical Monuments of England.

80 feet long, had been made for the symbolic purpose of conveying the king's body to a place of life after death. The ship itself had rotted away, but archaeologists were able to determine its size and shape. Armor, bowls, a purse full of gold coins, and a harp were buried with the vessel. These were found in good condition and demonstrate the elegance and imagination of Anglo-Saxon craftsmanship. A whetstone, apparently used like a scepter on ceremonial occasions, was one of the stranger articles excavated. Other objects, including a metal statue in the form of a fish and a pair of spoons inscribed "Saul" and "Paul," suggest belief in the Christian faith. It seems likely that the East Anglians of this time had recently accepted Christianity

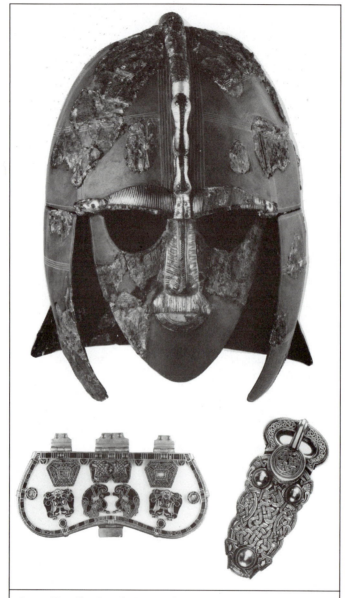

Sutton Hoo Ship Burial: East Anglians probably constructed the large wooden ship for the burial of Redwald, a king of East Anglia, who died in 625. The ship was made to convey the king's body symbolically to the afterlife. Top: the great helmet (partially reconstructed). Bottom left: the purse lid, ornamented with stylized figures of humans, birds, and dogs. Bottom right: a gold clasp, with intricate interlacing lines picked out with black enamel.
Reproduced by permission of the British Museum.

but had not yet abandoned all of their pagan customs. Ship burials of this sort are known at several sites in Scandinavia, but no others have been found in the British Isles.

Not actually made until after the Norman Conquest, the Bayeux Tapestry nevertheless belongs here because it sheds light on the end of Anglo-Saxon rule. Strictly speaking it is an embroidery rather than a tapestry, for its designs are stitched, not woven. Its panels, succeeding one another rather like a comic strip, depict the death of Edward the Confessor, the coronation of Harold, the preparations made in Normandy for the invasion of William the Conqueror, and the Norman fleet sailing across the Channel, as well as the actual events of the battle. This combat is shown in considerable detail, with pictures of the tight formations used at the beginning of the fighting, the disorganized hand-to-hand melee that occurred later in the day, and the rain of arrows falling from heaven. The tapestry shows clearly the sort of chain-mail armor worn by the fighting men and documents the use of horses in combat.

Historians have debated for centuries about the conditions under which the Bayeux Tapestry was made. There is now general agreement that Bishop Odo of Bayeux in Normandy, a half-brother of the Conqueror, commissioned the tapestry, but it was produced in England, probably near Canterbury, shortly after the Conquest. It was the work of professional embroiderers, probably men rather than nuns or courtly ladies. The tapestry has been displayed in Bayeux for centuries, at one time in the cathedral and now in its own special museum. Recently restored, it presents a unique visual record of an important chain of historical events.

The Bayeux Tapestry. The embroidered panels depict events that
marked the end of Anglo-Saxon rule. Top: shown here are
William's soldiers and horses crossing the English Channel.
Center: the battle of Hastings. In this early stage of the combat
the Norman cavalry (on the left) is attacking the shield-wall of
Anglo-Saxon soldiers. Bottom: the death of Harold. Harold is
depicted twice: at the center of the illustration, with an arrow in
his eye, and at the right, where he has fallen and is being struck
across the legs.
Reproduced by permission of the Tapisserie de Bayeux, with
special authorization from the City of Bayeux.

Suggested Reading

Ashe, Geoffrey, *The Discovery of King Arthur* (Garden City, N.Y.: Anchor Press, 1985).

Barlow, Frank, *Edward the Confessor* (Berkeley: University of California Press, 1970).

Bede, *Ecclesiastical History of the English People* (several modern editions available, including a Penguin paperback, 1968).

Blair, Peter Hunter, *Anglo-Saxon England* (Cambridge: Cambridge University Press, 1956).

Campbell, James, ed., *The Anglo-Saxons* (Ithaca, N.Y.: Cornell University Press, 1982).

Davies, Wendy, *Wales in the Early Middle Ages* (Leicester: Leicester University Press, 1982).

Deanesly, Margaret, *The Pre-Conquest Church in England* (New York: Oxford University Press, 1961).

Dickinson, W. C., *Scotland from the Earliest Times to 1603* (Edinburgh: Thomas Nelson, 1961).

Fell, Christine, *Women in Anglo-Saxon England* (Bloomington: Indiana University Press, 1984).

Henderson, Isabel, *The Picts* (London: Thames and Hudson, 1967).

Muntz, Hope, *The Golden Warrior* (London: Hodder & Stoughton, 1966) (a historical novel about King Harold).

Newman, Roger Chatterton, *Brian Boru, King of Ireland* (Dublin: Anvil Books, 1983).

Ó, Corráin, Donncha *Ireland Before the Normans* (Dublin: Gill and Macmillan, 1972).

Smyth, Alfred P., *Warlords and Holy Men: Scotland A.D. 80–1000* (London: Edward Arnold, 1984).

Stenton, Sir Frank, *Anglo-Saxon England*, 3rd ed. (Oxford: Oxford University Press, 1970).

Wilson, David M., ed., *The Archaeology of Anglo-Saxon England* (London: Methuen, 1976).

Wilson, David M., *The Bayeux Tapestry* (New York: Knopf, 1985).

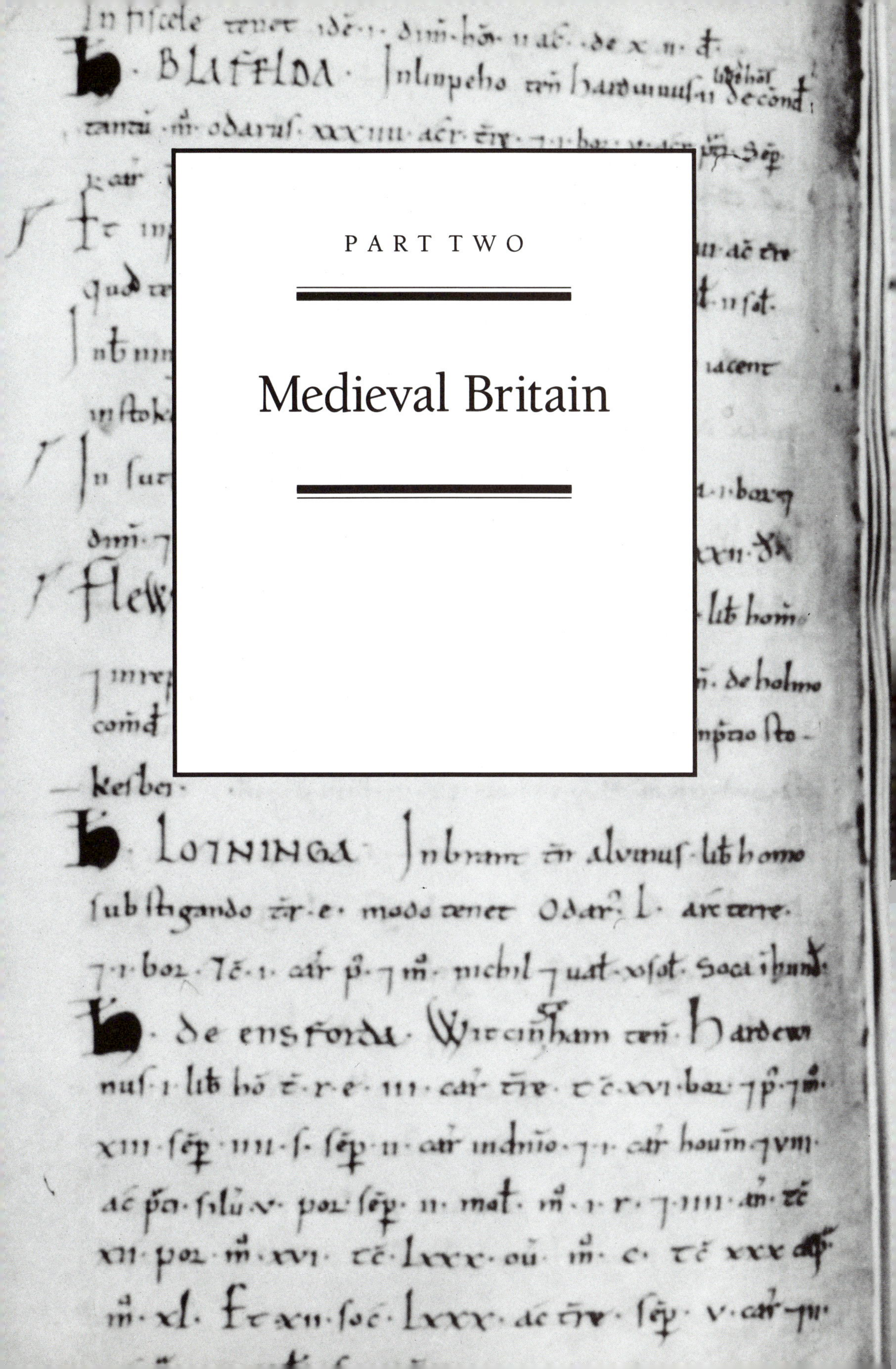

PART TWO

Medieval Britain

CHAPTER THREE

The First Century of Feudalism, 1066–1189

William I and English Feudalism

For the first five years of his reign, William the Conqueror was kept busy establishing his rule and wiping out pockets of opposition. There was relatively little difficulty in southern England. A few Anglo-Saxon leaders, most notably Hereward the Wake in the fenland near Ely, did attempt to resist Norman domination, but they were no match for the Conqueror.

The situation in the North and West was different. Here William faced a series of uprisings and secured control only after devastating much of the land. In 1068 there were disturbances on the Welsh borders and at Exeter, as well as a rebellion in northern England and the threat of a Danish invasion of Yorkshire. This did not materialize, and the northern earls submitted to William after he appeared in their land with a large army. Malcolm Canmore, the king of Scotland, had friends in the North of England; he had invaded Northumbria in 1061 and also controlled borderlands on the west coast. In 1070 he led a force into northern England again. He was unable to hold any territory permanently, but he did take a number of prisoners who became slaves or servants of the Scots. Two years later William in retribution invaded Scotland, with a navy supporting his land forces, and he secured a treaty that brought about a temporary cessation of hostilities. Although he was acknowledged to be Malcolm Canmore's overlord, William did not actually conquer Scotland, which thus remained free of the Norman institutions that he established in England. To ensure his hold on border areas, William built castles in the North, at Newcastle and Durham, and in the Welsh Marches, at Shrewsbury and Hereford.

Even before he finished dealing with his opponents, William had begun to turn his attention to the reorganization of society and government in England. The two-tier social system that he and his followers established resembled that of Roman Britain rather than that of the Anglo-Saxons. The Normans came in relatively small numbers with the intent of forming a new governing class. They did not wish to displace the Anglo-Saxons; indeed they needed them to till the soil and perform other menial tasks. For a century or more after the Conquest there were thus two social classes based on ethnic differences: the Normans functioning as aristocratic rulers and the old Anglo-Saxon inhabitants as the common people. Naturally, the change was felt most severely by members of the old Anglo-Saxon aristocracy, who lost their wealth and status.

The ethnic dichotomy was mirrored in a duality of languages, for French was spoken at court and in the homes of the wealthy Norman immigrants, while Anglo-Saxon remained the language of the masses. The form of English we now use owes much to this situation, for we have frequently inherited two words for the same thing, generally a more elaborate or acceptable term derived ultimately from Latin and brought to England by the Normans, and a shorter, more direct word of Germanic origin used by the Anglo-Saxons. The "four-letter words" not to be uttered in polite society today were the ordinary usage of the Saxons.

In organizing society and government, William brought feudalism to England. This complex system is perhaps easiest to understand if we imagine ourselves in William's place. His great asset was simply the possession of all the land in England: he regarded Anglo-Saxon land titles as being extinguished by the Conquest and held that everything was his, to be retained or distributed as he saw fit. On the liability side of the ledger were several serious problems. The king needed to establish a system of local government that would provide for law and order and ensure compliance with his orders, and he had to make provision for a strong military force that could be assembled whenever it was needed. His solution to these problems seems simple and obvious. He distributed lands to his followers, mainly leaders of the conquering army, but gave them the responsibility for local government and military service.

Such a system was already in place in France, and William was able to borrow its institutions and terminology. The land given by the king to a follower was called a fief. (The Latin term was *feudum*, and the word *feudal* was derived from it.) The king, as giver of the fief, became the lord in a personal relationship with the vassal, or recipient of the grant. A feudal contract was established whenever both parties entered into this relationship; the contract described the fief, provided that the lord would support his vassal in controlling it, and set out the obligations of the vassal in some detail. This included a specific statement about the number of fighting men he could be required to provide and the number of days a year, generally forty, for which they could be expected to serve. The contract was ratified in a personal ceremony called homage and fealty, in which the vassal promised to be the lord's man (*homme* in French) and remain loyal to him under all circumstances.

The system soon became more involved, as the king's vassals chose to enter into relationships with vassals of their own. A vassal of the king was called a tenant-in-chief, because he held his land directly from the monarch. In order to reduce his obligations, especially the need to have a substantial number of fighting men available for service, a tenant-in-chief might allocate parts of his fief to his own followers. In this context he would be their lord, they his vassals; there would be a feudal contract, and homage and fealty would be sworn. Such subinfeudation, as it was called, might continue until the land became subdivided into fiefs so small that each could support a single fighting man, although it seldom reached this point. Vassals who did not hold their land directly from the king were referred to as mesne tenants.

Monetary payments were not a basic part of the feudal system, which depended on personal service rather than money. Financial assistance (called a feudal aid) could be demanded by the lord on only three occasions: for ransom, if the lord were so unfortunate as to be captured by an enemy; for the knighting of the lord's oldest son; and for the marriage of the lord's oldest daughter. These last events were splendid festivities that vassals would be invited to attend, but the vassals had to help pay for them. Money was also involved when a vassal died. His oldest son, if he were of age, could ordinarily expect to inherit the fief, but he had to go through a new ceremony of homage and fealty with the lord and pay him a sum of money called a relief. If a male heir was not yet of legal age, he would become a ward of the lord, who would act as guardian, managing the fief and providing for the usual services during the period of minority. If there were no sons, a daughter

A ceremony of homage and fealty, as depicted
in a medieval English manuscript. This
ceremony ratified a contract in which a vassal
pledged loyalty to a lord.
Reproduced by permission of the British
Library.

might inherit, but the lord would arrange her marriage, often to a younger
son of another reliable vassal. In cases where there were no heirs, the fief
escheated to the lord, who might give it out as he wished, and it was possible
for vassals to forfeit their holdings if they failed to perform the duties required
by their contracts. In these instances too the lord could choose a new vassal
as he saw fit.

In France the feudal system often posed problems for the king, since
tenants-in-chief held large compact territories and could rival the king in
power. (William himself, as duke of Normandy, was a tenant-in-chief of the
French king, and he continued to divide his time between England and

France after 1066.) In order to prevent difficulties of this sort from arising in England, William gave scattered pieces of land as fiefs to his followers, so that they could not become territorial magnates. He also required all mesne vassals to swear that they accepted the king as their liege lord, the man to whom overriding loyalty was due should any conflict of interests arise.

The Manorial System

Feudalism was, among other things, a system that provided for land-holding. (We say landholding rather than land ownership, because in theory the monarchs retained ownership of all the land and others merely held it from them.) Feudalism did not include a set of arrangements for using the land or working the soil. Norman vassals did not perform such menial labor themselves—it would be degrading for persons of their social status to get their hands dirty—but they had underlings, generally of Anglo-Saxon stock, who did this work. These workers are usually referred to as villeins, although the terms *cottar* and *bordar* were also used to describe the poorest members of this group. Such agricultural workers can also be called peasants.

The unit of medieval farming was the manor. This was a compact, nearly self-sufficient piece of land, large enough to support a lord and his family as well as a number of villeins. A small fief might consist of a single manor. Larger fiefs included dozens of them, and a prominent feudal lord might divide his time among his various manor houses, leaving behind agents or "reeves" to manage affairs in his absence. In some cases a manor might be derived from an Anglo-Saxon village. The visible change would be the erection of a manor house for the lord; the underlying difference was the decline of independent Anglo-Saxon farmers into tenants.

Arable land in the manor was divided into a series of strips, so this system is sometimes referred to as strip farming. *Open-field farming* is another appropriate term, for the strips were not fenced in but merely separated by ridges or balks. Each strip was just the width that could be cultivated by a single plow, pulled by oxen led by a villein. A number of strips formed the lord's demesne. The lord was entitled to all the crops produced on this land; they were his principal source of income. Other strips were allocated to the villeins, who could take whatever they grew there.

Villeins were not paid for work on the lord's demesne, but they were not charged rent for the land allotted to them. As in feudalism, personal services

Open fields, still existing at Braunton, Devon, showing strip-farming patterns. In this type of farming, the land was divided into a series of strips separated by ridges. A number of strips formed a lord's demesne.
Cambridge University Collection of Air Photographs. British Crown copyright, Ministry of Defence, reproduced with the permission of the Controller of Her Britannic Majesty's Stationery Office.

rather than monetary payments prevailed. The peasants lived in small houses or cottages, often gathered together into a village. This would ordinarily have its own parish church, with a priest appointed by the lord of the manor. The manor might also include common pasture, a lake or pond where the villeins could keep geese and ducks, and woodlands, where they were allowed to gather fallen timber for use as fuel. There might be a mill, a bake house, or a blacksmith shop as well. This pattern, established throughout the Midlands, had to be modified in the Northwest, where the land was not suitable for intensive cultivation. The watery fenlands of East Anglia also required different arrangements, as did the county of Kent, where orchards and market gardening were more important than strip farming.

Continuity and Change

Historians have argued a good deal about some aspects of the feudal and manorial systems. A question often asked is whether these institutions existed in England before 1066. This may be thought of as an instance of the more general problem of the relationship between continuity and change. As we saw earlier, students of prehistoric times are coming more and more to emphasize the continuous development of indigenous institutions rather than sudden or catastrophic change resulting from foreign invasions. Somewhat similarly, some historians of the eleventh century now stress the presence of feudal institutions prior to the Norman Conquest. They also note that the open-field system antedates 1066. The fact that Edward the Confessor had such strong ties to Normandy has also suggested to some writers that Norman influence on English history began in 1042, not 1066.

Certainly there were elements resembling feudalism in place before 1066. In particular, the Anglo-Saxon thegns who were given land in exchange for assuming military obligations played a role much like the Norman tenants-in-chief. Still, it is appropriate to credit William with introducing the more elaborate institutions of fully developed feudalism. Among other things, there were no written feudal contracts in Anglo-Saxon society: what was new, one scholar has concluded, was the contract. Actually there were further novelties in both feudal and manorial organization. Both continuity and change can be traced, but 1066 remains a pivotal date when change dominated.

The Domesday Book

Late in his reign William undertook a survey of all the land in England, so that he would know who held the manors and how much income they produced. The results of this census were gathered into the famous Domesday Book, completed in 1087, the year of William's death. This great compilation lists the manors, names their lords, and enumerates (but does not name) the villeins, cottars, and bordars, as well as the farm animals (oxen, pigs, cattle, horses, and sheep). The annual income of each manor is also listed, as is the size, measured in a unit called the hide. (Hides seem to have varied from about 40 to about 120 acres.) The manor of Weston Colville near Cambridge, for example, had 22 villeins, 10 bordars, 8 serfs, 4 oxen, 373 pigs, 29 cattle, 3 horses, 765 sheep, and room for 19 plows. It was 10 hides in extent and had an annual value of 14 pounds and 5 shillings.

The Domesday Book. This was a detailed survey of the population, land ownership, and income in England, undertaken at the behest of William the Conqueror. British Crown copyright, Public Record Office, London. Reproduced by permission.

Some people resented the collection of such detailed information about their holdings—the name *Domesday* refers to their feeling that such an inquest was like the day of doom, or that its judgments were as final. They feared, quite correctly, that a desire to tax the manors lay behind a systematic valuation of their wealth.

Historians have found that it is necessary to use the information in the Domesday Book with some care, for the Norman scribes who collated the figures were not actually familiar with the lands in question and may have interpreted as normal manorial units some lands that were actually organized in different ways. Still, the survey is an exceedingly important historical source. No other European country possesses such a document, and no other comprehensive census was undertaken in England until the nineteenth century.

The Domesday Book provides one way of attacking the problem of continuity and change, at least as far as landholding is concerned. Analysis shows that pre-Conquest landlords still held as few as 5.5 percent of the manors listed in Domesday. Nearly half the land was in the hands of Norman invaders; the church possessed just over a quarter, sometimes under arrangements predating 1066; and the king and queen held 17 percent directly, including 2 percent in which Edward the Confessor's widow, Edith, had a life interest.

The Sons of William I

It is important to realize that William remained the duke of Normandy as well as king of England. He had responsibilities on both sides of the Channel and had to divide his time between his two territories. When he was in England his wife, Matilda, often administered Normandy for him.

Shortly before his death, William faced the question of succession. He had three sons (a fourth had died in a hunting accident) to whom he could bequeath two territories, the realm of England and the duchy of Normandy. He decided to leave Normandy in the hands of his oldest son, Robert Curthose, who was already active in political affairs there. William Rufus, the second son, was designated heir to England, and Henry, the youngest, was paid a sum of money in exchange for renouncing his claim to land. A daughter, Adela, had been provided for through marriage to a French nobleman, the count of Blois. (See Genealogical Table A.2 in the Appendix on page 335.)

William Rufus, or William II, succeeded to the English throne in 1087 and ruled until 1100. He soon gained control of Normandy as well, for his brother Robert wished to join the Crusades, that great medieval military movement to wrest control of the Holy Land from the infidels. Requiring money to fit out his forces as well as needing someone to rule Normandy in his absence, Robert mortgaged the duchy to William, who thus ruled all of his father's lands. Many Crusaders died of illness or wounds, and William may have hoped that his brother would never trouble him again.

William II was not a constructive monarch. He inherited little of the Conqueror's drive or sense of purpose. His younger brother, Henry, was far more able and much more ambitious. Disregarding his earlier promises, Henry began to covet the throne. He may have been responsible for William Rufus's death: in 1100 the king was killed in a hunting accident, the victim of an arrow shot by one Walter Tirel. Contemporary observers as well as later historians wondered whether Tirel was not Henry's agent. (In all probability he was not, and the shooting was truly accidental.)

Henry I (1100–1135)

Because Robert had not yet returned from the Crusade, Henry assumed the rule of both England and Normandy. Evidently he realized that he might be unpopular in England because his succession was suspect, so he set about to win the support of his people. He married an heiress of the old Anglo-Saxon House of Wessex (Matilda, the daughter of Malcolm

Canmore of Scotland), and he issued a document that is usually called his Coronation Charter or Charter of Liberties. In this he promised to uphold the provisions of existing feudal contracts, to respect the independence of the church, and to adhere to the laws and customs of Edward the Confessor. Because these provisions are vague and nearly meaningless, the Charter was mainly a piece of propaganda without any great significance in its own time. In later centuries, however, it came to be viewed as the first in a series of documents establishing a law above the king, ensuring that England possessed a limited monarchy rather than absolute or arbitrary kingship.

Soon after Henry's coronation Robert returned to Normandy. Believing that he, not Henry, should have succeeded to the English throne, he invaded England but withdrew without fighting. His rule of Normandy was so ineffectual that a number of his own tenants then invited Henry to invade France. At the Battle of Tinchebrai (1106) Henry conquered Normandy. Robert was kept in confinement for the rest of his life. Once again all the lands of William the Conqueror were in the hands of a single ruler.

Henry I was one of the great kings of the Middle Ages. He was sometimes called Henry Beauclerc, in tribute to his learning, or the Lion of Justice, in reference to his passion for improving the legal system. He was also intent on preserving the power to control the English church, which he had inherited from his father. He was fanatical about efficiency and honesty in government; when he heard that nearly a hundred officials of his mints were corrupt he ordered them to be castrated and their right hands struck off. The important constitutional and religious developments of his reign will be considered later.

Stephen and Matilda (1135–1154)

Succession to the throne became a problem at the time of Henry's death. His heir, William, had been drowned in 1120 when a ship in which he and some other young members of the royal family were traveling from Normandy to England struck a rock and sank in the English Channel. (They appear to have been drunk at the time.) Henry had no other legitimate sons, although he had fathered as many as twenty bastards, so he sought to provide for the succession of his daughter, Matilda. She was well acquainted with European politics, for she had been married to the Holy Roman Emperor and after his death to Geoffrey, the count of Anjou, a great feudal domain in southern France.

Initially Matilda did not press her claim as strongly as she might have, and many of the feudal magnates in England were unwilling to accept a woman as their lord. Instead, they secured the coronation of Stephen, the son of Henry I's sister Adela and her husband, the count of Blois. According to a contemporary chronicle, Stephen was "a mild man, soft and good, who did no justice"; he was simply not strong enough to manage the feudal system in England during a period of divided loyalties. Matilda and her followers invaded England in 1139, and a confused period of civil war lasted until 1153. In that year Stephen and Matilda accepted a compromise agreement, the Treaty of Wallingford. This provided that Stephen might rule unchallenged for the rest of his life but that Matilda's son Henry would be his successor. The arrangement satisfied both sides, for Stephen's oldest son, Eustace, had already died and Matilda was pleased with the assurance that her descendants would enjoy the throne.

Henry II (1154–1189) and the Angevin Empire

Stephen died shortly after the treaty was signed, and Henry II succeeded to the throne in 1154. Because his father was the count of Anjou, members of his family were called Angevins, or sometimes Plantagenets, a term derived from the broom plant (in French *plante genêt*), which was one of their armorial symbols. The Angevin or Plantagenet period in English history lasted from 1154 to 1399.

Henry II ruled a vast complex of territories in France, and he spent more time on the Continent than he did in England. From his mother he inherited Normandy and Brittany; from his father he inherited Anjou. His wife, Eleanor of Aquitaine, brought him possession of both Aquitaine and Gascony, the most important areas in southwestern France. Although Henry II was a vassal of the French king, he actually controlled far more land than the monarch did. Virtually all of the French coastline and most of southern France lay in his hands. Because these territories were not consolidated and had to be ruled according to a variety of local customs, they were difficult to govern. Their existence led to perennial conflict with the king of France and often to warfare. Only Henry's vast energy and domineering personality enabled him to hold his sprawling empire together.

Britain and France in the Middle Ages

Wales, Ireland, and Scotland

In somewhat different ways Henry II also came to dominate Wales, Scotland, and Ireland. Each of these areas had its own unique relationship with the Norman kings of England, and each had its own internal history.

English overlordship in Wales had already been asserted before 1066. Edward the Confessor was recognized as overlord of Wales in 1063, when the native leader Gruffud ap Llywelyn was overthrown by his own people after some years of conducting raids into English territory. William the Conqueror assumed the same role. The Normans enjoyed direct control of most eastern areas—lands adjoining Offa's Dyke—and gained greater influence in other places as a result of William's expedition into south Wales in 1081. Henry I enlarged the scope of English jurisdiction even more. He saw to it that the border lands, called the Marches, were securely in the hands of his followers; he built a number of castles, to serve as centers of military control over the native population; and he ensured Norman domination of the Welsh church, whose four dioceses were put in the hands of bishops chosen by the English monarch.

After Henry I's death, revolts broke out in several parts of Wales, especially in the South. The Welsh took advantage of the struggle between Stephen and Matilda to reassert their own independence; this was the most sustained rebuff to Anglo-Norman expansion in Britain since the Conquest.

Henry II sought to recover the ground lost since 1135. In 1157 he led an expedition into Wales, and in 1165 he mounted a larger campaign. His achievements were limited by bad weather, mountainous terrain, and his own lack of knowledge of Welsh circumstances, but he did succeed in striking an accord with native leaders in 1171. According to this settlement Henry was once again recognized as overlord. A native Welsh chieftain was appointed his viceroy or justiciar for Wales, and it was agreed that disputes among the Welsh would be settled according to their own law. In essence Wales had been divided, with the Marches and the South in the hands of Anglo-Normans, the North still controlled by Welsh natives.

The situation in Ireland was in some respects similar to that in Wales, for the land was divided between the natives and the Normans. The confusion was compounded by the ambitious designs of some Anglo-Norman lords from England, the greatest of whom was Richard de Clare, earl of Pembroke, usually known as Strongbow. Strongbow contrived to marry the daughter of a native leader, Dermot, king of Leinster. Although Dermot had sons alive, he named Strongbow his heir and joined with him in warfare against the high king, Rory O'Connor. When Strongbow failed to heed Henry II's order that he stop intervening in Irish affairs and return to his home in England, Henry decided to invade Wales himself. Some of the feuding Irish lords had asked him to intervene and initially welcomed his presence. His large military force, perhaps nearly five thousand men, proved invincible, and a short campaign secured the submission of Strongbow, Dermot, and other adventurers.

After Henry II's campaign, both the Normans and the native leaders were made to swear allegiance to the English king, who became overlord of Ireland. Some of the Irish were willing to do this because they believed it gave them an effective royal guarantee to the possession of their lands. Henry made it clear that he regarded the Anglo-Normans in Ireland as being subject to English laws, although local customs might be observed among the Irish natives. When he departed from Ireland, Henry II left a Norman, Henry de Lacy, as his viceroy or justiciar, but in 1175 he acknowledged the dominant position of the native high king. In a treaty signed at Windsor, the royal castle near London, Rory O'Connor became the king's vassal, and Norman overlordship was confirmed.

Henry's conquest of Ireland had important religious implications. Diocesan structure had never been fully accepted by the Irish church, which rejected rule from Canterbury and showed limited enthusiasm for the supremacy of Rome. After 1171 the Irish church was reorganized along lines normal in other parts of Catholic Christendom, to the delight of Pope Adrian IV. Henry II also secured a pledge that the Irish clergy would perform the Latin mass and other liturgies according to the Use of Sarum, a model based on the rites of Salisbury Cathedral, which had become the norm throughout most of England.

As we have seen, Scotland was forced to acknowledge the overlordship of the English kings shortly after 1066. A Scottish campaign into northern England took place in 1092, motivated by William Rufus's absence in France and his subsequent illness, but it was ruthlessly suppressed.

England's weakness during the quarrel between Stephen and Matilda provided another opportunity for Scottish invasion. The Scottish king at this time, and one of the greatest in all Scottish history, was David I (1124–1153). A distant relative of the English royal family, David had been educated in the household of Henry I, and he was later married to a rich Anglo-Norman, Maud de Senlis. Through her, David held a large complex of estates in England, but his chief interest lay in unifying Scotland and advancing its cause. The friendly relations he had enjoyed with England deteriorated after Henry's death, and David finally led a military force against Stephen in 1138. Scottish success was recognized in a highly favorable treaty signed at Durham in 1139; this confirmed the Scots' possession of some lands in what had been northern England and carefully avoided any reference to English overlordship. A cultivated and attractive man, David enhanced the prestige of the Scottish monarchy, provided notable patronage for the church, and endeared himself to his people. It is said that the name *David*, unusual in Scotland when he was crowned, soon became the most popular for Scottish males.

Henry II was fast to reassert his rights in Scotland, although he never set foot there himself. When warfare broke out again in 1174, English troops succeeded in capturing the Scottish king, David's grandson William. William was taken off to be imprisoned in Normandy and was forced to concede English feudal superiority once again.

In theory, relations between England and the outlying areas of Wales, Ireland, and Scotland were governed during these years by the feudal system, which provided an ideal framework for the overlordship of the English king. His vassals, sometimes Anglo-Norman lords and sometimes native kings or other leaders, could be allowed to govern their own areas in a variety of ways. In practice, the greater size and strength of England, coupled with the personal ambitions of kings like William I and Henry II, made it possible for England to dominate the British Isles.

Ecclesiastical History

Relations between church and state were of critical importance during the years between the Norman Conquest and the death of Henry II. It requires some leap of imagination for Americans to understand these, because our system of government provides for separation between church and state and because we are used to the notion that there are many different religious denominations, each individual being free to choose among them or to belong to none at all. The situation in England has always been different. Even today there is a state church, although only members of the royal family are required to adhere to it. Until the coming of the Reformation in the sixteenth century, there was but one church, that established following the Council of Whitby, recognizing the pope as its head and

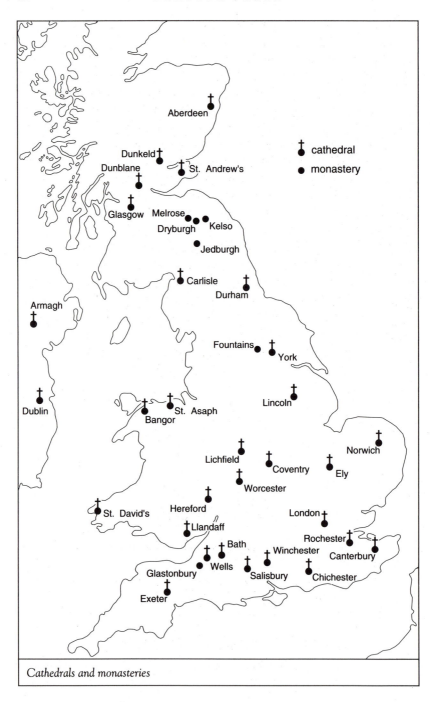

Aberdeen

Dunkeld

Dunblane

St. Andrew's

Glasgow

Melrose

Dryburgh

Kelso

Jedburgh

Carlisle

Durham

Armagh

Fountains

York

Dublin

Bangor

St. Asaph

Lincoln

Norwich

Lichfield

Coventry

Ely

Worcester

Hereford

St. David's

London

Llandaff

Rochester

Bath

Winchester

Canterbury

Wells

Glastonbury

Salisbury

Chichester

Exeter

† cathedral

● monastery

Cathedrals and monasteries

forming part of international Catholic Christendom. The men and women who lived in medieval England were born into both church and state; they could not opt out of either.

In England, church and state were especially closely intertwined. The king, as well as the pope and the archbishop of Canterbury, had considerable influence over the ecclesiastical establishment, and he was intent on preserving it. This situation led to a series of conflicts between the monarchs and the leaders of the church. Their relationship was always fluid, based on political realities rather than abstract theories. A strong king could dominate a weak pope; a powerful churchman could prevail over an ineffectual monarch. When both church and state had ambitious or inflexible heads, quarrels were almost inevitable.

The years immediately following the Norman Conquest witnessed a confrontation between William the Conqueror and one of the greatest of the medieval popes, Gregory VII, or Hildebrand. Arguing that only the church, not the state, could offer men and women the possibility of salvation, Gregory believed that the church was more important than the state and that it should be independent of secular control. He favored the introduction of ecclesiastical institutions that ran parallel to those of the state. In particular, he insisted that the church should have its own legal system, based on what was called canon law, and its own courts, which would have jurisdiction over all cases affecting the clergy as well as cases involving heresy, marriage and divorce, and the probate of wills and testaments. (Wills were to be proved in church courts because they generally included bequests to the church.) William I agreed to allow the establishment of ecclesiastical courts in England, where they remained important, even in the lives of persons who did not belong to the state church, until the nineteenth century. But he refused to accept the pope's claim to headship of an international feudal system. Even though William carried a banner blessed by the pope when he entered the battlefield at Hastings, he was convinced that his own actions were responsible for his acquisition of England. It was not a fief given to him by the papacy, and he was not the pope's vassal.

William I enjoyed cordial relations with his archbishop of Canterbury, a distinguished scholar named Lanfranc, who had previously been the prior of a great monastery at Bec in Normandy. One of Lanfranc's achievements was the rebuilding of Canterbury Cathedral in Norman style after much of the Saxon building was destroyed by fire. Lanfranc died in 1089, two years after the Conqueror, but William Rufus did not nominate a successor immediately:

by leaving the archbishopric vacant, he could enjoy its revenues and avoid possible conflicts with a new ecclesiastical leader. In 1093, however, William Rufus fell ill, and his chaplain suggested that his sickness was God's punishment for his failure to act. Seeking to appease the Almighty, William gave the archbishopric to another prior of Bec, a learned theologian named Anselm. The king then recovered, and he soon came to believe that God had tricked him into making an undesirable appointment. William II and Anselm never got along—they held divergent views about royal authority over the church—and Anselm was soon driven into exile in Normandy. When the tower of Winchester Cathedral fell following William's burial there, many churchmen regarded this disaster as showing God's judgment on an evil ruler.

Henry I brought Anselm back to England but proceeded to quarrel with him, although on a higher plane than his brother. The independence of the church remained the central issue of controversy. During this period it manifested itself in a dispute about arrangements for the appointment and installation of new bishops. It had been customary for the king to make a nomination and for the clergy attached to the cathedral where the vacancy existed to hold an election at which they accepted the royal nominee. The church would consecrate the designated man, and the king would invest him with a seal ring and a pastoral staff, the chief symbols of his office. The contention between Henry I and Anselm centered on this matter of royal investiture: Anselm believed that no layman should have a part in the induction of a new bishop, while Henry feared that he would lose the power to name his bishops if he abandoned the ceremony. (The issue of lay investiture loomed large throughout Europe during this period, and the quarrel in England was not an isolated event.)

After some years of dissension Henry was finally persuaded to accept Anselm's position and give up his right to investiture. As his sister Adela pointed out, the king retained the ceremony of homage and fealty in which new bishops became his feudal vassals; if the church were so perverse as to elect and consecrate a bishop who was not of the king's choosing, the monarch could always refuse to grant him the lands necessary to support his place in society. Henry I may appear the loser in the investiture conflict, but in reality he abandoned nothing more than an empty ceremony. The end of royal investiture, however, may mark a changed attitude toward monarchy. Earlier, kings were often regarded as consecrated agents of God, putting the divine will into operation. Now they were generally thought of as laymen holding a secular office.

Henry II and Thomas Becket

H enry II's troubles with the church were more serious. He realized that a cantankerous archbishop could be a source of trouble, so when a vacancy arose he named one of his closest friends, Thomas Becket. A brilliant administrator, Becket was already serving Henry as chancellor, and the two men had worked together without incident. But as soon as he became archbishop of Canterbury, Becket displayed a mind of his own. He resigned his position as chancellor, concentrated on ecclesiastical affairs, and demonstrated his adherence to the position that Hildebrand advocated.

The issue of ecclesiastical independence now came up in the form of a controversy about church courts. In 1164 Henry II issued a document called the Constitutions of Clarendon in which he attempted to restrict the activities of these ecclesiastical tribunals, especially their right to try clergymen accused of serious crimes. Becket admitted that the Constitutions merely restated English customs, but he said that such customs were unacceptable. Both Henry and Becket were strong-minded men, convinced that they were in the right and unwilling to budge from their positions. Becket went for a time to Normandy, then returned to England, where he proceeded to excommunicate some of the king's followers, including the archbishop of York, who had accommodated Henry II by crowning his oldest son as heir and joint ruler. Becket's action was too much for Henry, who swore angrily at four of his armed knights, "Will no one rid me of this turbulent priest?" The knights interpreted this outburst as a mandate to murder Becket, and they did kill him in his cathedral at Canterbury a few days after Christmas 1170. It was a horrible crime by any standard and was particularly appalling in the eyes of the church because cathedrals were held to be places of sanctuary where even criminals could find safe refuge.

When he heard of Becket's martyrdom, Henry II was overcome with remorse. His relationship with Becket had always been one of love for the man coupled with hatred for his policies. He insisted that he had never desired Becket's murder and went as a barefoot suppliant to Canterbury. He finally gained the church's absolution by agreeing to drop the Constitutions of Clarendon, so that criminous clerks continued to be tried by church courts. In his death Becket thus achieved a victory that would probably never have been his in life.

Soon after his death Becket came to be regarded as a saint—St. Thomas of Canterbury, the greatest English saint of the Middle Ages. Pilgrims thronged to see the place of his murder, and many of them believed that

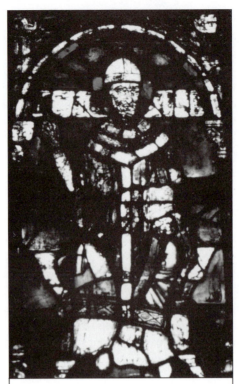

*Thomas Becket. Probably a depiction of
the saint in a later medieval stained glass
window at Canterbury Cathedral, this panel
escaped destruction by the iconoclasts of the
sixteenth century.
Reproduced by the kind permission of the
Dean and Chapter of Canterbury Cathedral.*

miracles occurred as a result of his intercession. Becket's shrine grew rich
with the offerings of these pilgrims; the east end of Canterbury Cathedral
had to be rebuilt to house the shrine more grandly. His martyrdom has given
rise to several famous pieces of literature. In the fourteenth century Geoffrey
Chaucer wrote his wonderful *Canterbury Tales*, a series of stories told by
pilgrims to entertain each other while on the road between London
and Canterbury. T. S. Eliot, the noted twentieth-century writer, also used
Becket's slaughter as the theme of his drama *Murder in the Cathedral*. Although Eliot violated historical fact in picturing Becket as a Saxon rather

than as a Norman and ascribing the conflict between him and Henry to ethnic roots, he may well have been right in thinking that the proud archbishop deliberately courted death.

The English Constitution Under Henry I and Henry II

Both Henry I and Henry II made significant contributions to the institutions of government in England, or to what historians call the English constitution.

Unlike the United States, England does not have a single written document as its constitution. Except for the brief period following the Civil War in the seventeenth century when there was no king, it has never had one. Instead, the English constitution is that collection of customs and precedents that determines how the government is constituted. Some written documents, like Magna Carta, are part of the constitution, but unwritten traditions are of greater importance. In studying the constitution, one examines mainly the development of organs of government.

Royal Advisors and Councils

Any ruler needs advisors, generally organized into a council of some sort. During the Anglo-Saxon period, the witan served this function. It was a gathering of prominent men, supposedly the wisest in the realm, who advised the king, assisted him in governing, and formally elected new monarchs. The witan disappeared with other Anglo-Saxon institutions after 1066; in the Norman period its place was taken by the Great Council, composed of the king's tenants-in-chief, and the Small Council, or Curia Regis, made up of professional civil servants.

The Great Council could meet whenever summoned by the king. One of the clauses in the feudal contracts of tenants-in-chief required them to attend at court when called. William the Conqueror introduced the practice of holding ceremonial meetings, called Crown Wearings, on the three great feasts of the Christian year. These occasions for regal splendor, intended as much to impress William's followers as for any other reason, normally took place on Christmas at Gloucester, on Easter at Winchester, and at Whitsun or Pentecost at Westminster.

The Curia Regis met much more frequently, eventually even daily, to handle the actual business of government. Its members were not great magnates in their own right but simply literate, able men—originally mainly priests—who were able to produce the written documents on which government more and more depended. Henry I is often credited with establishing the Curia Regis, although no precise date can be given, and one should probably regard it as taking shape gradually in response to an increasingly obvious need for effective administration.

One of the members of the Curia Regis was the chancellor. He headed the Chancery, or secretarial bureau of the government, and was responsible for writing important official documents called charters and writs. Royal charters recorded the grant of lands or privileges, usually in perpetuity. They required the signature of witnesses, and they were authenticated by the attachment of the Great Seal. Some charters date back to Anglo-Saxon times; Edward the Confessor is the first king known to have used the Great Seal. The chancellor had custody of the Great Seal, a double-faced matrix about 6 inches in diameter, which was pressed into sealing wax to create the impressions attached to important documents. Both sides of the Great Seal included portraits of the monarch: the front showed him in state, wearing a crown and seated on a throne, and the reverse generally depicted him on horseback, wearing armor as if ready for battle. Because they could sometimes find excuses for delaying the sealing of documents they disliked, the chancellors came to have considerable influence in the formation of royal policy, and they later became the king's chief advisors. The chancery also issued a variety of writs, documents less formal and elaborate than charters, which came to be of great importance in the English legal system.

Government Finance

Another member of the Curia Regis was the treasurer, who managed the financial department of the central government. Beginning with the reign of Henry I, this bureau was called the Exchequer.

The Exchequer received payments of money due the king from his estates and from taxation. The sheriff in each county was responsible for collecting these and physically transporting the gold and silver coins to the Exchequer office at Westminster. (There was no paper money and no system of bank drafts.) A checkered tabletop was used in counting the money. This was a difficult matter, since accounts were kept in Roman rather than Arabic numerals and since the coinage in pounds, shillings, and pence was not based

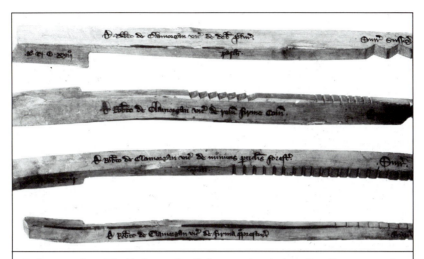

Exchequer tallies. The Exchequer handled money due the king from his estates and
from taxation. Tallies—sticks of wood notched to represent the amount of payment
received—were used as permanent receipts for money paid to the Exchequer.
British Crown copyright, Public Record Office, London. Reproduced by permission.

on units of ten. (There were twelve pennies or pence in a shilling and twenty
shillings in a pound; this monetary system lasted until the 1960s.) The title
"Exchequer" is derived from the accounting table. The Exchequer office also
kept permanent records of all transactions. The Pipe Roll listed all receipts
and expenditures: the earliest such account dates from 1130, and complete
records survive beginning in 1155, giving England the world's best set of
medieval financial documents. Tallies were also struck as permanent receipts
for money paid to the Exchequer. These were sticks of wood, precisely
notched to represent the amount received; they were split in half, one part
being given to the person responsible for the payment as an official discharge
of the obligation and the other retained in the Exchequer office itself. These
accounting procedures, very advanced for their time, continued in use until
the seventeenth century.

Henry II altered both government finance and feudalism by introducing a
new form of taxation called scutage. Vassals paid scutage (the term literally
means shield money) in lieu of providing fighting men. Earlier, churchmen
had sometimes been excused from military service on payment of a fee, but
Henry was the first to levy scutage regularly from laymen. The new arrangement was important for him, since feudal contracts generally stipulated that
English vassals and their followers could not be required to perform service

outside their own country while the king needed warriors to fight for him in France. Most tenants were pleased with this arrangement; it was expensive and troublesome to maintain the groups of armed men required by feudal contracts.

It has been argued that the introduction of scutage undermined the fundamental concept of feudalism, which was originally based on personal service rather than money. Something approaching a modern arrangement in which the tenants simply paid rent for their land gradually came into being, and feudal customs degenerated into antiquated traditions rather than living institutions. Some historians insist that the term *feudalism* should not be used once money was introduced; others call the new system "bastard feudalism." One writer has gone so far as to assert that genuine feudalism scarcely existed in England at all and to plead that the term be banished from the historian's vocabulary.

The Great Officers of State

During the Norman period, the highest-ranking official was the justiciar. He stood just below the king but above all departments of government while the king was in England, and he was usually the king's deputy or viceroy when the king was out of the realm, attending to affairs in France. William the Conqueror's half-brother, Bishop Odo of Bayeux, exercised such powers shortly after 1066; Ranulf Flambard was a famous justiciar of William Rufus's time. During the thirteenth century, the powers of the justiciar declined as those of the chancellor rose, and the office disappeared after 1265.

Below the justiciar, the so-called Great Officers of State were in fact officers of the king's household. These included the steward (responsible for the service of meals), the constable (who maintained order at court), the marshall (placed in charge of the king's horses), the chamberlain, and the butler. Some of these ceremonial offices still exist today, but the men appointed to them now serve only at the time of a coronation.

Local Government

As in late Anglo-Saxon times, the sheriff was the chief officer of local government under the Norman kings. Each county had a single sheriff, appointed by the king. Ealdormen, who had also been important in Anglo-Saxon local government, disappeared after 1066, although the name lingered on as the root of the new rank of earl. Earls formed an honorific group, eventually regarded as being holders of a title of nobility, and did not have specific administrative duties. Early sheriffs were chosen from among the ranks of earls holding large estates in each county.

Sheriffs had many duties. As we have seen, they were responsible for collecting taxes and paying the receipts to the Exchequer. Generally, they were charged with maintaining order and implementing the edicts of the central government within their counties.

In 1170 Henry II conducted an inquiry into the conduct of local officials. A number of them were found guilty of taking bribes or oppressing subjects in other ways. As a result of this inquest Henry II dismissed most of his sheriffs and made new appointments. He also transferred some duties to professional royal administrators.

At the beginning of the thirteenth century, another officer of loyal government appeared to serve alongside the sheriffs and to check on their loyalty. This was the coroner (a term derived from the Latin *corona*, or crown). Initially each county had four coroners, but the numbers increased as certain towns were granted the right to name coroners of their own.

Justices of the peace also came to be important agents of local government. It is impossible to fix a date at which they came into being. As we have seen, feudal lords were charged with maintaining law and order on their estates; a few of the more prominent landlords came to assume responsibility for keeping the peace within their counties. These peacekeepers did not become judges or justices until the fourteenth century, when they were given the right to hold courts (called Quarter Sessions because they convened four times a year) where petty offenders could be brought to trial. Justices of the peace gradually assumed the chief responsibility for enforcing orders of the central government, formerly held by the sheriff. The king named a panel of justices of the peace for each county. They were appointed annually and served without pay.

Sheriffs, coroners, and justices of the peace still act as officials of local government in both England and the United States, although their role is much less important than it was in the Middle Ages. Sheriffs remain law-enforcement officers, serving an entire county. Coroners are charged mainly with determining the cause of death in cases where foul play is suspected, and justices of the peace have the right to perform civil marriages.

Royal Courts and
the Common Law

T he greatest constitutional achievement of the twelfth century was
undoubtedly the development of a royal court system using the Common Law.

Both Henry I and Henry II were interested in creating a uniform legal
code based on the authority of the king, not that of individual feudal lords.
They may have had a passion for justice, but they also realized that royal
courts might be profitable, since fees could be charged when cases were heard
and fines could be levied against offenders. Ever since the Norman Conquest,
subjects had occasionally addressed petitions to the monarch, asking him to
redress their grievances. Initially these were referred to a high official at court,
the justiciar or the chancellor. But it would obviously be more convenient
for subjects if royal justices perambulated the country, settling cases in the
areas where they arose. The king appointed such officers. Itinerant justices,
moving about with no fixed circuit, came into being under Henry I; they
later developed into the justices of Assize, who held regular sessions in specified geographical circuits.

Henry II established two great central courts, which met at Westminster
to hear cases that were too important to be handled locally. The Court of
Common Pleas heard disputes between subjects—matters that later came to
be known as civil suits, largely turning on ownership of property—and the
Court of King's Bench considered cases to which the king himself was a
party. These included criminal offenses like murder. Because the king undertook to maintain law and order, a breach of the peace was an affront to his
government, not merely to the individuals who were wronged by it. Judges
in these courts were learned men with a specialized interest in legal matters.
In the later twelfth century, Common Pleas and King's Bench met sporadically, at the will of the king; their activities became more regular in the
thirteenth century.

The use of juries was ratified, if not initiated, by Henry II. His Assize (or
decree) of Clarendon, issued in 1166, provided for the use of twelve-man
juries to accuse persons believed guilty of serious crimes. These were the
ancestors of modern grand juries. Something like them may date back to
Anglo-Saxon times. Petty or civil juries could be employed in deciding certain sorts of actions, especially those concerned with ownership of land. The
Writ of Novel Disseisin, also promulgated in 1166, allowed suitors who

claimed that lands had been taken from them recently and unjustly to obtain a writ that guaranteed them a jury trial.

In dispensing justice, the royal judges gradually developed the Common Law. This was not based on statutes passed by a legislature but rather on custom, tradition, and precedent—on earlier decisions rendered by judges who had faced the same problems. Some elements of Anglo-Saxon law and local custom also found their way into the Common Law. It is perhaps easiest to understand the origin of the system if we imagine that we ourselves have been appointed judges, charged with making judgments based on equity and fair play but not yet provided with any legal code. As we heard cases, we would attempt to render justice as seemed best in each individual instance. When we heard similar cases we would naturally settle them in similar ways. Thus our earlier decisions would become precedents for later ones. As other judges followed us, they might look back at records of earlier verdicts so that they too could handle issues in a uniform manner. Eventually Common Law ensured that similar cases would be settled in similar ways, no matter who the judge might be. Such a system was of enormous importance to ordinary people, for they could plan their affairs knowing how society would react to their property arrangements and other actions. Indeed legal scholars sometimes maintain that it does not matter so much just what the law is but rather that the law is predictable.

Feudal courts and some Anglo-Saxon legal institutions continued to operate for several centuries after 1100 but gradually died out in the face of better justice provided more professionally by agents of the central government. Indeed the basic principles of Common Law have spread throughout the whole English-speaking world, including the United States. Some of our modern legal procedures can be traced, both in principle and in detail, directly to the innovations of the first two Henrys in England.

Suggested Reading

Barlow, Frank, *The English Church 1066–1154* (London: Longman, 1979).

Barlow, Frank, *Thomas Becket* (London: Weidenfeld & Nicolson, 1986).

Barrow, G.W.S., *Kingship and Unity: Scotland 1000–1306* (London: Edward Arnold, 1981).

Cannon, John, and Ralph Griffiths, *The Oxford Illustrated History of the British Monarchy* (Oxford and New York: Oxford University Press, 1988).

Chinball, Marjorie, *Anglo-Norman England, 1066–1166* (Oxford: Basil Blackwell, 1986).

Davies, R. R., *Conquest, Coexistence, and Change: Wales 1063–1415* (Oxford: Clarendon Press, 1987).

Dolley, Michael, *Anglo-Norman Ireland* (Dublin: Gill and Macmillan, 1972).

Douglas, David C., *William the Conqueror* (Berkeley and Los Angeles: University of California Press, 1964).

Flanagan, Marie Therese, *Irish Society, Anglo-Norman Settlers, Angevin Kingship: Interactions in Ireland in the Late Twelfth Century* (Oxford: Clarendon Press, 1989).

Lennard, Reginald, *Rural England, 1086–1135: A Study of Social and Agrarian Conditions* (Oxford: Oxford University Press, 1959).

Platt, Colin, *Medieval England* (London: Routledge & Kegan Paul, 1978).

Poole, A. L., *From Domesday Book to Magna Carta, 1087–1216* (Oxford: Clarendon Press, 1955).

Warren, W. L., *Henry II* (Berkeley and Los Angeles: University of California Press, 1973).

The Age of the Barons, 1189–1327

The Sons of Henry II

About a decade before his death Henry II decided to divide his territories among his four sons. The eldest, named Henry like his father, had already been crowned as heir and joint ruler in England. He was also to be duke of Normandy. Richard was to have Aquitaine and neighboring lands in southern France. Geoffrey was to hold Brittany. Because there was nothing left for the youngest son, he was sometimes called John Lackland. In fact Henry II hoped that John would assume the rule of Ireland. The old king intended to set up a sort of federated monarchy in which he would retain overall authority while passing direct regional rule on to his descendants.

It did not work. Perhaps the scheme itself, so similar to the plot of Shakespeare's *King Lear,* was bound to have a tragic denouement. But much of the trouble must be attributed to Henry's inability to maintain concord within his own family. His relations with his wife had always been strained, for Eleanor of Aquitaine was as hard-headed as Henry and was unwilling to be cast in a passive secondary role. She and Henry were often estranged, and she was seldom in England; in her French castles she presided over sophisticated establishments and provided patronage for courtly poets and musicians.

Henry's sons were equally independent. Knowing what lands they were to inherit, they could not wait for their father's death before attempting to seize power. Their rebellions began in 1173. Henry the Younger died in 1183 of dysentery caught on the battlefield. Three years later Geoffrey was fatally wounded while fighting in a tournament in Paris. In 1188 Richard swore an oath of homage and fealty directly to the king of France. The news that his youngest and favorite son, John, was disloyal was the final blow for Henry II. Already very ill, he died in 1189.

Richard I (1189–1199) and John (1199–1216)

On his father's death Richard assumed rule of all of Henry II's territories. A legendary figure, often known as Richard Coeur de Leon or the Lionheart because of his courage in battle, he had little to do with England. Instead, he was involved in French wars and then in the Third Crusade. Although his allies did not capture Jerusalem, they did secure a treaty allowing pilgrims to visit it. On the way home, traveling through Germany in disguise, Richard was apprehended and held for ransom. The enormous sum of 100,000 marks (two-thirds of the amount demanded) was paid, mainly by his English vassals, and Richard returned to England. Only a few months later he was called to the battlefield in France, where he was mortally wounded in 1199. That the English government ran normally without him is a tribute to the institutions put in place by Henry I and II and to the abilities of Hubert Walter, who was both the king's justiciar and the archbishop of Canterbury.

Richard was succeeded by his only surviving brother, John. King John is a controversial figure, ordinarily regarded as one of the worst kings in British history. He does not deserve the abuse heaped on him by the early chroniclers, for they were churchmen who had their own reasons to deplore his ecclesiastical policies. But John cannot be depicted as an effective ruler; he was exceptionally unlucky and unsuccessful.

John's troubles began in France. Here he had to face an able and ambitious king, Philip Augustus, who was intent on increasing his own royal power as a means of unifying what had been a very divided realm. Naturally Philip resented the fact that the territories held by the king of England were larger than those that he ruled directly. He sought every opportunity to make war on John or seize lands that were ruled by the Angevins.

John played into Philip's hands by marrying a young French woman, Isabella of Angoulême. She had previously been betrothed to one of John's French vassals, Hugh of Lusignan, who was angered by the marriage and appealed to the French king against John. Philip summoned John to appear at the French royal court to answer the charges; John refused to go; Philip then declared that John had violated his feudal contract and forfeited his lands. In the war that ensued, John was opposed by a number of his own vassals, who wished to replace him with his nephew Arthur, the son of John's brother Geoffrey. When John had Arthur murdered he became even less popular. He lost territory after territory. By 1205, when the fighting ended, he retained only Gascony and part of Poitou, remote lands in southern France near the Spanish border. The bulk of his great Angevin inheritance had slipped away.

Troubles in France were followed immediately by a bitter conflict within the English church. When Hubert Walter died the monks of Canterbury Cathedral proceeded to elect one of their own number as archbishop of Canterbury, ignoring the usual procedure of confirming a royal nominee. John was enraged at this attempt to deprive him of his traditional rights. He forced the clergy to accept his candidate, and the two rivals set off for Rome, each hoping to obtain the pope's blessing. Innocent III, one of the most aggressive popes of the Middle Ages, was shocked at this display of discord and took matters into his own hands, naming Stephen Langton as archbishop. Langton was well qualified, for he was an Englishman who had lived in Rome for some years and had been created a cardinal; he was a learned man and an able administrator. But John was unwilling to accept him or even to allow him to enter England. The pope used spiritual weapons against the king, first placing England under an interdict (so that the services of the church were suspended), then excommunicating John. He might have gone still further and called on faithful Christians to depose the king. Faced with this threat, and realizing (quite shrewdly) that he needed the support of the church for an impending struggle with his feudal magnates, John finally agreed to accept Langton. Indeed, he did more: he accepted the principle, rejected by William the Conqueror, that England was a fief held from the pope. In recognition of this subservience he agreed to pay Rome an annual tribute of 1,000 marks (about £667), but he gained the blessing of the papacy in his subsequent conflicts. Langton himself remained the king's enemy, however; he was a leader in organizing opposition to John.

The Barons and Magna Carta

J ohn's later troubles involved the barons. The term *barons* refers to the great men of the feudal system, both tenants-in-chief and those who held large fiefs in other ways. (As a result of subinfeudation the feudal system had by now become so complex that feudal magnates often held land from several different lords, and it was possible for a mesne vassal to accumulate larger properties than those held by some tenants-in-chief.) The barons scorned John because of his military failures, and they felt aggrieved because he had demanded and then wasted large sums of money, levied both as scutage and as a new tax on movable goods. They turned against him even more when his attempt to recapture some of his French territories ended in a disastrous defeat at the Battle of Bouvines (1214).

Early in 1215 the barons met secretly and decided to demand that John affirm a document based on the Coronation Charter of Henry I. Because this would have tied him to an earlier form of feudalism that did not include scutage, John felt that he could not comply; he asked for time to consider the matter. While he was doing so the barons gathered again and drew up a new document setting out their demands more fully. This has come to be known as the Great Charter or Magna Carta.

Under considerable pressure John agreed to meet the barons on June 15, 1215, at Runnymede, a watery meadow near Windsor Castle. Here he reluctantly agreed to accept the document.

Magna Carta is literally a great charter, for it is a long document, divided by modern editors into some sixty articles. Viewed in the light of thirteenth-century conditions, the actual provisions of Magna Carta are not especially important or progressive; it can be argued that the barons were conservatives who wished to turn the clock back to an earlier period of feudalism. It is also true that many of the clauses apply only to freemen, who were still a privileged group in society, of higher status than serfs, and thus the clauses do not guarantee the rights of all people.

Articles in the Charter call on the king to abandon the use of foreign mercenaries; they say, vaguely, that the church should be independent; they demand an end to extortionate feudal aids, like Richard's ransom; and they propose a system of uniform weights and measures. (It is said that the length of a yard was determined by measuring the distance from the end of the king's outstretched arm to the tip of his nose.) The most vital clause states that no scutage or other irregular payment should be levied without the consent of the Great Council. This contains the germ of the idea that was later expanded into the doctrine "no taxation without representation." A provision that no freeman could be imprisoned or dispossessed except by the lawful judgment of his peers or the law of the land foreshadows the American legal doctrine of due process. An impartial judicial system is also suggested by the famous statement "To no one will we sell, to no one will we refuse or delay right or justice."

The long-range implications of the Charter are thus more momentous than its actual meaning in its own time. Seen as a stage in the development of limited monarchy in England, Magna Carta possesses a significance that transcends the circumstances of its composition. Several copies of the document were signed at the same time and have equal authenticity; one, belonging to Lincoln Cathedral, was exhibited in the United States at the time of the American Bicentennial.

King John died in 1216, soon after accepting the Charter. Had he lived he would doubtless have repudiated it, arguing that he had signed it under duress. A contemporary account attributes his death to overindulgence in cider and unripe peaches. His nine-year-old son, Henry, succeeded to the throne.

Henry III (1216–1272)

Although his reign lasted for more than half a century, Henry III made few contributions to English government and society. He was well educated, cultured, and affectionate to his friends, but as a ruler he proved naive and ineffectual.

It was inevitable that other men would manage affairs during his minority. An old, experienced official, William Marshall, held the government together for a few years before retiring. Other influential figures were Pandulph, the papal legate; Hubert de Burgh, the justiciar; and Peter des Roches, the king's guardian and tutor. None of them had been born in England, and none was popular with the barons. Peter's penchant for giving office to his friends from southern France was particularly offensive.

In 1234 Henry undertook to rule personally, but without much success. He married Eleanor of Provence, whose French relatives thronged to the English court. He was extravagant, and his demands for money alienated members of the Great Council. His attempt to secure the throne of Sicily, the island in the Mediterranean, for his second son, Edmund, was particularly ill-advised: vast amounts of money were spent on a hopeless military campaign, which collapsed in 1257.

Angered by taxation and mismanagement, the barons resumed the activities they had begun under King John. They now found an extraordinary leader in the person of Simon de Montfort, a Norman knight who was Henry III's brother-in-law but had come to oppose his policies. In 1258 the barons forced the king to accept the Provisions of Oxford, in which he relinquished control of the government to a group of fifteen baronial magnates. Three years later he repudiated the document. The barons then made war on Henry, who had to give them power once again according to a new settlement called the Mise of Lewes (1264). The king was little more than a ceremonial figurehead during these periods of baronial rule.

Simon de Montfort's Parliament

In 1265 Simon de Montfort summoned a Parliament to discuss matters of concern to the barons and some other prominent men of the realm. The event has taken on special significance because Parliament was soon to develop as a permanent institution, eventually becoming the legislative body in the English constitution. In fact, some gatherings earlier than 1265 had been called Parliaments—the term is derived from the French verb parler, which means to talk, and Parliaments were essentially meetings at which prominent men talked about significant issues and problems. These Parliaments seem to have been attended only by members of the Great Council. Simon de Montfort's assembly was unusual because it included burgesses sent by some of the towns favorable to his cause, as well as the usual barons, knights, and churchmen. Although none of these men were actually elected, the Parliament of 1265 can be thought of as containing elements representing the politically active members of English society.

It would be interesting to know whether Simon could have maintained control of the barons and whether he would have made Parliament a regular part of the governmental system. As it was he had no opportunity to do so; he was killed in battle during the summer of 1265.

After Simon's death, Henry III was able to reassert his own right to rule, but he was in ill health and allowed his son Edward an increasing share of power. His chief interest turned to religion. He was primarily responsible for the rebuilding of Westminster Abbey in its present form, using the finest French architectural style of what was perhaps the finest century for church building.

Edward I (1272–1307)

D uring the Middle Ages the English royal family seemed to illustrate the biological principle of alternation of generations rather than normal heredity of shared characteristics. Several able kings sired children who proved much less effective, and they in turn sometimes produced exceptionally competent offspring. Such a phenomenon now manifested itself: the ineffectual Henry III was succeeded by an unusually creative and energetic ruler, who was himself followed by a disastrously inept son.

Edward I had grown up witnessing the attempts of the barons to strip the king of his power, and he had resolved never to permit such affronts to the monarchy once he himself was the ruler. He set out to strengthen the power of the central government in several ways and simultaneously to weaken the feudal magnates.

The Development of Parliament

B orrowing Simon de Montfort's innovation, Edward I held frequent Parliaments that generally included representatives of county and civic society. Parliament developed gradually rather than being created at any single time, but during the later thirteenth century it became a regular part of the English constitution. Edward I, more than any other king, can be credited with establishing its place.

As we have seen, Parliament in its early stages was more or less equivalent to the Great Council and served as a forum for discussion and debate, a point of contact between the king and his most influential subjects. It is interesting to note that the meeting at which Magna Carta was accepted was sometimes called a Parliament. Parliament was always a political body. In its formative period Parliament was also important as a court; indeed some historians regard this as its primary role throughout the thirteenth century. Even today the House of Lords is officially known as the High Court of Parliament, and it continues to have judicial functions that in some ways are akin to those of the Supreme Court in the United States.

Parliament's modern role as a legislature, approving taxes and passing statutes, was not so evident in its earliest years. During Edward I's reign, Parliament came to be the body that ratified taxation, under the principle enunciated in Magna Carta that those who would pay or their representatives had to grant consent. Edward's Confirmation of the Charters in 1297 contained a specific statement that extraordinary taxation was to be levied only

Edward I in Parliament. This is a later drawing by an artist of the Tudor period. Alexander, king of Scotland, is shown on Edward's right; Llywelyn, Prince of Wales, is on his left. Both are known to have attended an English Parliament, but not at the same time. Judges (with wigs) sit on the "woolsacks" in the center of the floor. Bishops may be recognized by their mitres (pointed hats), noblemen by the bars of ermine fur on their gowns.
Reproduced by permission of the Royal Library, Windsor Castle, copyright Her Majesty the Queen.

with the consent of the whole realm. Although Parliament was not specifically mentioned, it was the obvious forum for obtaining such approval.

Edward I also began using Parliament to make statutes. During his reign the initiative for these lay with the king, not with the members of Parliament themselves. Edward and his assistants drafted statutes intended to correct conditions that weakened the central government, and Parliament accepted them. The power of Parliament itself to devise and enact laws was not realized until the fourteenth century.

Edward I's Parliaments were attended by feudal magnates, who by this time were holders of titles of nobility (earls or barons), and by high-ranking churchmen (bishops and some abbots, the heads of large monasteries). These men came to receive official writs of summons, issued by the Chancery. Frequently, laymen of less elevated status were also included; Parliaments they attended are sometimes referred to as "full Parliaments." The so-called knights of the shire represented shires or counties (actually being knighted was not a requirement for being chosen), and men known as burgesses came from cities or towns. (The term *borough* refers specifically to towns that were entitled to parliamentary representation.) Full Parliaments were usually attended by two knights from each shire and two burgesses from each borough. We do not know just how these men were selected during the thirteenth century. Each sheriff was responsible for sending the Chancery a list of persons duly chosen within his county, and it is likely that thirteenth-century sheriffs had a good deal of freedom to handle local arrangements and to decide which boroughs were to be represented. This may account for some of the variation from session to session.

The Parliament that Edward I called in November 1295 has often been called the Model Parliament. Edward's motives in summoning this gathering were financial rather than constitutional. Faced with the coincidence of crises in Wales, Scotland, and his French territories, the king badly needed money. He was probably eager to spread the burden of taxation as widely as possible, and thus he sought representation from a variety of groups who might contribute. To this Parliament the king summoned seven earls and forty-one barons, all the bishops and archbishops, seventy heads of religious houses, two knights from each shire, and two representatives from each borough. He also called representatives of the lower clergy. These proctors of the clergy did not find a place in the structure of Parliament as it finally developed, for the rank-and-file clergy came to be represented only in their own gathering, the Convocation of the Clergy, held simultaneously with sessions of Parliament. Thus the Model Parliament did not actually provide the design for Parliament's later structure, nor were the representative elements invariably summoned to the sessions that met after 1295.

In one sense, however, the Parliament of 1295 did become a model. Those chosen to serve in it were told that they should come "with full powers," binding the groups they represented to pay whatever taxes Parliament might agree to. In establishing the doctrine of representation, with its corollary of general obedience to parliamentary enactments, the Model Parliament set a precedent of considerable significance.

By increasing the authority of Parliament as an organ of government representing the interests of a larger group of people, Edward I effectively curbed the barons' opportunities to dominate the country. He showed considerable skill in manipulating Parliament for his own ends; it remained a creature of the king.

Edward I and the Courts

Edward also initiated changes in the court system that were intended to clip the wings of the barons. It was his intention to eliminate many feudal courts and transfer their business to the royal judicial system. Originally Edward intended to force the closure of all feudal courts that could not prove that they had been instituted by royal charter. He used a new writ, called "Quo warranto," to inquire what warrant feudal lords had for holding a court. When the barons objected, quite justly, that feudal courts were based on tradition rather than written documents, Edward backed down, agreeing that those courts that had been in operation in 1189 could continue. (The term *year of legal memory* was used for 1189, to indicate that the law would not concern itself with "remembering" what had happened earlier. It applied to land ownership as well as the right to hold courts.)

Edward made significant efforts to improve the royal courts, so that suitors would prefer to have their cases adjudicated there. The predictable decisions made by juries or by learned judges naturally seemed more desirable than ordeal or the possibly biased orders of feudal lords.

Edward I's Last Years

Late in his reign Edward became involved in a further conflict between church and state. In 1296 Pope Boniface VIII, still intent on maintaining the independence of the church, issued a famous bull called *Clericis laicos*. (A papal bull—*bulla* in Latin—is simply an official pronouncement or proclamation issued by a pope; bulls are identified by quoting the first few words of their Latin text.) In this document Boniface ordered that the clergy pay taxes to the papacy, not to the secular rulers. Edward had no intention of losing the power to tax his subjects, regardless of their status as laymen or clerics. He was finally able to secure a compromise agreement that satisfied the king and the pope (but perhaps not the clergy!). This allowed both church and state to demand payments. To accommodate the idea that

*The Eleanor Cross at Hardingstone,
Northamptonshire. This is the earliest and finest
of the twelve large stone crosses that mark the
places where the coffin of Eleanor, the wife of
Edward I, rested on the way to Westminster
Abbey.*
*Reproduced by permission of the Royal
Commission on the Historical Monuments of
England.*

the church was independent of secular control, however, taxes paid by the clergy were regarded as gifts freely given to the king in times of emergency rather than as levies imposed on them by an outside authority.

Some years before he succeeded to the throne, Edward I had been married to a Spanish princess, Eleanor of Castile. The dynastic marriage strengthened English claims to land in southern France, and it seems to have been a happy union on the personal level as well. Eleanor accompanied Edward on a crusade; a contemporary chronicle says that she saved his life by sucking poison from a wound, but the story is probably untrue. When she died in the

English Midlands in 1290, Edward ordered the erection of twelve large stone crosses, elaborately decorated with pinnacles and statues, to mark the places where her coffin rested on its way to Westminster Abbey. Only three of these "Eleanor Crosses" survive. The earliest and finest remains in the village of Hardingstone, near Northampton. The most famous, Charing Cross in London, had decayed by the seventeenth century and was pulled down in 1647, but a replica was constructed in the nineteenth century and can still be seen in front of Charing Cross railway station. After Eleanor's death Edward married Margaret, the daughter of Philip III, king of France.

Edward II (1307–1327)

Edward I himself died in 1307. His heir was his fourth but oldest surviving son. Edward II had little experience in affairs of state and no real interest in them. A chronicler wrote that he was devoted to choristers, actors, grooms, sailors, and others who worked in similar vocations. Almost certainly homosexual, he was passionately fond of a young Gascon knight named Piers Gaveston and gave him lavish favors, including an English title of nobility. Distressed both by this relationship and by the lack of effective government, the barons once again appeared as an organized opposition, demonstrating that they had not been eliminated as a force to be reckoned with despite Edward I's efforts. Edward II was forced to give most of his power to a group called the Lords Ordainers, who ran England in accordance with the interests of the barons from 1311 to 1322. Gaveston's murder by one of the baronial leaders strained relations still further and brought out a vindictive strain in the king.

Early in his reign Edward had married Isabella, the daughter of the king of France. They did have children, but they never got on well, partly because Edward's new favorites, the Despensers, thought her extravagant. In 1325 Isabella traveled to Paris, ostensibly to renew English fealty to her brother, who had succeeded to the French throne. In fact, Isabella took advantage of the situation to plot the overthrow of her husband; she joined forces with an English nobleman, Roger Mortimer, who had become her lover and who hoped to dominate the government if Edward II could be forced to renounce the throne in favor of his teenage son. Edward had few friends and little choice. In 1327 his abdication was confirmed in Parliament and he was sent to imprisonment in Berkeley Castle, where he was murdered with a red-hot poker.

Wales and Ireland in the
Thirteenth Century

The thirteenth century was a crucial time in the history of Wales, Ireland, and Scotland.

As we have seen, Henry II secured recognition as overlord of Wales, but Celtic leaders remained powerful, especially in the North. Here Llywelyn ap Iorwerth (1195–1240), called Llywelyn the Great, developed a powerful position. He married King John's illegitimate daughter Joan and was recognized by the English monarch as the Prince of Wales. Llywelyn's son David also held the title "Prince of Wales," but David died suddenly, without heirs, and a period of confusion ensued.

Eventually Llywelyn ap Gruffydd, the grandson of Llywelyn the Great, succeeded in re-creating his grandfather's principality. In 1258 he too assumed the title "Prince of Wales." Most of the Welsh chieftains recognized him as their lord, and the Scots entered into an alliance with him. The weakness of the English government under Henry III allowed Llywelyn to consolidate his position. Edward I, however, had no intention of letting Wales slip from his grasp. He found various legal excuses for failing to render a decision regarding Llywelyn's right to the territory of Arwystli, in the central Welsh mountains, which Llywelyn claimed was his according to Welsh law. In 1282 this and other grievances felt by the Welsh precipitated a general revolt, led by Llywelyn and his brother Dafydd. Edward I then invaded Wales. Most of Llywelyn's territories were seized, and he was slain in battle in 1282. He is sometimes called Llywelyn the Last.

After a triumphal progress through Wales, Edward ensured permanent military control by erecting a series of well-fortified castles, including those at Caernarfon, Conwy, Beaumaris, and Harlech. Another great castle, Caerphilly, was built by Gilbert of Clare, one of Edward's followers. All of these remain as architectural masterpieces, embodying the latest ideas of medieval castle building. In 1284 Edward issued the detailed Statute of Wales, which provided the system under which Wales was governed until Tudor times. He did not completely oust Welsh customs, but he decreed that English law would prevail in all felony cases. He encouraged English colonization in Wales, and a number of new "plantation boroughs" were established, especially in the North. Edward then named his own oldest son Prince of Wales, ending the succession of native Welsh princes and establishing a tradition in the British royal family that survives today. Edward's conquest, coupled with heavy taxation, left a legacy of despair and bitterness among the Welsh. In

Caernarfon Castle, Wales. Edward I maintained military control in Wales by building a series of well-fortified castles, including the one at Caernarfon. National Monuments Record for Wales Collection, Royal Commission on Ancient and Historical Monuments in Wales.

Caerphilly Castle, Wales. National Monuments Record for Wales Collection, Royal Commission on Ancient and Historical Monuments in Wales.

1294 they attempted to revolt again but could not sustain a campaign against the English army.

In Ireland, the earlier conquest by Henry II continued to have repercussions throughout the thirteenth century. Henry had designated his favorite son, John, as lord of Ireland when the insolent lad was only seventeen. John invaded, built a few castles, granted away quantities of Irish land to his followers, and confirmed the holdings of some native leaders. After he succeeded to the throne, the lordship of Ireland was merged into the English monarchy; successive kings of England claimed both titles. As king, John ordered the building of Dublin Castle and attempted to extend English laws to Ireland. He also appointed Anglo-Norman bishops in an attempt to bring the Irish church into closer conformity with English and Roman practice.

Like England, Ireland witnessed a struggle between the monarch and the feudal barons during the reign of Henry III. Neither side gained decisive control. Native chieftains were unable to unite but remained powerful in several parts of the island. The Normans too were guided by their own ambitions rather than by a desire to support the English king. Edward I made persistent efforts to correct the chaotic situation by restructuring the Irish government according to the English model. He began holding Parliaments attended by Irish barons and sometimes also by representative elements. Because he could not stay in Ireland himself, he appointed resident deputies or viceroys, generally Englishmen, who were to rule on his behalf.

Edward II was too incompetent to continue his father's shrewd policies. When the Scots perceived that there was a power vacuum in Ireland, they tried their hand at invasion. This was the age of greatness for members of the Bruce clan. In 1314 Robert Bruce, the ruler of Scotland, annihilated an English army in the Battle of Bannockburn, and in 1315 his brother, Edward, invaded northern Ireland with a force of six thousand armed men, the largest army to set foot on Irish soil. Edward Bruce soon made himself master of the North. The Scots might have held Ulster indefinitely had he not died prematurely in 1318. With his death the dream of a Scottish monarchy in Ireland ended, but English rule was not securely reestablished at the time of Edward II's deposition.

Scotland

Unlike Wales and Ireland, Scotland succeeded in maintaining its independence during the age of baronial quarrels. Before he left for his crusade, and in exchange for a large sum of money, Richard the

Lionheart agreed to cancel the compact in which King William of Scotland had sworn homage to Henry II of England. The Scots also contributed to Richard's ransom. During John's reign there was some fighting in the border-lands, and Alexander II, the king of Scotland, gave some support to the revolt of the English barons. A dynastic marriage between Alexander and John's daughter Joanna (the sister of Henry III) helped produce a recon-ciliation between the two realms, and a treaty signed at York in 1237 fixed the border at the present Tweed-Solway line. There remained areas where the exact boundary line was debatable, however, and special wardens of the northern marches administered the borderland, settling complaints of raiding and cattle theft. Friendly relations continued under Alexander III (1249–1286), who was married to Margaret, the daughter of England's Henry III.

The children of Alexander III—two sons and a daughter—died before he did, so when the king accidentally lost his life while traveling to Edinburgh in 1286, the Scottish throne passed to his granddaughter Margaret. She was called "the Maid of Norway" because her mother (Alexander's daughter) had married the Norwegian king, Eric II. Although the Maid was only three years old, arrangements were made for her to sail from Norway to Scotland, but she died tragically during the voyage, perhaps of extreme seasickness.

After her death the succession to the Scottish throne was disputed, with members of the Bruce and Balliol families being the chief contenders. Edward I of England took advantage of the situation to assert his own claims, and in 1291 both Bruce and Balliol signed documents acknowledging that Edward was sovereign lord of Scotland. In 1292 John Balliol was declared to be the rightful king of the Scots, though a vassal to the king of England. He was crowned in Scotland and came to the border to do homage to Edward I.

Preparing for a military campaign in France during 1294, Edward de-manded the help of fighting men from Scotland. Balliol refused to cooperate and went so far as to enter into an alliance with the French king. Enraged, Edward marched into Scotland with a large force. He massacred many inhab-itants of Berwick, a border town, and defeated the Scottish army decisively at Dunbar. Over two thousand Scots were forced to acknowledge his feudal overlordship. On his return to England he took with him the Stone of Scone, a piece of rock on which Scottish kings traditionally sat during their corona-tion. This was incorporated into the English throne, as a symbol that the kings of England were also lords of Scotland, and it has remained part of the coronation chair at Westminster Abbey except for a short period in the 1950s when it was seized by Scottish nationalists. Because of his stern policies, Edward I came to be called "the Hammer of the Scots."

The English coronation chair, Westminster Abbey. The Stone of Scone—a piece of rock on which Scottish kings traditionally sat during their coronation—may be seen in the shelf below the seat. Edward I added the Stone as s symbol that kings of England were also lords of Scotland.
Reproduced by permission of the Royal Commission on the Historical Monuments of England.

Once Edward was off in France, the unhappy Scots reasserted their power. For some months William Wallace, a follower of Balliol, was virtual ruler of the country. But in 1298 Edward returned to England and then to Scotland, where he defeated Wallace disastrously. It was the end of Wallace's short but (in the eyes of the Scots) glorious career of resistance to English domination. Edward again tried to dominate Scottish affairs, but he was now too ill to succeed. The feeble old man died while beginning still another campaign against the Scots and their new leader, Robert Bruce. Edward's aggressive policies had not won Scotland but did create antagonisms that were to last for centuries.

rd II was no more successful in Scotland than he was at home. ᴴing his father's military campaign, he left Scotland briefly in the Robert Bruce, who had gained the support of almost all the native ᴸₐᵤₑrs. A forlorn Scottish tour mounted by the English in 1310 achieved nothing. Four years later, after coming to terms with the Lords Ordainers, Edward II marched into Scotland again, this time at the head of an enormous army numbering more than twenty thousand. Against all the odds, a much smaller Scottish force humiliated the English in what was to prove the greatest Scottish victory of the Middle Ages, the famous Battle of Bannockburn (June 24, 1314). Edward II was fortunate enough to escape from the battlefield, but many of his followers were killed, and others were captured and held for ransom. In this battle Scottish independence was reaffirmed, as was the Bruce clan's title to the throne. In 1328, weakened by the murder of Edward II and the minority of Edward III, the English abandoned all claims to jurisdiction in Scotland.

The Crisis of English Feudalism

The feudal system underlay many of the chief political events in all the territories of the British Isles during the period from 1066 to 1327. Initially useful to William I as a means of establishing secure control of England and to Henry II as a framework for asserting his overlordship of Wales, Ireland, and Scotland, the system began to unravel with the introduction of scutage and came apart during the weak reigns of John, Henry III, and Edward II. At such times the barons, sometimes referred to as "overmighty subjects," threatened to become more powerful than the king. Feudal arrangements, useful as they had been to the Norman conquerors, could be a curse if the monarch was unable to control his vassals.

Fortunately for the English monarchy, Edward III inherited the mentality of Edward I rather than that of Edward II. He understood the need to strengthen the authority of the central government and to unify his territories under his own personal leadership. During his reign the barons were again kept in their place by the king, and feudal institutions were molded by the monarchy into constitutional organs of government.

Suggested Reading

Butt, Ronald, *A History of Parliament: The Middle Ages* (London: Constable, 1989).

Curtis, Edmund, *A History of Ireland* (London: Methuen, 1936).

Gillingham, John, *Richard the Lionheart* (London: Weidenfeld & Nicolson, 1978).

Holt, J. C., *Magna Carta* (Cambridge: Cambridge University Press, 1965).

Otway-Ruthven, A. J., *A History of Medieval Ireland* (New York: Barnes & Noble, 1968).

Pounds, N. J. G., *The Medieval Castle in England and Wales* (Cambridge: Cambridge University Press, 1990).

Powicke, Sir Maurice, *The Thirteenth Century, 1216–1307* (Oxford: Clarendon Press, 1962).

Prestwich, Michael, *Edward I* (Berkeley and Los Angeles: University of California Press, 1988).

Sayles, G. O., *The King's Parliament of England* (New York: Norton, 1974).

Stones, E.L.G., *Edward I and the Throne of Scotland* (Oxford: Oxford University Press, 1978).

Vaughan-Thomas, Wynford, *Wales: A History* (London: Michael Joseph, 1985).

Warren, W. L., *King John* (New York: Norton, 1961).

CHAPTER FIVE

The Later Middle Ages, 1327–1485

Edward III (1327–1377) and the Hundred Years' War

Following his father's deposition in 1327, the fifteen-year-old Edward III succeeded to the throne. He was to rule England for half a century. For a few years Edward's mother, Isabella, and her lover, Roger Mortimer, were able to dominate the young king while they shaped the policies of the government. They hoped he would be a puppet ruler, willing to dance as they pulled the strings. Because Roger himself held land in both Wales and Ireland, he and Isabella were generally accepted there. They were responsible for England's abandonment of any claim to Scotland in 1328—many of the English regarded this as shameful—and for Edward's marriage to Philippa of Hainault in the same year. But Edward had been sickened at the way in which Isabella and Roger had treated his father. In 1330 he asserted his own right to rule; he placed his mother in honorable confinement and ordered Roger's execution.

Soon after assuming power, Edward III propelled England into what came to be called the Hundred Years' War with France (1337–1453). He had

Effigy of Edward III, Westminster Abbey.
Reproduced by permission of the Royal Commission
on the Historical Monuments of England.

several goals: he wished to assert his claim to the French throne, based on his mother's descent from the French royal family; he thought that English monarchs were under an obligation to regain control of the former Angevin empire; he was determined to maintain his authority in Aquitaine, where Philip IV was trying to advance his royal jurisdiction; he disliked the notion that the king of England could be a vassal of the king of France; he was concerned about rivalry between England and France in the lucrative wool trade with the Netherlands; he may have believed that the fastest road to fame was recognition as a chivalrous military hero. Perhaps most important, he knew how imperative it was for him to unify England under his sole leadership. The deposition of Edward II had left a legacy of bitter political and personal division among the barons. Very shrewdly, Edward III calculated that war against a common enemy could be an ideal way of ending these disputes. In Shakespeare's phrase, he wished "to busy giddy minds with foreign quarrels."

His initial campaigns were amazingly successful. He assumed personal control of the English forces and proved himself to be an excellent tactician and a charismatic leader. Luck seemed to be on his side as well. In 1340 the English navy achieved an important victory over the French fleet off the coast of Sluys, in northern France—it was essential for England to control the sea if men and matériel were to move unimpeded across the Channel. The Battle of Crécy (1346) gave instant glory to the English cause, as the English archers, armed with longbows, decisively defeated the French soldiers, who had adopted the more advanced but more cumbersome crossbow. French casualties were heavy and included the cream of chivalric society, whereas Edward claimed that the English lost only forty men and that they did not die fighting but rather while they were picking the pockets of the Frenchmen who lay dead on the battlefield. At Crécy and associated smaller engagements Edward gained control of much of northern France.

The major French port city of Calais fell to the English after a long siege in 1347. It was destined to remain in English hands for more than two centuries, longer than any other French territory. In 1356 English forces commanded by Edward III's oldest son, the Black Prince, gained control of much of southern France in the battle of Poitiers, a great engagement reminiscent of Crécy. John II, the king of France, was taken prisoner at Poitiers; the English were able to demand £500,000 for his ransom. In 1359 Edward III himself led a bold siege of Rheims, the traditional site of French coronations.

By 1360 the desperate French were driven to negotiate the humiliating Treaty of Brétigny. In this settlement Edward III obtained not only Calais but also a consolidated territory in southern France. The French now acknowledged that Aquitaine, Poitou, and Gascony were independent lands ruled by Edward III, not fiefs held from the French king. In exchange the English abandoned their claim to the French throne. The settlement was a dramatic sign of Edward's success, although it brought only a temporary truce in the fighting.

The Black Death

During the 1340s both England and France were struck by the most dreadful epidemic of the Middle Ages, the Black Death. Taking its name from the dark blotches that appeared on its victims, the Black Death is now known to have been the bubonic plague, most likely spread by fleas and rats. Contemporaries were not aware of the source of contagion, and without modern sanitation there was little that they could have done to contain the disease in any case.

France was hit first. Londoners first felt the plague in 1348. Then, according to a contemporary chronicler, "It attacked the whole of England so violently that scarcely one in ten of either sex was left alive. As the graveyards did not suffice, fields were chosen for the burial of the dead. . . . It was the young and strong the plague chiefly attacked; . . . it cleared many country villages entirely of every human being." Wales, Ireland, and Scotland were also affected, but by 1350 this first visitation had largely run its course. The epidemic returned between 1360 and 1362 and again in 1369 and 1375.

The death rate was very high everywhere, although it was not so disastrous as contemporary writings suggest. Exact figures will never be obtained, but most historians think that at least a quarter of the population of the British Isles succumbed, and some would put the death toll as high as half. Forty percent is perhaps a good guess. Mortality probably never exceeded 10 or 12 percent in any single year. It varied greatly from place to place. For some reason certain trades, among them textile workers and bakers, seem to have suffered more than others.

The Black Death had significant effects in the areas of morality, religion, and economics. Realizing the uncertainty of life, some people abandoned all moral scruples, believing that they should "sing, dance, and be merry, for tomorrow we die." Others were driven to fanatical extremes of piety and asceticism, fasting and performing other penances in the hope of being spared or gaining salvation if they were not. The probability of death was higher among the clergy than among laymen, since the priests were expected to visit the sick and bury the dead. Those who lived in monasteries, too, were exposed to contagion, since the monks ran the only hospitals of the Middle Ages. It is often argued that young men who had no real vocation for a religious life were forced into the church so that its essential services could still be performed. However this may be, it does appear that the English church generally and English monasteries more specifically became less spiritual and more worldly in the later years of the fourteenth century.

In terms of economic and social conditions the result of the Black Death was to reduce the number of laborers available to till the soil and perform other basic functions. Because there was still the same amount of land to be cultivated by a diminished number of workers, the laborers were able to demand better working conditions, including the abolition of serfdom or villeinage. It is probable that the gradual introduction of a money economy would soon have eroded the basis of manorialism, as labor services were commuted into money payments for labor and for rent of land, but the Black

Death may have hastened the process. Landowners tried to block change by having Parliament pass the Statute of Laborers in 1351. This act attempted to freeze wages, prices, and working conditions, but it proved impossible to enforce.

Scotland and Edward III

Despite the treaty of 1328 in which England abandoned its claim to overlordship in Scotland, the fourteenth century proved a troubled time for the Scots. The Scottish monarchy was particularly weak during the years of Edward III's reign in England. In 1331 David II, the five-year-old son of the Scottish hero Robert Bruce, was crowned king at Scone. His minority, as was so often the case, was marred by dissension and violence, culminating in the coronation of Edward Balliol as a rival king. Edward III supported Balliol and persuaded him to hold a Parliament in which the Scots acknowledged the king of England as paramount lord of Scotland. Balliol also gave England the border town of Berwick and transferred several counties in southern Scotland to English rule. In so doing he unwittingly committed Scotland to a hundred years of warfare, in which the Scots struggled to regain their lost territories.

Balliol became so unpopular that he could not remain in Scotland; he spent some time in northern England, then went to the Continent to advance a claim to the French throne. During this time the Hundred Years' War began, and David II, who had regained the Scottish throne, decided to take advantage of English preoccupation with the campaign in France. Eager to display his military might, the twenty-two-year-old monarch undertook a new building program at Edinburgh Castle, a great fortification that was already centuries old. In 1346 he led a Scottish force into northern England, penetrating as far south as Durham. But some English lords who had not accompanied Edward III to France were able to gather an army that defeated the Scots decisively in the Battle of Neville's Cross. David II was taken prisoner. He was not released until 1357, and when he was freed the English demanded a large ransom, to be paid in annual installments over the next ten years.

Finding it impossible to deal with the financial burden these payments imposed, David II went to London in 1363 and offered to name Edward III and his descendants as heirs to the Scottish throne if the debt was cancelled. Because he had no children, the arrangement did not distress him personally. The Scottish Parliament refused to accept this capitulation, however, and

Edinburgh Castle. An earlier fortification on Castle Rock in Edinburgh was rebuilt beginning in the reign of David II, about 1361. Some of the buildings seen here are of later date.
Reproduced by permission of the Royal Commission on the Ancient and Historical Monuments of Scotland.

arrangements were made for further payments to England that continued until the death of Edward III.

David II died in 1371. All in all his reign had been a disaster. Scottish historians find it difficult to say anything good about him, either personally or as a national leader. The only positive feature of these years was the rise of Parliament in Scotland as a regular part of the governmental structure.

Edward III and Ireland

Because the kings of England were already recognized as lords of Ireland, the situation there was different. An English colony survived in Ireland during the later Middle Ages, attempting to operate as a smaller mirror image of England itself. But the Anglo-Norman settlers always found themselves under pressure from the Celtic natives, and their situation seems to have deteriorated in the fourteenth century.

Edward III made preparations for a personal expedition to Ireland at the beginning of his reign but canceled his plans after the outbreak of the war with France. He later sent his son Lionel, duke of Clarence, to Ireland as chief governor. Lionel was largely responsible for the important Statutes of Kilkenny, passed by the Irish Parliament in 1366. They attempted to codify and regulate the government of Ireland and began by acknowledging that there were two groups of people in the island—the English and their natural enemies, the "wild" Irish. These ethnic groups were ordered to live separately, follow separate legal systems, and even worship separately. Irishmen were not to minister in churches that served the English population. The Statutes went so far as to express concern about "degeneracy" on the part of the colonists, who were commanded not to adopt the language, dress, customs, or laws of the natives. Through this settlement, the English government hoped to ensure the loyalty of the colonists and a sort of peaceful coexistence with the natives, but it was not always able to achieve even these limited goals.

Richard II and the Revolution of 1399

In England, the end of Edward III's reign proved considerably less successful than its beginning. After the death of his wife in 1369, the king came more and more under the influence of his mistress, Alice Perrers, and her disreputable relatives; he withdrew to Windsor Castle and after suffering a series of strokes became senile some time before his death in 1377. Despite the weakness displayed during his last years, Edward III should be remembered as a great king, a brilliant soldier, and a great leader of men, renowned for his bravery and chivalry. He was the founder of the famous honorary Order of the Garter. It is easy to criticize him for spending so much money and sacrificing the lives of so many men for the sake of personal ambition and national prestige, but we may be judging according to twentieth-century attitudes when we do so.

During the last year of Edward's life it became obvious that succession to the throne would be problematic. It was one of the duties of rulers to beget sons who could follow them on the throne, and considering the high mortality rates among medieval infants and adolescents, a wise king would not rest content with one or two male offspring. Edward III and Philippa, however, had such a large progeny that their offspring eventually formed rival branches of the royal family, fighting among themselves for more than a hundred years. Five of their twelve children were daughters, and two of their sons died in infancy, but five sons survived to maturity and played prominent roles in politics.

Throughout most of Edward III's reign, his heir apparent was his oldest son, Edward the Black Prince, who was widely respected for his military successes in the Hundred Years' War. But the Black Prince died in 1376. Although two younger brothers of the Black Prince—the dukes of Lancaster and York—were still alive when Edward III died in 1377, the rules of primogeniture prevented them from succeeding to the throne. Instead the crown passed to Richard II, the ten-year-old son of the Black Prince, who had the hereditary right as the eldest son of Edward III's eldest son.

Richard II was an intelligent, sensitive king whose reign was marred by his extravagance, love of personal luxury, and inability to hold together the disparate elements of noble factions and ordinary people. The characterization of Richard in Shakespeare's famous play is basically accurate, although not all of Shakespeare's details are derived from known fact.

During Richard's minority the government rested in the hands of Parliament and came increasingly under the control of his uncle, John of Gaunt, the duke of Lancaster. The second phase of the Hundred Years' War, a sequence of minor engagements fought between 1369 and 1396, continued during this period, with little success but at considerable cost. In an attempt to shift some of the expense from the shoulders of the landowning classes, who were the ordinary subjects of taxation, Parliament experimented with a poll tax, a levy of a shilling a head on every person over age fifteen. This hit many people who had never been taxed before, and when a third poll tax was collected some of the poor decided to show their opposition by joining in the Peasants' Rising of 1381.

Resistance was first encountered in Essex, but the later stages of the rebellion centered in Kent. The rebels were inspired by the radical views of a priest named John Ball, whose denunciation of the rich was encapsulated in the couplet, "When Adam delved and Eve span, who was then the gentleman?" (His point was that there were no class distinctions in the Garden of Eden.) Ball had been imprisoned in Canterbury, but the insurgents secured his release, although they accepted Wat Tyler rather than Ball himself as their leader. When men from both Essex and Kent marched on London, the fearful government leaders sent the young king to meet with them. An ugly confrontation could have developed when Wat Tyler was killed in a scuffle with the mayor of London; it was headed off by the quick-witted teenaged king, who jumped on horseback, proclaimed himself the new leader of the common

*Tomb and effigy of Edward the Black Prince, Canterbury
Cathedral.*
*Reproduced by permission of the Royal Commission on the
Historical Monuments of England.*

people, and promised that their demands would be given serious consideration. The rebels then dispersed, having caused no serious damage to London
itself. Their radical proposals were soon forgotten by those in authority but
have remained of considerable interest to historians, some of whom regard
them as the earliest significant expression of class animosity in England.

Richard's precocious ability to deal with the Peasants' Rising suggested
that he would be a successful king when he reached maturity. Such a predic-
tion, however, proved false. For a time he did preside over a brilliant court,
assisted by a wife to whom he was deeply devoted, Anne of Bohemia, and he
succeeded temporarily in implementing a policy of peace abroad. He was also
responsible for rebuilding Westminster Hall, where the chief courts of law

*Effigy of Richard II, Westminster Abbey.
Reproduced by permission of the Royal
Commission on the Historical Monuments of
England.*

met until the nineteenth century. But he was always a willful ruler. He quarreled bitterly with Parliament. He allowed noble factions to arise, then ordered or countenanced the execution or banishment of prominent noblemen. One of the magnates he exiled was the future King Henry IV, son of John of Gaunt, the duke of Lancaster.

Factional problems came to a head in 1387, when a group of noblemen calling themselves the Lords Appellant brought treason charges against some of the king's friends. Richard referred the matter to a Parliament, the "Merciless Parliament" of 1388. Despite the king's efforts to save them, two earls and an archbishop who had supported the king were condemned to death, a monumental injustice perpetrated by one of the most discreditable assemblies in English history. Nine years later Richard retaliated by using Parliament as a forum for bringing charges against his enemies, several of whom were executed or exiled.

It sometimes appeared that Richard was more concerned with Ireland than with England. He was distressed that real control of Ireland still eluded the English, and he resolved to recover the authority he believed was his. In 1394 he sailed to Ireland with a large army—the expensive expedition was financed by taxes granted by the English Parliament, a further grievance as far as the king's opponents were concerned—and he called on the native

Westminster Hall. The original building, erected by William Rufus about 1097, was rebuilt by Richard II after 1394. The oak hammer-beam roof rises to a height of 92 feet and has a span of remarkable width, not supported by columns.
Reproduced by permission of the Royal Commission on the Historical Monuments of England.

leaders to do homage to him as their ruler. He attempted to clarify the racial divisions by turning the area in eastern Ireland, surrounding Dublin, into an English "pale" where all land would be held by English settlers of reliable loyalty. He left Roger Mortimer behind as his lieutenant and returned to England, but when Mortimer was slain in 1398 Richard found it necessary to go back himself, seek vengeance, and reassert his power. He was again successful, but his absence from England at a critical moment played into the hands of his enemies.

While Richard II was in Ireland, Henry, duke of Lancaster, returned from exile. His father, John of Gaunt, had just died. Henry was infuriated by Richard's confiscation of his Lancastrian estates. He was determined to unseat the unpopular king, and he quickly gained the support of many influential Englishmen. When Richard returned to England he found the government already in Henry's hands. Richard had no alternative but to abdicate. Parliament listed the deeds that justified his deposition: he had broken his coronation oath, misused Parliament, set aside the laws, terrorized the judges, and given possessions of the Crown to unworthy persons. Richard was promised his life if he stepped down but was imprisoned at Pontefract Castle in Yorkshire, where he died, probably violently, in February 1400.

The Revolution of 1399, as these events came to be called, marked the end of the Angevin or Plantagenet period in English history. Although the new king, like Richard II, was a grandson of Edward III, he is always referred to as a member of the Lancastrian branch of the royal family. The Lancastrians ruled England from 1399 to 1461, but members of the Yorkist line, descended from the third and sixth sons of Edward III, were eventually to contest the kingship and gain the throne. The years between 1399 and 1485 are thus called the period of Lancaster and York.

Parliament in the Fourteenth Century

The long reign of Edward III witnessed significant developments in the history of Parliament. His half-century on the throne may be regarded as Parliament's chief formative period. In the main it was an age notable for remarkable harmony between the king and the parliamentarians.

The most significant development was the establishment of Parliament's right of initiative in making statutes. This became possible because Edward III did not control Parliament as tightly as Edward I had. Edward I had proposed laws that Parliament accepted or ratified; by the time of Edward III, Parliament presented acts passed by its two houses for assent by the monarch. Parliament thus gained greater political independence and fuller control of its own proceedings.

In this evolution, parliamentary petitions served as forerunners of statutes. Early in the fourteenth century, Parliament framed a number of petitions asking for changes in law or government. These were sent to the king; if he accepted them, they came to have almost the same force as statutory law.

The movement from petitions to statutes came gradually, but by the end of the century something approaching the present procedure was in place.

Contemporary interest in the development of parliamentary procedure is evinced by the famous treatise *Modus Tenendi Parliamentum* ("the manner of holding Parliament"), composed about 1320. The *Modus* describes Parliament as being divided into two houses, the Lords and the Commons, but this separation may have been less certain than the document suggests. If the *Modus* can be trusted, the Commons were growing in importance, perhaps because they were used by the kings as a counterbalance against the weight of the barons. The treatise also contains valuable evidence that the knights of the shire and the burgesses were thought of as repesenting the whole community of the realm, whereas the lords spoke only for themselves "and no one else." An unusual feature of fourteenth-century Parliaments was the frequency of meetings between leaders of the two houses, to coordinate activities and sort out differences in drafts of pending legislation. This practice was called "intercommuning."

Sessions of Parliament were summoned almost annually during this period. Indeed, an act passed in 1330 required annual Parliaments, but it was not always observed. Generally meetings were held in Westminster, where parts of the royal palace (mainly the "Painted Chamber") and Westminster Abbey (the chapter house and the refectory) provided adequate space. But Parliament's meeting place was not yet fixed, and some gatherings took place in York, Lincoln, Gloucester, Salisbury, Northampton, Worcester, Winchester, and even such an out-of-the-way spot as Carlisle, almost on the Scottish border.

Burgesses continued to be chosen according to a variety of local arrangements. Most often the mayor and aldermen designated the members, although other rich merchants might be involved. Almost invariably the electorate was small and privileged. Nearly 150 different towns and cities were represented at one time or another in the later Middle Ages, but only about half that number were likely to send burgesses to any single session. Large landowners came to have a voice in the election of the knights of the shire, which was managed in each county by the sheriff.

The most important Parliament of this period was the so-called Good Parliament of 1376. It met while Edward III was in his dotage and earned its name because it effectively represented the concerns of the people. Its members were severely critical of military failures in the Hundred Years' War, high levels of taxation, the inept political leadership of John of Gaunt, and the evident corruption of some government officials. Indeed, two such officers were impeached: the Commons brought charges against them, and the Lords acted as a court, determining their guilt. This procedure, once established, was used occasionally during the later Middle Ages. It fell into abeyance under the Tudors but was revived in the early seventeenth century. The last impeachment in England took place in 1805. The American Congress inherited the legal procedure, and impeachment is still possible in the United States. The House of Representatives actually brought impeachment charges against one American president, Andrew Johnson, although the Senate failed to find him guilty, and there was also serious discussion of impeaching Richard Nixon. A number of American government officials, especially judges, have been removed from office by impeachment.

The Good Parliament is also memorable because it is exceptionally well documented (by the "Anonimalle Chronicle," not its own records) and because in it we have the earliest reference to a Speaker of the Commons (Peter de la Mare).

In a different way the volatile political situation under Richard II also led to growth in Parliament's influence. Both the king and his enemies used Parliament as the agent of their vindictive policies, and when Richard's opponents succeeded in overthrowing him everything was done in the name of Parliament. In 1399 Parliament even designated the heir to the throne, creating a situation that at least in theory was quite different from that following the deposition of Edward II, who was immediately followed by his son.

Parliament in Scotland

The early history of Parliament in Scotland is strikingly similar to that of its English counterpart. During the thirteenth century the Scottish Parliament evolved out of the Great Council. Only high-ranking clergy and noblemen attended the earliest sessions, but by the early fourteenth century lesser landowners and burgesses were occasionally summoned. After 1360 they were always present. Parliament acquired the power to enact statutes, ratify treaties, supervise military and judicial affairs, and grant taxation; it was the supreme court of law, able to hear appeals from lower tribunals. It met irregularly but generally gathered once a year.

In several significant ways, however, the Scottish Parliament differed from the English body. It was not divided into two houses: all three estates—clergy, nobility, and burgesses—continued to meet together. Scottish lairds (the equivalent of the landowning gentry in England) were regarded as belonging with the greater nobles to the second of the three estates.

Representation in Scotland was not limited to two knights from each shire and two burgesses from each enfranchised town. All tenants-in-chief were summoned, on the theory that the entire realm was therefore represented. In practice few of the lesser landowners bothered to attend, and medieval Scottish Parliaments were dominated by relatively small numbers of magnates. Scottish Parliaments never experienced the political conflicts that were common in late medieval England; the Scottish kings were generally able to live within their regular revenue, without demanding special parliamentary grants, and constitutional issues rarely arose.

Henry IV (1399–1413) and Henry V (1413–1422)

Henry IV, the beneficiary of the Revolution of 1399, immediately faced very serious problems in governing England. Even those who had come to dislike Richard II were prone to disapprove of the way in which he had been deposed, for he held the throne by hereditary right and had been crowned king in a religious ceremony that conveyed the blessing of God and the church. During the coronation ceremony, English kings were annointed by the archbishop of Canterbury with holy oil, called chrism, and some political theorists held that this gave them an indelible mark of legitimacy. Shakespeare again produced the words that summarize this position: "Not all the water in the rough, rude sea can wash the balm off from an annointed King," he wrote.

Henry IV's problem, then, was to unify England under his leadership, to convince as many of his subjects as possible that he was indeed the lawful ruler, and to eliminate his most obstinate enemies. His problems were compounded by his lack of money, for he was poorer than his Plantagenet predecessors. He did succeed in gaining the immediate support of Parliament and of the church—indeed, the churchmen produced some specially sacred oil for his coronation, supposedly given by the Virgin Mary herself to Thomas Becket and recently discovered in Normandy.

Troubles in outlying areas were more persistent. Henry's short reign saw the king fighting in northern England, in Wales, in Scotland, and in Gascony, against such prominent opponents as the Percys (Henry Percy, known as "Hotspur," and his son, the earl of Northumberland). Ultimately Henry IV succeeded, and his success proved his legitimacy in the eyes of many of his subjects.

Effigies of Henry IV and his queen, Joan of Navarre, Canterbury Cathedral. Reproduced by permission of the Royal Commission on the Historical Monuments of England.

During the final years of Henry IV's reign, England was at peace but the king himself, perhaps worn out by his earlier efforts, was in declining health. At this time he may have worried less about his opponents and more about the character of his heir, for Prince Hal appeared dissolute and fun-loving. Stories of Prince Hal's youthful escapades in the company of Sir John Falstaff provide some of the most delightful passages in Shakespeare's plays. These tales should be viewed as fictional comedy rather than as genuine history— Falstaff himself was not a historical character, although he may have been based on one—but they do incorporate what seems to have been the contemporary judgment that the heir to the throne was irresponsible.

Accession to the throne appears to have brought new seriousness to Henry V, for he handled his new duties with efficiency and purpose, soon proving

*Henry V, portrait by an unknown artist.
Reproduced by permission of the National
Portrait Gallery.*

himself an exceptional leader. One of his first acts was to reopen the Hundred
Years' War, which had been bogged down in unproductive skirmishes for
years. Henry probably believed, as had Edward III, that England could be
united by focusing attention on a common enemy, and he may have sought
glory and fame as a charismatic commander of England's youthful forces. He
had little regard for the inevitable drain on English resources and loss of
English life in a conflict that was not essential to England's national interests.
His dazzling victory at Agincourt in 1415 certainly established his reputation—the English fought under such disadvantages that a professional strat-
egist would probably have abandoned the field, but Henry V whipped up his
followers to defend their position and ultimately prevailed against all the
odds. His longbowmen brought down the French cavalry, primarily by slaugh-
tering the horses, and his swordsmen then dismembered the armored soldiers
who were lying helplessly on the rain-soaked ground. In 1419 Henry also
captured the important city of Rouen, the chief port in Normandy.

The extent of Henry V's military success was evident in 1420, when the
French king signed the Treaty of Troyes. In this document Charles VI made
amazing concessions: he agreed that Henry should marry Charles's daughter
Katherine, and he recognized Henry as the heir to the French throne, thus

disinheriting his son the dauphin. The marriage did take place, and Katherine soon bore Henry a son. But Henry V did not live to enjoy the dual monarchy that lay within his grasp; he died in 1422, probably of dysentery, while engaged in a minor military campaign.

Wales Under the Lancastrians

W ales proved a special trouble-spot for the earlier Lancastrians. Two-thirds of Wales was organized into about forty Marcher lordships, held by prominent families like the Mortimers. This area was virtually self-governing; only the so-called principality (mainly bordering the coast) was ruled directly by the king and his son, the Prince of Wales. Some of the once-great Welsh families had died out, and many of the Welsh now had ties to the English government, as members of the civil or military establishment. English settlers extracted huge profits from Wales, partly through their operation of the local judicial system. There was no Welsh Parliament, and Welsh representatives appeared only occasionally at the English Parliament in Westminster. Wales seemed at peace but was actually a land of festering grievances.

The Revolution of 1399 presented an opportunity for Welsh nationalism to come to the fore under the leadership of Owain Glyn Dwr (or Owen Glendower, as he appears in Shakespeare's *Henry IV*). Owain was descended from two prominent Welsh families. He had studied law in London, served Richard II in the Welsh borderlands, and acquired a position of considerable importance. In 1400 his followers proclaimed him Prince of Wales. Many men, including Welsh students at Oxford, flocked to his side. Allying with the Percys in northern England, Owain took part in a conspiracy that came close to driving Henry IV from the throne. He survived the defeat of the Percys, captured several of the great Welsh castles, and summoned two Welsh Parliaments. For a time it appeared that he might succeed in establishing an independent Wales.

But Henry IV was too strong for Owain. After dealing with his enemies in England, Henry turned his attention to Wales. He recaptured Owain's strongholds at Harlech and Aberystwyth. Owain himself fled into the hills. No one knows what his end was, though Welsh legends have grown up around him. He is still regarded as a great hero by Welsh nationalists.

Henry IV reacted against the Welsh rebellion by issuing a series of statutes and ordinances in 1401. These denied Welshmen the right to buy land in England or the English boroughs established in Wales itself, to hold major offices in Wales, to carry arms in any town or on any highway, or to marry Englishwomen. The statutes also stated that no Englishman could be convicted according to Welsh law, or at the suit of a Welshman. In their attempt to segregate the two races and relegate the natives to an inferior position, these acts are reminiscent of the Statutes of Kilkenny in Ireland. They left a blighting legacy of resentment and mistrust.

Henry V's appoach was in some ways more positive. He appreciated that one way to gain the support of the Welsh was to employ them in his armies. More than three thousand Welshmen had taken part in the battle of Crécy, and a large number were also present at Agincourt. The Welsh were excellent archers and had a reputation for bravery and directness. They tried to kill their enemies without regard for their social standing or the ransom they might bring if they were taken prisoner.

Henry VI (1422–1471)

The hero of Agincourt was succeeded by his nine-month-old son, who was recognized by the English as Henry VI. His claim to the French throne was never taken seriously: Charles VI died in the same year as Henry V and was followed by his own heir, the dauphin. The dauphin, however, was not immediately crowned.

Long periods of royal minority always brought troubles to the English government. As usually happened, younger brothers of the former king now acted as regents for their nephew. For the first years of Henry VI's reign, internal affairs were handled by Humphrey, duke of Gloucester, and the Duke of Bedford was left in charge of matters in France.

Neither was successful. The final phase of the Hundred Years' War saw the French victorious under the leadership of Joan of Arc. A peasant girl, Joan believed that she heard voices sent by God instructing her to arrange the coronation of the dauphin as King Charles VII and to assume command of the French army, despite her gender and lack of experience. Amazingly, she broke the English siege of Orleans in 1429. Then her voices deserted her; she was captured, tried by church courts as a heretic, and finally burned at the stake in Rouen when she was only nineteen. (The charges against her included the fact that she had dressed in men's clothes.) Her reputation as the savior of the French nation grew over the centuries, and she was finally recognized by the Catholic church as a saint in 1919.

Despite Joan's demise, military affairs continued to run badly for the English. Northern France slipped out of England's grasp rapidly, and the last

Henry VI, portrait by an unknown artist.
Reproduced by permission of the National
Portrait Gallery.

strongholds in the south were lost with the fall of Bordeaux in 1453. This proved to be the last gasp of the war, which ended (to borrow the words of T. S. Eliot) "not with a bang, but with a whimper." England's great French empire was now gone forever; only the port of Calais remained English.

At home, Humphrey, duke of Gloucester, was discredited when his mistress, Eleanor Cobham, was charged with practicing black magic. Aspiring to the throne, she obtained a wax image of Henry VI and exposed it to the heat of an open fire, hoping that the king's health would wane as the doll melted. Eventually she was arrested and died in prison. Humphrey escaped, but he lost the respect and power that had been his earlier. In later life Duke Humphrey became a great collector of books and manuscripts. The oldest part of the library at Oxford University is named for him and still contains part of his bequest.

During the years between 1436 and 1453, Henry VI ruled directly. He was intelligent and pious, and he deserves to be remembered as the founder of two great educational institutions, Eton (the great "public" school near Windsor) and King's College, Cambridge. But he was suspicious, extravagant, and not gifted at politics. General discontent with the corruption and inefficiency of his officers was manifest in 1450, when a young man named

Jack Cade led an uprising of landowners from Kent. The rebels—respectable members of society, including mayors and prominent gentlemen—were able to enter the city of London, where they had numerous sympathizers, and to free prisoners held in the jails there. They secured the execution of several members of the king's council. Eventually the king marshaled a force that turned the insurgents back. Cade was captured, died on the way to trial, and was posthumously beheaded as a traitor. Historians have only recently come to realize the full significance of the episode. It was not a protest by unorganized peasants but rather a political rebellion with specific proposals for remedying misgovernment.

In 1453 Henry suffered a psychological collapse—he withdrew into himself and became unable to communicate with others. By 1456 he had recovered to some extent, but he continued to suffer from melancholy and was never able to grasp the seriousness of the problems that surrounded him. It is possible that he inherited mental problems from his French grandfather, Charles VI.

The Wars of the Roses,
1455–1485

Henry VI's inability to govern brought to a head dynastic conflicts that had been brewing throughout the fifteenth century. Open warfare erupted in 1455 and continued, sporadically, for thirty years. These events have come to be known as the Wars of the Roses, although that name was never used during the fifteenth century itself. It is based on the fact that Henry's opponents, the Yorkists, had long used a white rose as their armorial symbol. The Lancastrians, whose coats of arms had originally been quite different, came to adopt the red rose as their contrasting sign. Shakespeare and other Tudor writers did refer to the symbolic conflict between the red rose and the white, but the term *Wars of the Roses* was invented by nineteenth-century historians and novelists, mainly Sir Walter Scott.

The Wars of the Roses had several causes. Most obvious was the breakdown of government, which could be laid at the feet of an incompetent monarch. Social conditions also contributed to the drift toward anarchy. For some time barons and other feudal magnates had been employing bands of followers or "retainers." These men were given "livery" (apparel ornamented with their lord's badge or coat of arms) and "maintenance" (the lord's personal support, both financial and political). The system of livery and maintenance had been criticized by Parliament as early as 1400, and the

Lancastrian kings had attempted to control its spread. Nevertheless it became an established part of fifteenth-century political society.

Through retaining, many wealthy Englishmen came to have what were essentially private armies. If these magnates chose to make war on the king, or if they formed rival political groups, civil war was likely to result. The situation became more volatile after the end of the Hundred Years' War, when a number of fighting men who had been employed in France returned to England and attached themselves to noble households.

Henry VI's nervous breakdown, if one may describe his condition with such modern terminology, provided the spark that ignited this tinder. A rival member of the royal family, Richard, duke of York, served briefly as the "protector" of the incapacitated king but then was persuaded to fight for the throne itself. Some feudal magnates flocked to his banner, and open warfare between the Lancastrians and Yorkists began in 1455.

Both of these branches of the royal family traced their ancestry back to Edward III. The Lancastrians were descendants of Edward's fourth son, John of Gaunt, the duke of Lancaster. King Henry VI represented this line. Richard, duke of York, could claim descent from two sons of Edward III: on the female side he was descended from the old king's third son, the duke of Clarence, and his male forebears sprang from the sixth son, the duke of York. In seeking the throne the Yorkists advanced two genealogical claims. They insisted that the Lancastrians were usurpers who had illegally seized the crown in the Revolution of 1399, and they argued that their family, tracing its antecedents to the third son of Edward III, took precedence over the descendants of the fourth son. The second point was moot, for constitutional experts had never decided whether a claim to the English throne could be transmitted through a female. Such descent was explicitly barred in France by the so-called Salic Law, but it was unclear whether this restriction applied in England.

Bloodshed and property damage in the Wars of the Roses were minimal; actual fighting occupied only twelve or thirteen weeks out of more than thirty years. But the battles had important political repercussions. After being defeated at St. Albans in 1461, Henry VI, his wife, Margaret of Anjou, and his young son fled to Scotland. Richard, duke of York, had died the previous year, but his son took advantage of the situation and was crowned king as Edward IV.

A decade later Henry VI partially regained his sanity and fought his way back to the throne, but he was finally defeated at the Battle of Tewkesbury in 1471. His son was killed, and Henry himself was murdered soon after. It appeared that the Wars were over, although they were in fact to be reopened later.

Edward IV (1461–1483)
and the Yorkists

E dward IV was not quite twenty years old when he assumed the throne. The earliest years of his reign were marred by his unpopular marriage to Elizabeth Woodville and the defection of one of his chief supporters, the earl of Warwick, called Warwick the Kingmaker because he had been so influential in placing Edward on the throne. Like Henry VI, Warwick was killed in 1471, and Edward's control of the government grew more secure.

As the first king of a new branch of the royal family, Edward IV faced the same problems as Henry IV. He proved an able monarch, and most of his subjects came to accept his rule, which seemed a relief from the incompetence and strife the realm had experienced. Edward's management of government finance, in particular, represented a notable improvement.

The Yorkists were particularly interested in Ireland, where English influence had declined badly after 1399. Richard, duke of York, won the hearts of the Irish as few Englishmen ever did, and Edward IV was also quite popular. But he was too busy in England to give Ireland much personal attention. For a time the native earl of Desmond virtually ruled the country, but in 1467 Edward IV sent over an English deputy, John Tiptoft, earl of Worcester. Tiptoft was noted for his cruelty; he ordered the execution of Desmond and two of his infant sons. After Tiptoft's brief stay the Irish earls of Kildare became dominant. The supremacy of the Kildares lasted until 1540, and the Irish were essentially allowed to manage their own affairs during this period.

Had he lived longer, Edward might have been able to pass the crown to his descendants without incident. As it was, his children were still young when he died in 1483. He wished his older son to be king, and Edward V was indeed recognized as the successor. But he was only twelve; his younger brother, Richard, duke of York, was but nine. Supposedly to ensure their safety, the two boys were sent to live in the Tower of London, while their uncle, Richard, duke of Gloucester, ruled as regent.

Richard III (1483–1485)

N o other English monarch poses such problems for the historian as does Richard. All evaluations of his character are controversial. He was depicted by Shakespeare as a thoroughly evil man, deformed in

Richard III, portrait by an unknown artist. Reproduced by permission of the National Portrait Gallery.

both body and soul, whose eyes were always fixed on the crown. The play *Richard III* contains famous scenes in which the duke of Gloucester contrives to obtain the murder of his older brother, the duke of Clarence (he was charged with treason and drowned in a vat of malmsey wine), and his young nephews, the "princes in the Tower," merely because they stood between him and the throne. Shakespeare also describes the political chicanery and bribery involved in Richard's assumption of the throne himself.

But we know that Shakespeare was biased. He took much of his historical material from sources that were unfriendly to Richard, and he manipulated it in ways that led to dramatic tension and conflict. Recent historians have tried to discard his picture of Richard and to form a more accurate one, based primarily on original sources that document the work of his government.

It is true that Clarence was executed, but he was probably actually guilty of treason against Edward IV. It is true that Edward IV's sons never reappeared after being sent to the Tower. We will probably never know precisely what their fate was. When skeletal remains of two young men were excavated in the Tower during the eighteenth century, these were assumed to be the bodies of the princes, and they were reburied in Westminster Abbey, but the identification is uncertain and would in any case not tell us when the boys died or under what conditions. Some circumstantial evidence, recently discovered, does indeed suggest that their murder was ordered by Richard III, or at least that it was done under the assumption that he would be pleased by it, just as the knights who killed Thomas Becket supposed that their deed would satisfy Henry II. If the boys were not killed in 1483, it is entirely possible that they would have met their death early in the Tudor period, for they would have threatened Henry VII as much as Richard III.

It is true, too, that Richard was more than willing to become king, despite the rights of his nephews. Here again there could be compelling reasons: he may have come to believe his own propaganda, which insinuated that the princes were not legitimate sons of Edward IV, and he may have become convinced, as he read the history of earlier reigns, that royal minorities were such a disaster for the realm that virtually any action to prevent them was justifiable.

In any case the claims of the princes were put aside. Richard III was crowned in 1483, the last of the Yorkist kings. His nephews were not seen alive after that summer.

Richard's unpopularity, and questions about the legality of his position, revived the factionalism that Edward IV had tried so hard to eliminate. It became clear that the Wars of the Roses had not really ended. Another descendant of Edward III, related to the Lancastrians, reopened the fighting and undertook a military campaign that was to lead him to the throne and Richard III to the grave.

Richard's rival was Henry Tudor, an ambitious man with an ambiguous claim to the throne. The Tudor family itself was not royal, or even distinguished; it sprang from relatively minor Welsh gentlemen. Early in the reign of Henry V, Owen Tudor had left Wales to seek his fortune at the court. Ultimately he became an attendant, and perhaps an advisor, to Henry, and after Henry's untimely death he became a close friend of the king's widow, the French princess Katherine. Owen and Katherine finally married, and they had a son, Edmund, who was thus a half-brother of Henry VI. Edmund also married well: his wife was Lady Margaret Beaufort, whose ancestors were descended from John of Gaunt and his mistress, Katherine Swynford. Their son Henry Tudor could thus claim English royal blood, though through a female line and one that was tainted with illegitimacy. Henry was as close to the Lancastrian line as anyone living in the 1480s. Through his mother he was also descended from the French royal family, though he made little of this claim.

In the summer of 1485 Henry Tudor invaded England. He had been living in France, where he gathered a small force of friends and mercenaries. They landed in Wales, marched to the English Midlands, and engaged Richard

III's army near the town of Market Bosworth. Here, at Bosworth Field, a decisive battle was fought on August 22. The forces on both sides were small and were dominated by a handful of noblemen. The outcome can be attributed largely to Richard's fatal decision to attack Henry personally and to the defection of two powerful magnates, the earl of Northumberland and Sir William Stanley. Stanley had promised to support Richard (largely because Richard held his son hostage) and did remain neutral during the earlier stages of the combat, but when he saw that Henry might be victorious he ordered his retainers to fight for him. By sundown Richard lay dead on the battlefield, and Henry VII had been proclaimed king by his followers. Although no one could have known it at the time, the Wars of the Roses had finally ended; the Tudor age had begun.

Parliament in the Fifteenth Century

B ecause these great political struggles were fought out on the battlefield, not in the Parliament chamber, Parliament was less prominent in the fifteenth century than it had been in the fourteenth. Parliament also met less frequently; on several occasions there were intervals of three or four years between sessions. Nevertheless, some significant changes occurred during this time.

Probably the most important change was the growth of acknowledged parliamentary privilege. The right of the two houses to initiate legislation and to give their assent to petitions presented to them by subjects or by the king was now unchallenged, and Parliament also began to claim the privilege of judging instances of disputed elections. (This power was not clearly in the hands of Parliament until the seventeenth century, however.)

Fifteenth-century Parliaments also saw the introduction of bills of attainder. Under this procedure a royal officer accused of malfeasance could be found guilty of treason without a trial, by using legislative rather than judicial machinery. Attainder was used frequently in the political squabbles of these years: Richard II's Parliaments had attainted first his friends, then his enemies, and those who were on the wrong side at the wrong time during the Wars of the Roses might also become victims of attainder. Confiscation of all property was the usual punishment; royal finances improved notably under Edward IV because so much land had come into his hands in this way.

The election of knights of the shire was regularized in 1429, when a uniform property qualification was introduced. Following this date only free-holders whose lands produced an annual income of forty shillings (£2) or more were allowed to vote. This limited the franchise to fairly substantial landowners and probably disenfranchised some persons who had voted earlier. The effect of the new rule was limited, however, by the fact that rival candidates were seldom presented to the voters. The great magnates within each county generally determined who the knights of the shire would be, and the actual election was little more than a formality. Borough elections continued to follow various nondemocratic patterns. Under Edward IV about one hundred boroughs enjoyed representation, and London's importance was recognized by its right to send four burgesses rather than two.

Provision for the payment of members of Parliament began in the fifteenth century. Knights of the shire were entitled to collect four shillings a day, burgesses two shillings. The earliest fragment of a parliamentary journal also dates from this time. It records the actions of the House of Lords in 1461.

The Early Stewarts in Scotland

The fifteenth century in Scotland, as in England, witnessed weak rule and dynastic strife. A new dynasty gained the Scottish throne in 1371, when David II died without heirs. In accordance with an act of settlement passed earlier by the Scottish Parliament, the Stewart family, descended from the hereditary high stewards of the realm, succeeded to the throne. The first king of this line was Robert II. He was already middle-aged at the time of his coronation, and there was some question about the legitimacy of his son John, who took the name Robert III when he became king. But the real problem with both rulers was their temperament; their rule was weak and ineffective, and the disarray of the monarchy gave rise to factionalism among the noblemen. As one chronicler wrote, the strong oppressed the weak, and the whole kingdom became a den of thieves.

The early Stewarts did attempt to regain some of the territory that Edward Balliol had unwisely ceded to England, but their campaigns were not very successful. Indeed, Richard II of England brought a considerable force into Scotland in 1385, humiliating the Scots by burning their great abbeys at Melrose and Dryburgh and even invading Edinburgh. The Stewarts entered into alliances with France, and French soldiers did come to the aid of the Scots. But their military tactics were different—the French favored large-scale pitched battles, whereas the Scots had learned that guerrilla operations were more effective given their terrain and limited resources—and the French presence proved to be of little value.

In 1404 Robert III arranged for his heir, a seven-year-old son named James, to go to France. The English succeeded in capturing the boy while he was at sea and held him prisoner for twenty years. When Robert died in 1406 his brother, the duke of Albany, became regent for James, and sometimes claimed to be king himself, since James could not be crowned. Finally the English, during the minority of Henry VI, allowed James to return to Scotland, but they demanded a ransom that strained the resources of the disordered Scottish state.

With the coronation of James I in 1424, the Scots finally gained a monarch who was young, energetic, and determined to restore peace and the rule of law. He cut down the power of the nobility, arresting a number of Highland chiefs who resisted his authority and even executing a few. He worked effectively with Parliament in strengthening the legal system. Although he was harsh and vindictive, he might have done much to bring stable rule to a troubled realm if he had been granted a long reign. But in 1437 he was murdered by a group of disaffected conspirators.

Once again a royal minority brought chaos to the realm. James II was only six when he was crowned. His regents were incompetent, and the central government disintegrated rapidly. By the 1450s James II had reached maturity and eliminated some of the overmighty noblemen who had usurped his authority. His promising reign was cut short in 1460: he was killed accidentally when one of his own guns exploded.

By this time England was engaged in the Wars of the Roses, and Henry VI's intrepid wife, Margaret, came to Scotland to seek help in combating the Yorkists. She agreed to cede the important border town of Berwick to Scotland and promised to surrender some lands in northwest England as well. Her concessions were of no permanent value; after the Yorkists had gained secure control of England they recaptured Berwick, which has remained in English hands ever since.

Scotland reverted to virtual anarchy during the minority of James III (1460–1488). Even when he became twenty-one he was incapable of running the country. He was more interested in religion and the arts than in government and spent his time in the company of musicians and architects, despite repeated demands from Parliament that he "put forth justice" throughout his realm. By 1485 Scotland, like England, badly needed stability and efficiency in government.

Suggested Reading

Cosgrove, Art, ed., *A New History of Ireland, Vol. II (1169–1534)*. (Oxford: Clarendon Press, 1987).

Goodman, Anthony, *The Wars of the Roses* (London: Routledge & Kegan Paul, 1981).

Grant, Alexander, *Independence and Nationhood: Scotland, 1306–1469* (London: Edward Arnold, 1984).

Griffiths, Ralph A., *The Reign of King Henry VI* (Berkeley and Los Angeles: University of California Press, 1981).

Hatcher, John, *Plague, Population, and the English Economy* (London: Macmillan, 1977).

Jacob, E. F., *The Fifteenth Century, 1399–1485* (Oxford: Clarendon Press, 1961).

Kendall, Paul Murray, *Richard the Third* (London: George Allen & Unwin, 1955).

Kendall, Paul Murray, *The Yorkist Age* (London: George Allen & Unwin, 1962).

Kirby, J. L., *Henry IV of England* (London: Constable, 1970).

McKisack, May, *The Fourteenth Century, 1307–1399* (Oxford: Clarendon Press, 1959).

Ross, Charles, *Edward IV* (Berkeley and Los Angeles: University of California Press, 1974).

Ross, Charles, *Richard III* (London: Eyre Methuen, 1981).

Storey, R. L., *The End of the House of Lancaster* (London: Barrie & Rockliffe, 1966).

Tey, Josephine, *The Daughter of Time* (New York: Macmillan, 1952) (a classic murder mystery about the princes in the Tower, probably coming to the wrong conclusion).

Wilkinson, Bertie, *The Later Middle Ages in England, 1216–1485* (London: Longmans, Green, 1969).

CHAPTER SIX

Medieval British Society, 1066–1485

The Population

The preceding chapters dealing with the period following the Norman Conquest have attempted to narrate the chief developments in the monarchy and government. Important as these matters are, they do not in themselves form a full history of the Middle Ages in Britain. It is essential to discuss medieval society, in order to obtain some picture of the lives of ordinary men and women who lived during the years between 1066 and 1485.

Statistics about the actual size of the population are hard to obtain. The most useful sources relate only to England; these are the Domesday Book of 1086 and the poll tax returns of 1377. It is easy enough to add up the tenants listed in William the Conqueror's survey—the number is about 275,000—but not so simple to calculate the total population, including women and children. Allowance must also be made for evasion and omission. An educated guess at the population of England in the years immediately following the Conquest is two million. Similar estimates put the number of inhabitants in 1377 between 2.5 and 3 million.

The figures for 1377, however, reflect the great mortality associated with the Black Death, in which (as we have seen) about 40 percent of the inhabitants of the British Isles died. If one makes allowance for this loss, it seems likely that the population of England had risen to five million or a bit more before the plague struck. The first two centuries after the Conquest, then, saw a very significant increase in population, in which the number of English men and women more than doubled, finally approximating the maximum population attained under Roman rule. The late fourteenth century witnessed a sudden decline.

If one realizes that land area remained constant, one can easily appreciate the significance of the changing conditions. As the population grew during the decades before the Black Death, it created serious pressures on available resources, probably lowered the standard of living, and forced a number of people to seek employment in areas unrelated to agriculture. After the plague there were not enough laborers to till all the soil that had been cultivated; many towns and villages shrank in size, and some were even abandoned. Although the Black Death is always regarded as a tragedy, it did reduce a population that must have strained England's resources. There are good reasons for believing that the standard of living for working people rose between 1350 and 1485.

The only really large city was London. Its population in 1300 has been estimated at thirty to forty thousand. If these figures are correct, medieval London was no larger than Roman London at its peak, but the number of inhabitants had declined severely during the earlier Middle Ages. York, the most important city in northern England, probably had about ten thousand residents in 1300. Flourishing ports like Norwich and Bristol may have boasted populations of five thousand each. Most other towns, even those that were county seats and trading centers, had fewer than three thousand inhabitants during the Middle Ages. Comparison with modern towns of this size will help one appreciate how small they were.

Statistics for the outlying parts of the British Isles are much less reliable. There were probably about 400,000 people in Scotland in 1300. It is impossible to make valid estimates of the populations of Ireland and Wales, except to say that they were smaller than that of Scotland. There were only four major cities, or "burghs," in Scotland, and the only true city in Ireland was Dublin. No urban center had developed in Wales.

Social Structure: The Peasants

A lthough medieval men and women did not use modern terminology in describing social classes, they were familiar with the concept of order and degree. Medieval society was clearly stratified, with the king at the top, then feudal magnates or members of the nobility, followed by lords of manors, merchants, and clergy, all resting on the large, solid base of the peasantry. The interlocking relationships between these groups were ratified by the feudal concept of homage and fealty, by the manorial custom of villeinage, and by the church, which preached the importance of each member of society performing the appropriate services so that the whole body politic might flourish. Historians have often used the pyramid as a symbol or model of medieval society, mainly because its tapering form emphasizes the large number of laborers at the bottom and the fact that each higher group was smaller than the one below it, until finally the monarch occupied the highest pinnacle in solitary eminence.

The agricultural workers who formed the bulk of English society were legally separated into two groups, the free and the unfree. Those who were unfree were not slaves, but as villeins or serfs they were bound to remain on the manors where they had been born, performing compulsory labor services in exchange for modest housing and minimal amounts of land. They needed their lord's permission to marry and to educate their children. Unless he agreed, they could not move to cities or other manors, or enter religious orders. They were not legally free to buy, sell, or bequeath land or other property. Indeed they had no legal rights in the royal system of Common Law; disputes were to be settled by the lord of the manor. Free peasants did have access to the law. They were able to move, buy and sell land, and manage their own affairs largely as they chose, but their economic conditions were not necessarily much better than those of the villeins. The Domesday Book suggests that most manors had both free and unfree tenants, but there was some regional variation, and not all estates fit a single pattern.

During the later Middle Ages the status of the peasants became more complex; a great variety of specific conditions applied in individual cases. In particular, it became more common for villeins to "buy out" their disabilities, so that in exchange for a money payment they were permitted to move, alienate land, or send sons away to school or to monasteries. The blurring of the line separating villeins and the freeborn is emphasized by the frequency of intermarriage between the two groups.

Peasant families were generally nuclear units composed only of a husband, wife, and unmarried children; it was rare for extended families including several generations to live together. It used to be believed that marriage was generally delayed until the couple had an assured livelihood, most often through inheritance of land following the death of parents. Recent studies, however, suggest that this was not the case, at least in the later Middle Ages. Couples most often married in their early twenties, or even (following the Black Death, which opened up new opportunities) in their late teens.

As many as 94 percent of the peasant farmers were married. Their households were small, usually including between one and three children. Although some form of birth control may have been practiced, infant mortality probably played a more significant role in keeping down the size of families. The average life expectancy was no more than thirty-three years, and (in contrast to the situation in the late twentieth century) only 10 percent of the population was over fifty, although some people did live into their eighties or nineties. Because of their short life spans, most medieval men and women spent the majority of their lives unwed, either single or widowed; the average marriage lasted little longer than a dozen years. A recent writer has described these marriages as economic and emotional partnerships—flexible institutions that worked to the benefit of both husband and wife.

It was during the Middle Ages that the use of family names became common in England. Many surnames were derived from occupations. Examples, which tell us a good deal about the major medieval crafts and trades, are Miller, Baker, Brewer, Butcher, Shepherd, Carpenter, Thatcher, Smith, Taylor, Weaver, Wheeler, Franklin (a freeman), and Fuller (one who "fulls" cloth, to improve its texture following weaving).

Social Structure: The Aristocracy and Middling Groups

The upper groups in society—we may term them the aristocracy—became more clearly differentiated in the fourteenth and fifteenth centuries. Earlier, the feudal concepts of tenants-in-chief and more generally of feudal magnates set aside an upper class. With the rise of Parliament came the notion of parliamentary peerage, carrying with it the right of noblemen to be summoned to meetings of what developed into the House of Lords. We have already noted the origins of the earls and barons. Additional ranks of nobility were recognized by the end of the Middle Ages, producing the honorific structure that still applies today.

The highest title of nobility was that of duke. There were only a few dukes; originally most of them were related to the royal family. Then came the orders of marquess, earl, viscount, and baron. In fact there were never very many marquesses or viscounts, perhaps because the titles were originally French and thus suspect in England. Dukes, marquesses, and earls used territorial names for their titles as, for instance, duke of York or earl of Cambridge. The wife of a duke was a duchess; an earl's wife was called a countess, because earls were at the same level of society as counts in France or Germany. Barons, the most numerous group of noblemen, were often merely called "lord," like Lord Dacre or Lord Mountjoy. Almost all the noblemen were very rich and owned vast landed estates with hundreds of tenants and retainers. In general the members of each group were richer than those in the group below it; a duke was likely to have a larger estate than an earl, and he certainly enjoyed greater prestige.

Ranking just below the noblemen in wealth and status were the gentlemen—landlords who were not prominent enough to be ennobled but not poor enough to have to work the soil with their own hands. Collectively known as the gentry, they formed a group that soon came to be the most important element in English society. Although not noble, they are sometimes regarded as members of the landed aristocracy, clearly set apart from those below them in society.

Some members of the gentry could claim the title "knight." During the first century or so after the Conquest, knighthoods were conferred, often on the battlefield, when the monarch wished to recognize outstanding military service. Later, knighthoods were given to those who had aided the government in other ways, or simply as recognition of the wealth and social status of the richer gentlemen. Knights could be elected to the House of Commons in Parliament but were not automatically summoned, as were the peers. Knights were identified by the title "sir" preceding their own Christian name; their wives were called "dame," or sometimes merely "lady," a title that could be confusing because the wife of a baron was also a "lady." Knighthood was not hereditary, although it was not unusual for a knight's heir to be knighted in his own right. Peerages, on the other hand, did descend to the oldest surviving son of the nobleman.

Several middling groups (it is premature to view them as a single modern middle class) can be identified in medieval English society. Yeomen (the next group below the gentry) might be defined as working landlords; they owned

land and cultivated it themselves, perhaps with the assistance of a few peasant tenants. Medieval writers sometimes idealized the yeomen and their
wives, emphasizing their industry and sturdy independence.

Among urban dwellers, merchants grew increasingly important in the
later Middle Ages. Some of them, especially those involved in foreign trade
or in selling luxury articles, amassed considerable wealth. Many merchants
dreamed of buying land and acquiring the social status that went with it, and
a few succeeded in doing so. Lawyers already formed an important professional group by the fifteenth century. As today, the practice of law was a
means by which clever young men could rise in society. They often hoped to
enter the ranks of the gentry if they prospered.

Churchmen fitted into the social scheme at all levels. The bishops and
archbishops were as aristocratic as the peers; they held landed estates and
were summoned to Parliament as Lords Spiritual. Parish priests were supported by the tithes of their parishioners: as rectors, the clergy were legally
entitled to a tenth of the produce of agricultural estates and to an equivalent
share in the income of urban dwellers (though this was more difficult to
collect). Some parish priests were well-off and lived comfortably, like minor
gentry, whereas others were closer to the status of the yeomen or peasants to
whom they ministered. Like the bishops, the heads of the larger monasteries
were summoned to Parliament as Lords Spiritual and enjoyed substantial
incomes from their estates. Even ordinary monks generally had better food
and housing than the peasant households from which most of them came.
The church, like trade and the law, offered an opportunity for intelligent,
enterprising young men to rise in society; it was largely staffed by those whose
parents had been common people, rural laborers or urban artisans.

Medieval Women

Medieval society was dominated by men, and women were seldom
involved in government, warfare, land management, or the professions. The life of peasant women might include milking cows,
keeping poultry and pigs, and working in the fields as well as the essential
domestic chores of cooking, sewing, and child care. Women were also heavily
involved in cottage industries, especially spinning and carding thread—
weaving itself was more often done by men. Aristocratic ladies had challeng-
ing responsibilities in managing large households of servants and retainers as
well as large families of their own, and their presence graced the banquets,
dances, and other social events held at the court or in the castles of the

nobility. Occasionally widows took over the management of their husband's estate or business, and some of them seem to have had considerable freedom to exercise their talents in these areas.

Brief examination of the lives of three exceptional medieval women will dispel any notion that their lives were inevitably dull or unimportant. We may consider the careers of England's greatest medieval queen, Eleanor of Aquitaine; one of the most fascinating religious mystics, Margery Kempe; and an exceptionally articulate and able gentlewoman, Margaret Paston.

Eleanor of Aquitaine was born in southern France, the daughter of a duke of Aquitaine, whose properties she inherited. By her father's arrangement she was married to the king of France, Louis VII, and she went with him on a crusade. Their marriage was annulled in 1152, probably because it had not produced a male heir but in theory because of a distant kinship between husband and wife. Eleanor almost immediately married Henry II of England, thus bringing Aquitaine into his far-flung empire. A headstrong woman, she never got on well with Henry. For a time she was kept under arrest in one or another of Henry's English castles. Finally allowed to establish her own residence at Poitiers, in southern France, she created one of Europe's most sophisticated courts, with elegant private chambers, tournaments fought by armed knights, visits by aristocrats making pilgrimages, and music and poetry composed by troubadours—indeed, all the trappings of chivalry and courtly love. Eleanor was deeply involved in the political machinations of her four sons against their father. After the death of Henry II she was virtually the ruler of England while Richard the Lionheart was gone on his crusade. Dying in 1204, she was buried alongside kings of France at Fontevrault Abbey in Normandy.

Margery Kempe was the daughter of a rich merchant, the mayor of Lynn in East Anglia. Intimate details of her life are known because she dictated her autobiography, *The Book of Margery Kempe*. Strangely enough, the book did not come to light until the 1930s. In it she relates her marriage to a husband of lower status, her immediate pregnancy, and the sicknesses and difficult labors that attended the birth of all of her fourteen children. Finally, religious meditation led her to reject her husband's sexual advances. An extraordinary scene in the autobiography describes how she and her husband—over cakes and a beer—agreed that she might take a vow of celibacy, although they would share the same bed and eat together on Fridays. Despite this agreement they lived apart until his old age, when she took him in and nursed him. Claiming to be visited by visions of Christ, Margery came to believe that she had a special vocation to weep for sinners and pray for the salvation of their souls. She died about 1440.

The famous Paston Letters, an extraordinary collection of more than one thousand items dating from the fifteenth century, give us a remarkable insight into the interests and exertions of Margaret Paston. She was married to Sir John Paston, a prominent member of the gentry in the county of Norfolk. Because her husband had to spend a good deal of time conducting business in London and attending Parliament there, Margaret often assumed responsibility for managing the family estates and dealing with difficult legal problems that arose at home, and she handled everything with notable efficiency. She helped arrange the education of her sons—they attended Eton and Oxford, and one of them entered the church—as well as the marriage of her daughters. When her husband fell ill she prayed for him and promised to undertake a pilgrimage to the famous shrine at Walsingham if he recovered. Her affectionate relationship with Sir John and her special love for her son Walter come out clearly in their letters to each other.

Among other fascinating women of this era one might single out Dame Julian of Norwich, a nun who became a mystic recluse and the author of the striking *Revelations of Divine Love,* and Countess Ela of Salisbury, who after her husband's death in 1226 founded a nunnery at Lacock and served as its abbess for nearly twenty years. At least two women—Katherine "the Surgeon" of London and Ann "the Medica" of York—are known to have practiced medicine, with more professional skill than the hundreds of women who served as midwives. Elizabeth de Burgh, lady of Clare, was involved in high politics during the unsettled years of the early fourteenth century but is remembered chiefly as the founder of Clare College at Cambridge. Henry VII's mother, Lady Margaret Beaufort, was another notable patron of Cambridge University, the founder of not one but two colleges, Christ's and St. John's. Her statue may still be seen over the entrance to these houses of learning.

Inheritance Patterns

The legal system known as primogeniture determined inheritance patterns among the upper classes. In order to keep estates together, so that a family could retain its status over a period of more than a single generation, the oldest surviving son inherited both his father's title (if there was one) and his lands. Some provision was made, of course, for other members of the family. Widows generally received the revenues from about a third of the estate during their lifetimes, or until they remarried. Because women often outlived their husbands by several decades, these jointures could be a considerable continuing burden on the heirs. Daughters were usually provided with a substantial dowry at the time of their marriage. This was controlled by their husbands during the duration of the marriage, but it could be reclaimed by the woman should the husband die. Similar portions were sometimes given to nunneries if daughters chose a religious life instead of marriage, or if their parents arranged for them to enter a religious house because a suitable husband could not be found. Because of the expense of dowries, some fathers did not even look for suitable husbands for their daughters, especially younger ones.

Younger sons were unfortunate victims of the system of primogeniture, but they were frequently able to marry heiresses who had no brothers and thus assume control of their wives' estates. They could also seek respectable careers in the church or the law. It was thought to be less acceptable for descendants of the aristocracy to enter commerce, but some did become merchants nonetheless.

The county of Kent was unique in having the custom of partible inheritance, called "gavelkind," in which sons received equal shares of their father's property. This system may go back to the traditions of the Jutes, who settled the area. Partible inheritance was also usual in Wales and Ireland, although it gradually died out as English law was introduced.

Until the sixteenth century only personal property could be willed away; except in special circumstances, lands passed according to primogeniture and other established legal precedents. It was common for those who made wills to bequeath some property to the church, so as to procure prayers for the souls of the dead. Indeed, wills were prefaced by "testaments," professing faith in God. For this reason church courts, rather than the Common Law, oversaw the administration of wills and testaments until the nineteenth century. Judgment that the testament was not heretical was part of the procedure. Landless laborers were less likely to be involved with the law and could generally dispose of their meager goods as they wished.

Farms and Towns

B ecause most people throughout the British Isles lived off the soil, it is useful to have some understanding of medieval farming practices.

Reference has already been made to the system of open-field or strip farming that characterized Anglo-Saxon agriculture and the manorial system. It would be a mistake, however, to assume that all land was cultivated in this way. Much of England, and most of Scotland and Wales, was better suited for grazing than for plowing and planting, and most manors included both arable land and pasture. The animals most frequently kept were sheep, cattle, oxen, and pigs. Wheat was the most usual cereal crop, though rye and oats were also grown. Fruit orchards were also common, especially in Kent and Worcestershire. Where the land was plowed, the soil was usually easy to work and could be turned over by a light plow pulled by two oxen—horses were rarely used. In Scotland, however, eight- or even twelve-ox teams were needed to propel the cumbersome plows used for breaking up heavier soils, especially those not previously cultivated. A number of well-built timber barns dating from the later Middle Ages survive; one of the best preserved is at Widdington in Essex.

Expansion was necessarily a constant theme in British society between the Conquest and the Black Death, since the population increased so rapidly during this period. In terms of actual land, expansion meant cutting down trees and creating what were called "assarts," or open spaces, in forests, in order to increase the amount of land available for cultivation. Fen and marsh lands could also be drained for agriculture. All in all, more land in England was cultivated during the twelfth and thirteenth centuries than at any other time in the realm's history, except for World War II. New lands were won for farming in Scotland and Ireland as well.

Economic expansion could also take other forms. Existing farmland could be cultivated more intensively, by using manure as fertilizer and by modifying the custom of crop rotation, so that fields were planted two years out of three rather than only in alternate years. More intensive trade and urbanization could also provide a livelihood for an expanded populace. New towns in England were often created by royal charter; by the fourteenth century there were at least three hundred identifiable urban areas. Some urbanization occurred, too, in Scotland, Ireland, and Wales.

Many existing towns and farming villages grew in size and importance during the later Middle Ages. Most of them served as markets for agricultural produce and for those commodities that farmers could not provide themselves. A large number of English towns still have their marketplaces— generally, large central squares where open-air stalls can be erected to display a variety of goods. In some places, like Chichester, beautiful stone market crosses were erected to provide some cover for transactions during inclement weather. Markets were usually held only one day a week, but some towns had more than one. King's Lynn, for instance, had both a Saturday market and a Tuesday market, held in different places. Ipswich, also in East Anglia, had separate markets for cloth, wool, fish, meat, cheese, wood, utensils, and livestock.

Prior's Hall Barn, Widdington, Essex, a fine example
of a large fifteenth-century timber barn.
Reproduced by permission of English Heritage.

The larger cities were surrounded by high stone walls, intended to keep
out intruders and ensure the safety of merchants and citizens. Only small
portions of the London city wall survive, but place names like Barbican,
Moorgate, and Bishopsgate still serve as reminders of its existence and its
great portals. Much of the medieval wall remains at York and Chester, and a
walk along the top of the wall helps one appreciate the size and layout of
these medieval cities.

Many towns benefited from the right to hold fairs, a privilege that was
usually granted by royal charter. Itinerant traders brought luxury goods and
other unusual items, often imported, to these fairs, which were held only
once or twice a year, and families might travel some distance to purchase
commodities that were not ordinarily available. Sometimes fairs were held

some distance outside towns because of the possibility of disturbances at them. At Cambridge, for example, the famous Stourbridge Fair took place at Barnwell, a village several miles away from the town center. Special courts, called courts of pie powder (the phrase is derived from the French *pie poudré* or "dusty feet"), were sometimes held to deal speedily, on the spot, with disputes that arose at these fairs.

Foreign goods were sold at fairs, as well as at settled locations in the larger cities like London and York. Luxurious textiles, including silks, velvets, and cloth of gold, were the most valuable imports, but French wines did not lag far behind. (Water was not thought to be a healthful drink in the Middle Ages; the poor drank beer or ale and the rich drank wine.) Furs from the Baltic were prized, as were metalwork from Germany and the spices, rare fruits, sugar, and rice that came from more distant lands, often aboard Italian galleys. The British exported wool, grain, fish, and dairy products to help pay for these imports.

The Wool Trade

Throughout the Middle Ages England's most important export was wool. Even poor peasants might own a few sheep, but most wool came from the substantial estates held by the gentry and aristocracy. Church lands, especially those owned by monasteries, also provided pasture for large flocks. By the end of the thirteenth century, England was exporting more than thirty thousand sacks of wool a year—nearly 6,000 tons. Wool produced in England was made up into finished cloth on the Continent, primarily in Flanders, and large quantities of cloth were imported by the residents of the British Isles. Luxury fabrics, of higher quality than those produced in England, were especially popular with members of the aristocracy.

The wool trade was handled largely by foreign merchants. Italians, some of them papal tax collectors, dominated during the earlier Middle Ages. In later centuries German traders from the Hanseatic League were also impor- tant. They secured special privileges in England, including the right to have their own guildhall in London as well as exemption from some customs duties. During the fourteenth century, English merchants controlled more of the wool trade themselves; they gained royal charters that allowed them to set up monopolistic centers on the Continent, called staples, as centers of their activity. The staple at Calais was especially important. Trading here was regulated by a small group of Englishmen known as merchants of the staple.

The wool trade declined during the second half of the fourteenth century, in part because of a great increase in the quantity of cloth being made within England. Indeed, England began to export finished cloth as well as raw wool. Trade with the Netherlands continued to flourish in the fifteenth century, but elsewhere the sale of both wool and cloth declined.

Guilds

G uilds were important institutions in medieval towns and cities. They were originally established for religious and social purposes: guild members, sometimes including women, made small annual payments in exchange for which they received prayers offered by a guild chaplain in the local parish church, or in a special chapel at a cathedral. Their funerals would be handled by the guild, whose members would attend, and financial assistance might be provided for survivors. (Medieval funerals were often costly, and the expense might be a great burden for those who did not belong to guilds.) Such a guild is known to have existed at Canterbury as early as the ninth century. A London guild founded in the tenth century had the additional purpose of maintaining the peace.

Merchant or craft guilds came slightly later. They arose when guilds dominated by merchants, like the Trinity Guild of Coventry, began to regulate conditions of manufacture and trade. In this case the cloth trade came under the control of the Trinity Guild, and one of its members was routinely chosen mayor. In London, guilds were organized to represent such groups as the mercers, fishmongers, goldsmiths, and tallow chandlers (candle makers). In the fourteenth century a number of guilds were incorporated; because of their special insignia, they came to be called livery companies. Some still survive, though they are now merely honorary social organizations, and their halls are frequently used for civic ceremonies.

Guilds commonly enforced a seven-year apprenticeship for young men wishing to enter organized crafts or trades. Apprentices lived in their master's household and served him without pay while they were learning special skills. On completing this period of training they could become journeymen, able to work in the employ of masters. Eventually (if they prospered) they might become masters themselves, with their own apprentices and journeymen. Guilds were sometimes criticized because they created monopolies, but it is

The guildhall at Lavenham, a prosperous wool town in East Anglia. The half-
timbered style was commonly used for houses as well as civic buildings.
Reproduced by permission of the Royal Commission on the Historical Monuments
of England.

also true that they were creative forces, providing education, control over the
quality of products, mutual assistance in time of need, and good fellowship
for their members.

Housing

Ordinary men and women of the Middle Ages lived in very simple
houses, sometimes no better than huts. These were built of wood:
often two large curved pieces of oak, called crucks, formed the basic
framing, and the walls might be filled with earth or mud in what was called
wattle and daub construction. Roofs were frequently thatched with straw or
reeds; floors were generally compacted earth, perhaps covered with straw.
Because fireplaces were uncommon, fires were often lit in the middle of
rooms, with at least some of the smoke escaping through a vent in the ceiling.
Glass was too expensive for ordinary use, so windows were small and openings were sometimes covered with wood shutters, thus excluding light as
well as air.

Haddon Hall, a medieval fortified dwelling later converted into a Tudor country house. Only wealthy members of medieval society could afford large, substantial homes such as this one.
Reproduced by permission of the Royal Commission on the Historical Monuments of England.

Medieval houses were small and crowded, seldom more than two rooms. Furnishings were sparse, often consisting of no more than a few stools, a trestle table, and a chest. It was common for a number of people, not just husbands and wives, to sleep together in the same bed; indeed travelers, putting up at inns or taverns, might share beds with complete strangers. In rural areas it was not uncommon for farm animals to share a building with their owners. Such buildings were generally elongated rectangles, called longhouses, separated in the middle into quarters for humans and beasts.

Wealthier members of society had larger, more substantial homes. Feudal noblemen needed great stone castles, both for defense and to house their numerous retainers and servants. Originally these castles were moated and protected by drawbridges, portcullises, and watchtowers. By the fifteenth

century, castles had become more comfortable, with large windows and fireplaces in their great dining halls and separate suites of rooms for their owners.
Tapestries often adorned the walls, helping to keep out drafts as well as
providing beauty and color. A quest for greater privacy is one of the chief
characteristics of the life of the upper classes in late medieval Europe, and
many of the finer houses in England, like Haddon Hall in Derbyshire, reflect
the success of such efforts. Private chapels, too, are a common feature of the
homes of noble men and women.

Even in London and other cities, most houses were built of wood and thus
were susceptible to fire. Modern concepts of sanitation were unknown; filth
and squalor were constant companions of urban life. Streets were narrow and
unpaved, but water was often supplied, sometimes through conduits, to public pumps and fountains. As the authority of mayors and aldermen expanded,
civic buildings were erected to house council meetings, courts, and markets.
A substantial guildhall, part of which survives, was built in London in the
fifteenth century, replacing an older structure from the twelfth century. Such
town halls were generally made of stone, as were the homes of some of the
richer merchants. A surviving example in London, now much altered, is
Crosby Hall, originally built in the 1460s for a prominent grocer, Sir John
Crosby, and now moved upstream to a site in Chelsea.

Some attempt was made to control the intramural growth of London and
a few other cities. As a result, suburbs of substandard houses grew up outside
their walls. The first stone bridge across the Thames in London was under
construction at the time of the Norman Conquest. In medieval and Tudor
times the chief recreational areas for Londoners lay near its south end, in
Southwark rather than London proper, since city officials feared the disorders
that sometimes arose at bear pits and theaters.

The Church

Christianity was a more powerful force in medieval society than it is
today. Throughout western Europe, until the Reformation of the
sixteenth century, there was a single church, acknowledging the
headship of the pope but managing many of its affairs on a national basis.
Earlier chapters have described the quarrels between kings and popes that
were such a common feature of the Middle Ages in England.

Medieval men and women were born members of the church, just as they
were born subjects of the monarchy. They had no choice of denominations,

Durham Cathedral. This view of the nave shows the round arches and massive columns characteristic of the Norman style. Reproduced by permission of the Royal Commission on the Historical Monuments of England.

and they were not free to decide where to attend services, since parishes were geographical units and men and women were expected to worship regularly in their own parish church unless they were traveling. As we have seen, they were required to pay tithes for the support of their parish priest—these were legally established payments rather than voluntary contributions. They often made bequests to the church in their wills, ensuring the continuity of prayers for the dead and sometimes providing for educational and social services as well.

The period between 1066 and 1530 was the great age of church building in Britain. Most of the villages in England, Wales, Scotland, and Ireland

Salisbury Cathedral. This was built in the Early English style and displays
features unique to England. This external view shows lancet windows and the
great spire.
Reproduced by permission of the Royal Commission on the Historical
Monuments of England.

have parish churches that were erected during these years, and the great
cathedrals that survive throughout England date to the later Middle Ages
as well.

The Normans were great builders. They had constructed sophisticated
churches in Normandy before the Conquest, and they were dissatisfied with
the small, rude buildings they found in England. As a result they frequently
demolished Anglo-Saxon churches and replaced them with more substantial
edifices. The Norman style in architecture is easily recognizable, for it is
characterized by small windows and doorways that terminate in round-headed
rather than pointed arches. Walls were massive, giving a great sense of

Wells Cathedral. Shown here is the façade with its extraordinary display of medieval sculpture.
Reproduced by permission of the Royal Commission on the Historical Monuments of England.

stability and permanence. The roofs of parish churches were constructed of wood, but because wood roofs were liable to catch fire, the Normans contrived a method of providing stone vaults for some of their cathedrals. This involved the use of diagonal stone ribs strong enough to carry the weight of lighter masonry that was used as infilling. All of these features, together with enormous circular pillars decorated with various ornamental patterns, may be seen in the Norman cathedral at Durham, which is one of the world's greatest ecclesiastical structures.

On the European Continent the Norman style is referred to as Romanesque. About 1200 it was superseded by the Gothic architecture in which the great French cathedrals were built. Gothic buildings can most easily be identified by their use of pointed arches in windows, doorways, and arcades. The

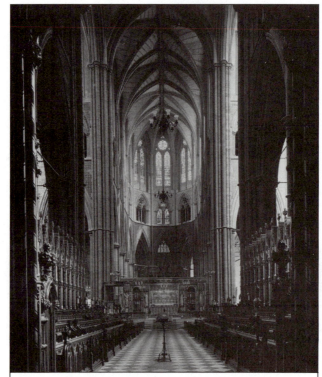

*Westminster Abbey. The choir was rebuilt by Henry III in the
Early English style. Coronations take place at the high altar
shown here.
Reproduced by permission of the Royal Commission on the
Historical Monuments of England.*

thirteenth century is often regarded as the finest period for ecclesiastical
architecture. In England the style of this age is called Early English, since it
exhibits certain features that are unique to the country. Salisbury Cathedral
is perhaps the best example of an Early English cathedral, since it was constructed during a relatively short span of time and exhibits few features from
any other period. It has large numbers of tall, narrow windows, called lancets
because they resemble a surgeon's instrument. Flying buttresses were used to
help carry the weight of the stone vaults down to the ground. The buttresses
made it possible to have thinner exterior walls, with more space given over

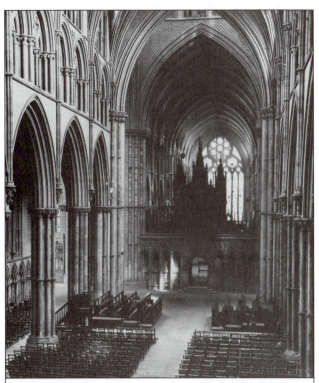

The nave of Lincoln Cathedral. This is another fine example of the Early English style.
Reproduced by permission of the Royal Commission on the Historical Monuments of England.

to windows. The great spire of Salisbury, visible for miles around, was not part of the original plan but was added in the fourteenth century. Its weight created structural difficulties that still present problems, but few would deny its exceptional beauty or its importance as a symbol of the cathedral's presence. The cathedral at Wells, in southwest England, is notable for the three hundred magnificent statues carved in the thirteenth century to adorn its façade. Much of Westminster Abbey was rebuilt in the Early English style during the reign of Henry III. Lincoln Cathedral is another great edifice of this era.

The Church of St. Peter and St. Paul, Lavenham, Suffolk, one of England's largest parish churches. Built in the Perpendicular style, this is an example of a "wool church"—one built by the wealth gathered through the wool trade.
Reproduced by permission of the Royal Commission on the Historical Monuments of England.

The earlier part of the fourteenth century saw the introduction of the Decorated style. Buildings of this age, like Exeter Cathedral and the choir of Wells, display larger windows with elaborate, fanciful patterns of stone tracery. More elaborate vaulting patterns were also developed, with subsidiary stone ribs called liernes added simply to create elegant designs, without regard to their structural function.

The final phase of medieval church building witnessed the introduction of the Perpendicular style, a form that is unique to the British Isles. The architects of this age (about 1350–1530) possessed very advanced engineering skills that permitted them to open up vast areas of wall space for windows. They were able to construct lofty buildings with supremely elegant fan vaults,

King's College Chapel, Cambridge. This is often regarded as the finest example of Perpendicular Gothic architecture. The royal arms of the Tudors are displayed above the west door.
Reproduced by permission of the Royal Commission on the Historical Monuments of England.

so called because they resembled the shape of a lady's fan. Hundreds of Perpendicular parish churches dot the English landscape. It was the responsibility of parishioners to build and maintain the naves of these churches, and the clergy were held responsible for the choir or east end. Some of the great Perpendicular churches are called "wool churches" because the wealth created by the wool trade made their erection possible; a contemporary couplet ran, "I thank the Lord and always shall, it is the sheep has paid for all."

King's College Chapel from the south. Most of the wall space has been opened up for stained glass windows; the weight of the roof is carried on buttresses set at right angles to the main axis of the building.
Reproduced by permission of the Royal Commission on the Historical Monuments of England.

The churches at Lavenham in Suffolk and Northleach in the Cotswolds are spectacular instances of such buildings.

Many cathedrals were partially rebuilt in the Perpendicular style. The great nave of Canterbury is an outstanding example. The finest of all the Perpendicular buildings is the chapel of King's College, Cambridge, the result of Henry VI's inspiration and Henry VIII's continuing interest and financial support. Although it is sometimes asserted that medieval architects were anonymous, that is untrue. Their names are often known. The greatest builders were perhaps William of Sens, a Frenchman who worked at Canterbury in the twelfth century and was seriously injured when he fell from scaffolding there, and John Wastell, a native Englishman who designed much of King's College Chapel.

Most of the medieval churches contain stained glass windows, which on sunny days flood the buildings with color as well as light. Thirteenth-century glass is surpassingly lovely; the gemlike brilliance of its reds and blues has

King's College Chapel, an interior view showing the fan vaulted ceiling.
Reproduced by permission of the Royal Commission on the Historical Monuments of England.

never been equaled. But the larger windows created in the fourteenth and fifteenth centuries have their own special merits. Unfortunately, much medieval stained glass was destroyed in later centuries, some of it by pious but misguided persons who regarded all pictorial art as blasphemous or superstitious, but enough remains, especially at Canterbury and York, for one to appreciate its quality. Pictorial windows were useful as teaching devices in the Middle Ages, when most people were illiterate and could not read the Bible itself. The large biblical scenes incorporated in Perpendicular-style windows were obviously ideal for this didactic purpose.

St. Andrew's Cathedral, Scotland. Only ruins of this great church survive. Reproduced by permission of the Royal Commission on the Ancient and Historical Monuments of Scotland.

Outside England, styles were similar but churches were built on a smaller scale. In Scotland, large cathedrals were erected at St. Andrew's and Glasgow, with more humble churches sufficing for the bishops of Aberdeen, Dunkeld, Dunblane, and Moray. The fine Gothic church of St. Giles in Edinburgh did not attain cathedral status until the seventeenth century. By the end of the Middle Ages there were four cathedrals in Wales. St. David's was (and is) an exceptional structure, but the others were no larger than English parish churches. Among the finest churches in Ireland are a handful of Norman buildings put up in the early twelfth century; the ruined cathedral of Ardfert shows thirteenth-century lancets used in Ireland as well as England.

St. David's Cathedral, Wales. Elements of the Early English and Decorated styles can be seen in this photograph. The ruined building at the left was the bishop's palace.
National Monuments Record for Wales Collection, Royal Commission on Ancient and Historical Monuments in Wales.

Monks, Friars, and Nuns

It is difficult for persons living in the twentieth century to recapture a sense of the significance of monasticism in medieval society. Monasteries, in which groups of men lived a common life regulated by a common rule, provided a home for thousands of people and spiritual leadership for the entire church. They were often centers of learning: illuminated manuscripts were copied in their scriptoria, historical chronicles were written, and theological treatises were composed and discussed. The monastic liturgies, which consisted of eight daily offices as well as a daily mass, came to include elaborate polyphonic music as well as the unison chanting of psalms and prayers. Sometimes boys were educated, sick persons were given nursing care, and travelers were lodged in monasteries.

Monastic buildings were generally well constructed and displayed great concern about sanitation and the supply of water. Arranged around a monastic cloister would be the monks' dormitory; the dining hall, called the refectory; kitchens; the scriptorium and library; guest rooms; an infirmary; a warming room (often the only room in which fires were allowed); and special quarters, sometimes spacious and elegant, for the abbot or prior who had been chosen as head of the house. Some monastic churches were as large as cathedrals (indeed, half the cathedrals of medieval England were also monasteries and were staffed by monks) and, despite regulations intended to limit their grandeur, they ranked among the greatest buildings in Britain.

Because the monasteries were dissolved at the time of the Reformation, most monastic buildings survive only as ruins, sometimes very romantic ones, as at Glastonbury in Somerset or Fountains in Yorkshire, although Henry VIII did convert a few of the greatest monastic churches into cathedrals. Monasteries were also of great importance in Ireland, where the chief leadership for the church came from monks, and in Scotland, where the borderlands contained flourishing houses with beautiful buildings at Melrose, Jedburgh, and Kelso. These too remain as ruins.

British monks lived according to several different rules. The most important houses were Benedictine; these black monks (so called because of the color of their habits) followed the sensitive, liberal rule of St. Benedict. The Cistercian order, founded in France, had a number of large houses in England, of which Fountains was perhaps the greatest. The most austere monks were the Carthusians, whose abbeys were called Charterhouses. More than members of other orders, the Carthusians practiced silence, fasting, and self-denial.

Friars also played a major role in the medieval British churches. Not bound to reside in a monastery, as were the monks, and not allowed to own individual property, the friars wandered the country, preaching and teaching. Sometimes caricatured as jolly vagabonds, like Friar Tuck in the Robin Hood legend, they were often popular preachers who interacted with ordinary people more easily than did members of the established ecclesiastical hierarchy.

Because women could not be ordained as priests, the only role the church offered them was that of nuns. The women's religious houses or nunneries never housed large numbers of people, but they performed a valuable function in medieval society. They made communal life possible for single women, including some widows, who otherwise would have found it difficult to establish suitable living arrangements. The nunneries produced some abbesses of marked administrative ability and a few mystics with great spiritual insight. Most nuns followed the Benedictine rule, although the native English order of Sempringham was popular in the early fourteenth century and the Bridgettine house at Syon was the largest and most important nunnery during the century before the dissolution.

The Church in Medieval Society

Two more points must be made. First, one must recognize the financial importance of the church in medieval society. By the end of the Middle Ages the church had come to own at least a quarter of the land in the several countries of the British Isles. If one adds to this the income from tithes and special offerings, it is clear that at least a third of the national revenue was used for religious purposes. Churchmen were great landlords, and their involvement with other groups in society was monetary as well as religious.

The church was also involved in the daily life of ordinary people because its liturgies were designed to follow an annual cycle that related to the changing of the seasons and the phases of farming activity. The church blessed the planting of crops, prayed for their success, and held services of thanksgiving at harvest time. It brightened the bleak midwinter days with joyous celebrations at Christmas, Epiphany, and Candlemas. It allowed women to identify with the cult of the Virgin Mary and to join in her festivals, especially the Feast of the Annunciation (March 25, one of the most important days in medieval church calendars). It provided for times of penitence (Advent and Lent) and seasons of rejoicing (Easter and Pentecost). It did much to bring warmth, color, and intellectual activity into lives that otherwise would have been cold, drab, and full of drudgery. It is impossible to know how many people regularly attended services during medieval times, but the proportion of the population was certainly higher than in our own day. For many people in the British Isles, the Middle Ages were truly an age of faith.

Wycliffe and the Lollards

During the fourteenth century the English church was unsettled by the activities of John Wycliffe. A theologian who taught at Oxford, Wycliffe became distressed at what he regarded as the worldliness and corruption of the clergy, who were often ignorant, selfish men with little genuine spirituality. He hoped that the pope would reform the church; when this did not happen, he looked to the state for change. For a time he gained the favor of John of Gaunt and some other lay magnates, but in the end they too disappointed him.

Wycliffe was finally driven to question the most fundamental beliefs of the medieval church. He came to reject the doctrine of transubstantiation (which holds that during the communion the priest transforms bread and wine into the substance of Christ's body and blood) because he thought it gave the clergy too great control over the salvation of individual men and women. He argued that papal power had no scriptural justification. He wanted as many people as possible to read the Bible themselves, not merely hear portions of it expounded by the clergy. He was one of the first scholars to translate the Scriptures into English. He and his friends produced the first complete English Bible.

The pope condemned Wycliffe's teachings in 1377. A few years later he was suspended from his university post. He was not executed, perhaps because his orthodox enemies did not wish to make him a popular martyr, but a number of his followers were later burned as heretics, particularly after Parliament passed the statute *De haeretico comburendo* in 1401. His disciples came to be known as Lollards—the term originally meant "babblers"—and Lollardy attracted a considerable following, mainly among urban craftsmen and the poorer gentry. After the failure of a Lollard rising in 1414 the movement went underground, but many of its ideas survived and came to the fore again in the sixteenth century, at the time of the Protestant Reformation.

The Jews in England

The Jews formed a special minority community in medieval England. They first crossed the Channel from Normandy soon after the Conquest, settling initially in London. This always remained their center; the area where they lived is still called Jewry Street. By the thirteenth century there were communities of Jews in more than twenty towns and cities, including Norwich and Lincoln, where one of the finest surviving medieval homes is still called the Jew's House. The Jews were active in financial dealings, especially as moneylenders and pawnbrokers. Sometimes they were called on to lend money to the king, to bishops, and to religious houses. Part of the rebuilding of Westminster Abbey was financed with money borrowed from the Jews. Their services were especially valuable, since in theory the Christian church condemned taking interest on loans as being usury. Jews also dealt in land and in grain.

For a time the Jews enjoyed the special protection of the monarch, but they were also liable for special taxes, and the king was regarded as their universal heir. In theory they could not own land, since all their property was destined to revert to the monarch. In practice they did occasionally hold estates when foreclosure followed nonpayment of loans, but they were always urban in orientation and never joined the ranks of landed gentry.

Christians seem to have grown less tolerant of the Jews during the thirteenth century, when there were unpleasant episodes in which Jews were accused (unfairly) of murdering a Christian boy and (more plausibly) of clipping coins. Because of these problems, and perhaps also because Italian bankers were beginning to supply the financial needs of the aristocracy, Edward I expelled the Jews from England in 1290, reaping a handsome profit from confiscating their property.

Schools and Universities

The growth of education was one of the most significant phenomena of the later Middle Ages in Britain. Although most peasants remained illiterate, those involved in trade, government, and the professions needed to be able to read and write. Churchmen had to know at least a smattering of Latin. It has been estimated that as many as 40 percent of the male householders in late medieval London could read some Latin; the number who could read English would of course have been substantially higher. But these figures are extraordinary rather than typical. In outlying areas, among women, and among lesser working people, literacy rates were much lower.

The most important schools of medieval England were the grammar schools, intended to teach Latin grammar to boys who were destined for careers in the church or, perhaps, in government. (Many medieval government officials were men in holy orders; the words *clerk* and *cleric* have a common root.) The most prestigious grammar schools were Winchester, founded in 1382 by William of Wykeham, the bishop of Winchester, and Eton, nestled in the shadow of Windsor Castle, established by King Henry VI in 1440. (They survive as two of the great "public schools" of England, so called because, although private, they made some places available to poor scholars.) The ability to dispute in Latin was highly prized. Boys also spent time in games, including football, tennis, and cockfighting.

Some boys were able to proceed from the grammar schools to the universities of Oxford and Cambridge. These great centers of higher learning grew up gradually, almost spontaneously, in the twelfth century. It is often said

Oxford University. A photograph of High Street, taken early in the twentieth century, shows buildings of several of the medieval colleges.
Reproduced by permission of the Royal Commission on the Historical Monuments of England.

that Oxford was founded by scholars from Paris who had experienced diffi-culties with the authorities there and that Cambridge began when unruly Oxford students were expelled and forced to move elsewhere. Although these tales may have some basis in fact, the actual origins of the universities were less dramatic. Initially, groups of scholars congregated in favorable environ-ments—Oxford may have seemed desirable because of the existence of several large religious houses there—and groups of students came, at first individually and informally, to study with them. In the next stage of development, hostels or halls were established to provide housing for students; some of these were then transformed into colleges, which undertook responsibility for supervis-ing the students' studies as well as providing room and board. The actual universities themselves were at first no more than collections of colleges. Their chief role in the Middle Ages was to administer examinations and award degrees.

Three of the Oxford colleges (Balliol, University, and Merton) trace their origins to the thirteenth century. William of Wykeham established New

College, Oxford, in the fourteenth century. Its link with his school at Winchester remains important even today. King's College, Cambridge, was founded by Henry VI and enjoyed a special tie to Eton. Peterhouse, founded in 1284, is the oldest college at Cambridge. A number of additional colleges were established at both universities during the fourteenth and fifteenth centuries.

The curriculum of the grammar schools and universities was based on the seven liberal arts of classical antiquity. These included the *trivium*—grammar, rhetoric, and logic, subjects that would be pursued in school—and the more advanced, less "trivial" studies of the *quadrivium:* arithmetic, geometry, astronomy, and music (here considered as a theoretical, mathematical exercise, not in terms of actual performance). Medieval students might go up to the universities when they were still quite young. Normally they spent six years mastering the liberal arts (the Master of Arts degree was intended to certify their proficiency and was evidence that its holders were qualified to teach). Higher degrees were available in theology, medicine, and law. Cambridge, for instance, had a graduate faculty in theology as early as 1250.

The theology studied at the great medieval universities of England and France is often referred to as scholasticism (literally, the theology of the schools). Anselm, the Franco-Italian scholar who became archbishop of Canterbury in 1093, was an important figure in the early development of scholasticism. In his writings, human reason was brought to bear in defining the teachings of the church, especially the doctrine of the Incarnation.

The so-called Renaissance of the twelfth century, which included a fresh interest in the Latin classics and the writings of Aristotle, helped shape the progress of scholastic thought, in particular the movement to annex philosophy to theological study. During the thirteenth century the chief exponents of scholasticism were Thomas Aquinas, probably the most influential theologian in the history of Christianity, and Peter Lombard, whose *Sentences* applied refined logical arguments to theological debate. Both Aquinas and Lombard worked on the Continent, not in England, but their ideas permeated instruction at Oxford and Cambridge for centuries. Two British thinkers, Duns Scotus and William of Ockham, did dominate scholastic thought during its final flourishing in the fourteenth century. Often criticized as an arid intellectual exercise with scant relationship to real life, scholasticism at its best did stretch the horizons of the human mind and provide a tightly reasoned intellectual framework for Christian belief.

Legal studies also became institutionalized during the later Middle Ages, not in the universities but in the Inns of Court. These foundations sprang up in London, near the royal courts of justice, during the late fourteenth and early fifteenth centuries. Practicing lawyers had chambers in the four great

Inns (Gray's Inn, the Inner and Middle Temples, and Lincoln's Inn). Students were able to take meals with them, attend lectures, and assist barristers in their work. By the end of the Middle Ages the Inns of Court really constituted a third, specialized university. Like Oxford and Cambridge they retain many of their early traditions even today.

The three ancient universities of Scotland—St. Andrew's, Glasgow, and Aberdeen—were founded during the fifteenth century. A few Scottish students were also drawn to Balliol College, Oxford (as the college's name suggests). Wales had no university, though a number of Welshmen went to Oxford. Surprisingly, Ireland had no university until Trinity College, Dublin, was established in 1592. There had been an attempt to found a university in Dublin during the early fourteenth century, but it came to nothing.

Chaucer and the
English Language

Linguistic developments in the fourteenth century are of crucial importance in the history of the English tongue. During the first three centuries after the Norman Conquest, English was little used as a written language. The church kept its records in Latin, and the Chancery, the law courts, and Parliament used French—often a bastardized form, sometimes called "law French." Not until the second half of the fourteenth century was English recognized as a serious literary language, in no way inferior to French or Latin.

The language in use during the later Middle Ages is referred to as Middle English. Although it is not easy for twentieth-century students to read, since it includes both vocabulary and word forms that are different from our own, it is the direct ancestor of modern English.

More than any other single person, Geoffrey Chaucer may be credited with establishing the position of Middle English. Chaucer was a major figure in politics as well as literature. The son of a London wine merchant, he received patronage and government office from Edward III, Richard II, John of Gaunt, and Henry IV; he served abroad as an ambassador and at home as a financial administrator and member of Parliament. The most famous of his several writings, and the one most important in the formation of the English language, was the *Canterbury Tales*, completed about 1390. Here Chaucer used the form of English spoken in London, which came to dominate the dialects common in other parts of the country.

Wycliffe's English Bible, which dates from almost exactly the same time, was also influential in establishing standard Middle English. The coming of printing in the fifteenth century helped spread the acceptance of English texts. William Caxton, the first English printer, set up his press at Westminster in 1477 and published nearly eighty separate books, including the *Canterbury Tales* as well as his own translations of French romances.

The End of the Middle Ages

English historians sometimes argue about the date assigned to the end of the Middle Ages. For centuries the year 1485 was used as a matter of convenience, since it marked a break in the history of the English monarchy. Now most scholars believe that the decade of the 1530s should be singled out as the turning point between medieval and modern times in Britain, if such a division is worth identifying at all. Certainly the personal monarchy and the universal church, two characteristic institutions of the Middle Ages, were still intact in 1485.

In a broader perspective it does not matter greatly whether one thinks that the Middle Ages ended in the late fifteenth or early sixteenth century. What is important is to realize how fully developed British society had become by this time. Despite turmoil in the monarchy, both in England and in Scotland, quite sophisticated systems of government had been instituted, with financial, legal, and parliamentary organs securely in place. Towns had grown; trade had expanded; royal mints produced the coins that were required in a money-based economy. Fine parish churches and great cathedrals had been erected. An educational system that included schools and universities of international stature had been established. Learning and literature flourished, as did music (plainsong, polyphony, and carols) and drama (especially mystery plays). It would be a serious mistake to imagine that medieval society was less vital and creative than what came later.

Suggested Reading

Bennett, H. S., *The Pastons and Their England* (Cambridge: Cambridge University Press, 1970).

Bennett, H. S., *Six Medieval Men and Women* (New York: Atheneum, 1962).

Bennett, Judith M., *Women in the Medieval English Countryside* (New York: Oxford University Press, 1987).

Dyer, Christopher, *Standards of Living in The Later Middle Ages* (Cambridge: Cambridge University Press, 1989).

Hanawalt, Barbara, *The Ties That Bound: Peasant Families in Medieval England* (New York: Oxford University Press, 1986).

Kelly, Amy, *Eleanor of Aquitaine and the Four Kings* (Cambridge, Mass.: Harvard University Press, 1950).

Labarge, Margaret Wade, *Women in Medieval Life* (London: Hamish Hamilton, 1986).

Leader, Damian Riehl, *A History of the University of Cambridge*, Vol. 1 (Cambridge: Cambridge University Press, 1988).

Miller, Edward, and John Hatcher, *Medieval England: Rural Society and Economic Change, 1086–1348* (London: Longman, 1978).

Orme, Nicholas, *English Schools in the Middle Ages* (London: Methuen, 1973).

Postan, M. M., *The Medieval Economy and Society* (Harmondsworth, Middlesex: Penguin Books, 1972).

Power, Eileen, *Medieval People* (New York: Doubleday, 1956).

Richardson, H. G., *The English Jewry Under Angevin Kings* (London: Methuen, 1960).

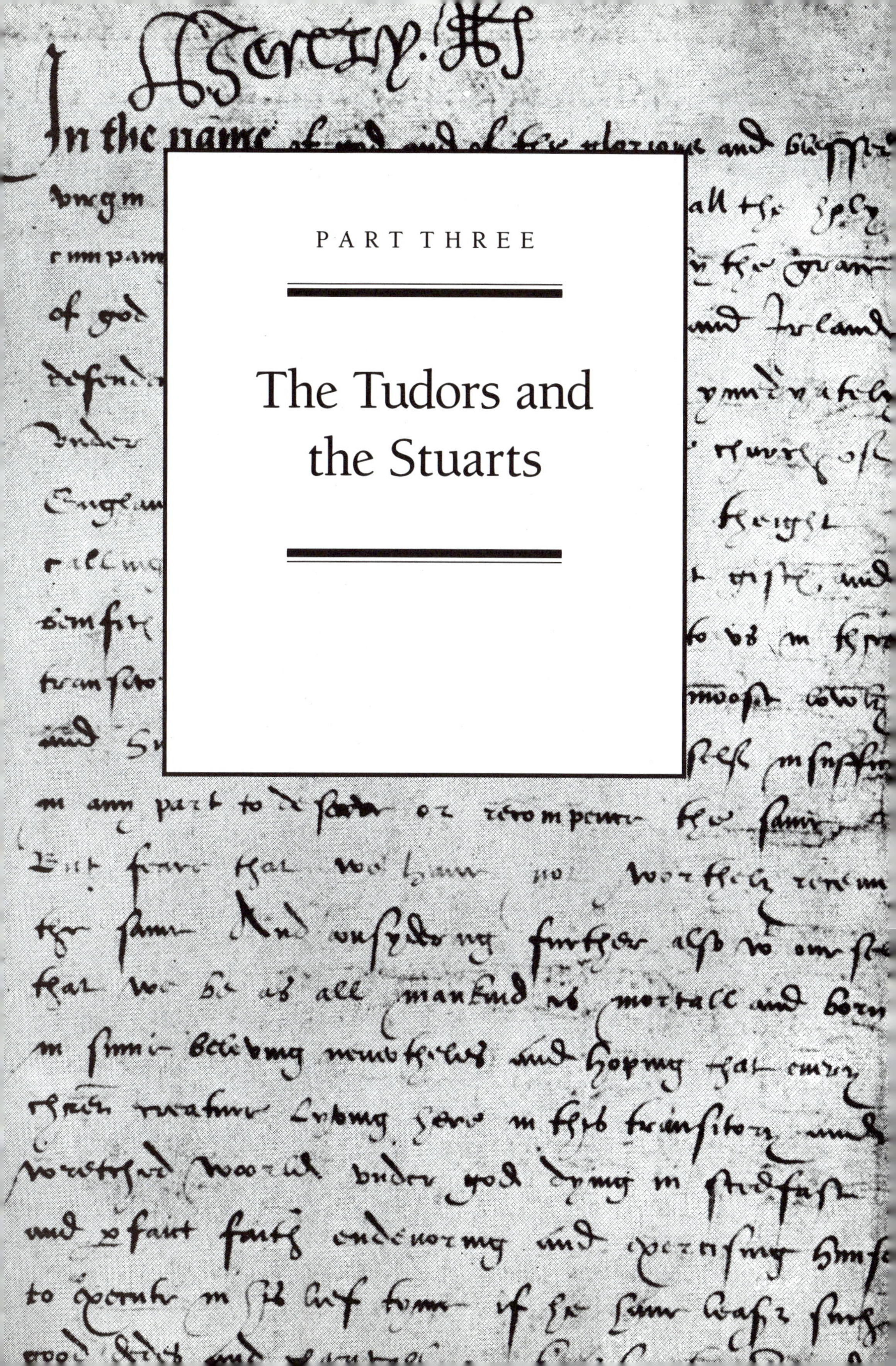

PART THREE

The Tudors and the Stuarts

CHAPTER SEVEN

The Earlier Tudors,
1485–1547

Henry VII (1485–1509)

Henry VII gained his crown on Bosworth Field, in the battle that ended the Wars of the Roses. As the first ruler of the Tudor dynasty, he shared the problems that had faced Henry IV and Edward IV, the first Lancastrian and the first Yorkist. He needed to unify a realm that had been split by past quarrels, convince his subjects that he was entitled to the throne, and reestablish sound central government, which had inevitably suffered during the dynastic conflicts of the last quarter century.

Henry could advance a genealogical claim that superficially seemed compelling, since he was related to the earlier Lancastrian kings. His mother, Lady Margaret Beaufort, was a descendant of Edward III, and his grandmother was Katherine of Valois, the French princess who became queen of England as the wife of Henry V. His father, Edmund Tudor, was a half-brother of Henry VI. But there were flaws in this lineage. The original Beauforts were born out of wedlock, before John of Gaunt married his mistress, Katherine Swynford, and when the family was legitimized by an act of Parliament, a specific provision excluded the right of succession to the throne. Katherine of Valois gave Henry Tudor an inheritance of French royal blood (which he

*Henry VII and Elizabeth of York. Effigies from their tomb in
Henry VII's Chapel, Westminster Abbey. The Italian
sculptor Pietro Torrigiano was brought to England to create
this monument.*
*Reproduced by permission of the Royal Commission on the
Historical Monuments of England.*

seldom mentioned) but no actual descent from the English monarchy. The
Lancastrians could argue that the Yorkists had been usurpers and that their
genealogical claims were faulty because of female links, but the Tudor line
also depended on a female link, and one of dubious legitimacy. Henry VII
was the closest living relative of the former Lancastrian kings, but his title
was imperfect if scrutinized carefully.

Before he sailed from France in the summer of 1485, Henry had vowed to
marry Elizabeth of York, the daughter of Edward IV, if he was successful in
becoming king. The marriage was celebrated soon after Henry's coronation.
One might have expected Elizabeth to be wary of wedding the man who

overthrew the Yorkist line, but she seems to have been disenchanted with her uncle, Richard III, and happy enough to see him defeated. (One cannot help wondering if she knew more than modern historians about the fate of her brothers, the princes in the Tower.) Although the marriage was clearly a political one, intended to unite the red rose and the white and thus help end old animosities, it came to be a happy personal union. One of the few occasions when Henry VII publicly expressed grief was when Elizabeth died, in 1503.

Henry VII's kingship gained additional support from Parliament, which passed an act accepting him as England's lawful ruler, and from the pope, who blessed both his marriage and his succession. In the eyes of common people it may have gained favor, too, as a result of the lavish ceremonies and banquets that accompanied his coronation: surely only a lawful ruler would be crowned so grandly. But when all was said and done it was really Henry's victory on the battlefield and the fact that his opponent had been killed that won the crown for him, and it was his own skill in governing that set the seal of success on his reign.

The Impostors

The earlier years of Henry's rule were marred by several minor threats to his position. In 1486 Lord Lovell, who had been Richard III's chamberlain, led a rebellion seeking to regain power for the Yorkists. He was easily defeated and was executed as a traitor. His extensive lands were confiscated by the king and formed an important addition to Henry VII's estates.

A lower-class lad from Oxfordshire attempted to unseat Henry in 1487. Named Lambert Simnel, he had been coached by an unscrupulous priest to impersonate a member of the Yorkist family, the earl of Warwick, who was a cousin of the young princes. Simnel gained support from Ireland and from Margaret of Burgundy, Edward IV's sister who had married into the French nobility, but his attempt at invading England was pathetic. After his igno-minious defeat in the Battle of Stoke, Henry VII took pity on him and, rather than executing him, made him a scullion in the royal kitchens. The king knew that Simnel was an impostor, since the actual earl of Warwick was secretly being kept prisoner in the Tower of London. The earl was feeble-minded and not likely to advance a Yorkist claim himself.

The final attempt to reopen the Wars of the Roses came in 1496, when Perkin Warbeck invaded England pretending to be Richard, duke of York, the younger of Edward IV's sons. Because few people knew what had become of the princes, it was often supposed that they had fled into exile, so the claim seemed plausible enough. Perkin's story is an interesting one. Born on the Continent, he was apprenticed to a Flemish cloth merchant who traveled to Ireland selling his luxury wares. In the city of Cork, Perkin was taken to be a member of the Yorkist family. He soon agreed to foster the deception. He gained support from the Irish, from Margaret of Burgundy, from the Emperor Maximilian I, and from James IV of Scotland. For several years he lived regally in Scotland, and he married there. He would probably have been happy enough to continue such a life, but his advocates insisted that he invade England. A laughably small effort in Cornwall resulted in his capture in 1497 and his execution in the Tower two years later. Henry VII took the precaution of beheading the true earl of Warwick at the same time. Warbeck's invasion was to prove the last serious challenge to the legitimacy of the Tudors.

Dynastic Marriages

Once he had ensured security at home, Henry turned his attention abroad. He realized that England was regarded as a second-rate country that had lost its Continental holdings and subsequently taken little interest in European affairs.

Involvement in the endemic European wars might focus international attention on England, and Henry did undertake a war with France in 1492, sending an English force to assist the duke of Brittany in his conflict with the French king. Parliament gave Henry tax money to finance the campaign, not all of which was actually spent, but Charles VIII of France was eager to sign a truce and agreed to pay Henry an annual pension in exchange for a pledge of peace and friendship.

Henry thus made a profit on this military venture, the only one of his reign. Perhaps he came to realize that dynastic marriages might enhance his prestige more easily than warfare and that they could be lucrative as well.

Henry VII and Elizabeth of York had four children, all of whom were potentially useful as marriage partners. The heir to the throne, Prince Arthur, was obviously the most important, and Henry was determined to see him wed to a member of one of the great European royal families. In the late fifteenth century, Spain appeared to be the rising power on the Continent. The country had just been unified by the marriage of Ferdinand of Aragon and Isabella of Castile, the queen who financed Christopher Columbus's voyage to the New World in 1492. Their daughter, Catherine of Aragon, was bethrothed to Arthur by the Treaty of Medina del Campo, signed in 1489. Arthur and Catherine were still young children at the time, but by 1501 Catherine was old enough to come to England, and the marriage took place. A substantial Spanish dowry was promised as well, but not all of it was paid immediately.

Plans for a long-lasting Spanish alliance were dashed in 1502, when Arthur died. He seems to have contracted a respiratory illness, perhaps both pneumonia and tuberculosis, while staying with Catherine at Ludlow Castle in Wales. Catherine remained in England, an unwanted teenage widow. Her parents were not eager to have her return to Spain unless her dowry was repaid, and Henry VII was loath to give up the treasure. But eventually Henry VII realized that all the benefits he had anticipated as a result of her union with Arthur might still be realized if she married Prince Henry, the king's younger son and new heir. The marriage was postponed because of Henry's youth, but Henry VII's dying wish was that it take place at the beginning of his son's reign.

Henry VII and Elizabeth also had two daughters. The younger, Mary, was not old enough to be used as a marriage pawn during Henry VII's lifetime; had he been alive he would have been well pleased, however, when she was married to the king of France in 1514. Margaret Tudor, the older daughter, was wed, somewhat unwillingly, to James IV, the Stewart king of Scotland, in the hope that the union would end the hostility that had poisoned Anglo-Scottish relations for centuries and thus usher in a new era of peace and cooperation. This marriage alliance was not successful in the short run, for James was slain fighting the English in 1513, but its longer implications were enormous, since the Stuarts who ruled England in the seventeenth century were descended from Margaret and James.

Financial Administration

Henry VII is sometimes regarded as a financial genius. He began his reign in debt, since he had been obliged to borrow money to pay for his invasion of England. But the indebtedness was quickly cleared, and Henry began to save part of his revenue. By the end of the reign his savings, mostly invested in jewels, amounted to £300,000, or about two years' income. This was not an enormous sum, but because few rulers left the country in better condition than they found it, Henry's policies do deserve analysis.

Henry was nearly unique among English kings in finding government finance personally interesting. Apparently he enjoyed examining the records of his revenues and expenditures, occasionally correcting his clerks' errors in arithmetic. He found the old Exchequer inconvenient, since it was bureaucratically organized and not physically part of his own household, so he followed Edward IV's lead in channeling most of his income into the King's Chamber. Originally no more than a royal petty cash fund, the Chamber now became the principal national treasury. It instituted modernized accounting procedures and was easily amenable to direct royal supervision.

The Exchequer continued to receive tax revenues voted by Parliament. Henry VII was not so dependent on Parliament as his recent predecessors had been, for he enjoyed a larger income from other sources and was actually able to "live of his own" if necessary. But the king did persuade six of the seven Parliaments called during his reign to grant taxes. These were always justified by citing specific purposes, like the suppression of the rebellions of Simnel and Warbeck or the invasion of France. On one occasion Henry proposed to collect feudal aids for the knighting of his son Arthur (who had been dead for two years!) and the marriage of his daughter Margaret. Unhappy about seeing these feudal traditions perpetuated and fearful of having their land titles examined, members of Parliament offered a tax grant of £40,000 in lieu of the aid, and the king, with a rare show of generosity, agreed to accept only £30,000. The Exchequer also continued to receive customs duties, and these increased substantially during Henry's reign. Henry was always interested in encouraging foreign trade, and he was responsible for negotiating a favorable commercial treaty, called the Magnus Intercursus, with the Netherlands.

The King's Chamber oversaw the collection of revenues from the king's lands. Because of forfeitures by rich subjects who were on the losing side at various times during the Wars of the Roses, these lands were now larger in extent than they had been earlier in the fifteenth century. This change, coupled with more efficient administration, substantially enhanced Henry's income. The Chamber managed the estates of minor heirs of tenants-in-chief and greatly increased the profit from these wards' lands. It received income from fines, from the sale of offices and pardons, and even from the rent of ships from the Royal Navy to merchants when they were not needed for military service.

A recent controversy among Tudor historians concerns the question of Henry VII's greed. The debate springs from a statement in Sir Francis Bacon's seventeenth-century account of the life of the king: "Hearing of the bitter cries of his people against the oppressions" of his ministers, Bacon wrote,

Henry "was touched with great remorse" as he lay on his deathbed. More recently a leading Tudor scholar (Sir Geoffrey Elton) argued that Henry took no more than his due. He had not been rapacious, and so he had no reason to be remorseful. One may conclude that all of his exactions were indeed lawful, but some involved payments that subjects had earlier been able to evade. Efficient enforcement therefore appeared harsh, and Henry's popularity may indeed have suffered. It is not easy to find anything warm or endearing about Henry's personality, as it is revealed in surviving documents. He appears as a successful but cold monarch.

The Early Reign of Henry VIII

Henry VII died in April 1509, and his sole surviving son succeeded as Henry VIII. Although the young king was a few weeks shy of his eighteenth birthday, no one insisted on a period of minority and regency. On June 11, Henry married Catherine of Aragon; the coronation took place June 24. The early years of their marriage were happy. One of the great ceremonial occasions is depicted in the Westminster Tournament Roll, which shows Henry jousting for Catherine's entertainment in 1511.

Henry VIII's position was much stronger than his father's. Because he was descended from both the Lancastrians and the Yorkists, there was no longer any question about the legitimacy of his title. He benefited, in two opposed ways, from the events of his father's reign. Henry VII's success in establishing the Tudor dynasty eased his accession, and the old king's aloofness and miserly ways made many people eager for the excitement that a dashing, open-handed monarch might provide.

Because he was inexperienced in governmental affairs and not greatly interested in them, Henry VIII initially relied heavily on advisors who already held high office, especially the archbishop of Canterbury, William Warham, who was also lord chancellor, and the bishop of Winchester, Richard Fox, who was keeper of the Privy Seal. (A foreign ambassador referred to Fox as "alter rex," or the "other king.") One of Henry VIII's first actions, however, was to dismiss two of his father's chief financial administrators, Sir Richard Empson and Edmund Dudley. Although they were guilty of nothing more than carrying out the old king's directions with exceptional efficiency, Empson and Dudley were charged with extortion and were executed in 1510. Clearly Henry VIII believed that his father's fiscal demands had made him unpopular, and he wished to shift the blame to scapegoats who were not members of the royal family.

*Part of the Westminster Tournament Roll, showing Henry VIII taking part
in a joust. Catherine of Aragon can be seen among the spectators, sitting under
a canopy of state. The rose and portcullis used for decoration of the viewing
stand were symbols of the Tudor dynasty.
Courtesy of the The College of Arms, London.*

Shortly after his accession Henry VIII became involved in European diplomacy and warfare. During this period Italy was not a single nation—it was
not unified until the nineteenth century—but rather was a collection of
duchies and city-states. Such division made it weak and a prey to stronger
invaders, especially France and Spain. In the early sixteenth century the
French invaded northern Italy and posed a serious threat to the security of
the papacy, in Rome. Pope Julius II (nicknamed the "Warrior Pope" because
of his involvement in military affairs) tried to repulse the French by putting
together a Holy League, composed primarily of Ferdinand of Aragon and the
Emperor Maximilian. In 1512 Henry VIII agreed to join the League. He was
a devoted son of the church, and Catherine of Aragon's position as a member
of the Spanish royal family helped cement the alliance.

One suspects that Henry welcomed an opportunity to demonstrate his
military prowess as well as his piety. Young, handsome, and athletic, he had
already proved his skill at jousting. In 1513 he personally led an English army

Henry VIII. This portrait is copied from a
painting by Hans Holbein the Younger.
Reproduced by permission of the National
Portrait Gallery.

into northern France, as Henry V had done. His forces defeated French troops at the town of Thérouanne (the French rode off so speedily that the English referred to this as the Battle of the Spurs) and subsequently captured the larger city of Tournai as well.

As an ally of France, Scotland was also drawn into the fray. Local border troubles joined with international concerns in persuading James IV to invade northern England while Henry VIII's troops were preoccupied elsewhere. The English were not taken by surprise, however; Henry VIII's close friend the earl of Surrey led an English force that repulsed the Scots in the bloody Battle of Flodden. James IV (Henry VIII's brother-in-law) was killed, along with ten thousand Scottish soldiers. The power of Scotland was broken for a generation.

Militarily, Henry VIII had been stunningly successful. Diplomatic success, however, eluded him: the European powers concluded a peace settlement without consulting him, and he failed to secure the French territories to which he believed he was entitled. (Tournai did remain English for a few years, but it was never profitable and Henry abandoned it in 1519.) Henry concluded that his chief ministers were too naive to understand the power politics of the European courts, and he turned against his Spanish allies as well. The shift to a pro-French, anti-Spanish foreign policy became obvious when Henry arranged a marriage between his sister Mary and the French king, Louis XII. Naturally enough the teenage English princess disliked the thought of union with the aged foreign monarch, but she agreed to cooperate when she was promised the right of selecting a subsequent husband herself. In fact Louis died almost immediately, and Mary was then able to wed a handsome English nobleman, Charles Brandon, the duke of Suffolk.

Cardinal Wolsey

The king's dissatisfaction with his chief ministers provided the opportunity for the rise of Thomas Wolsey, who within a few years consolidated his exceptional control of both church and state in England.

Wolsey's career is fascinating, especially because it provides an unusual instance of social mobility. Wolsey's birth was undistinguished—his father was a butcher in the country town of Ipswich—but his intellectual powers were recognized early on, for he went to Oxford at the age of fifteen and graduated while still so young that he was dubbed "the boy bachelor." His education was financed by the church, in which he had taken minor orders. He became a priest as soon as he was old enough, and he remained at Oxford as a fellow and treasurer of Magdalen College, only to be turned out in disgrace when it was discovered that he had ordered the erection of a beautiful but costly belltower without proper authorization.

He soon migrated to court, where he became one of Henry VII's chaplains. He held the same office under Henry VIII and was increasingly employed in secular matters as well. During the French campaign he distinguished himself for the speed and efficiency with which he dispatched his duties (he was in charge of providing food for the troops), and it seemed evident that he possessed a shrewder sense of politics and diplomacy than did Warham and Fox.

After 1513 Wolsey's ascent was meteoric. He succeeded Warham as chancellor, thus assuming control of the Chancery and the courts and the right to preside over the House of Lords in Parliament. Within the church, he held a series of bishoprics, each more lucrative than the one before. Finally he became archbishop of York, second in dignity only to the archbishop of Canterbury. Warham did not accommodate Wolsey by dying or retiring, but Wolsey did gain honors that Warham did not have. In 1515 the pope named him a cardinal (a signal sign of favor), and three years later Wolsey was designated papal legate. In this position he was the direct personal representative of the pope within England and thus could claim precedence over the senior archbishop.

Henry VIII, who was more interested in hunting and dancing than in ruling, left the government more and more in Wolsey's hands. The cardinal continued to demonstrate amazing intellectual ability and attention to detail, and he displayed some interest in reform. Within the church, he dissolved a number of monasteries and diverted their revenues to educational institutions, particularly a college at Oxford that survives as Christ Church. In the state, he announced his intention to use the new Court of Star Chamber, over which he presided, as a means of aiding weak subjects who had grievances against powerful persons; he issued the Eltham Ordinances, with regulations that overhauled the operation of the royal household; and he tried to stem the tide of the enclosure movement, a new form of land management that was putting many agricultural laborers out of work. His collection of offices yielded enormous revenues, second only to those of the king himself.

Wolsey was greatly interested, too, in foreign policy and diplomacy. In 1520 he arranged a glamorous conference between Henry VIII and Francis I, king of France, held in a city of tents erected in Flanders, about halfway between London and Paris, so that both monarchs would be on neutral ground. At this famous "Field of Cloth of Gold" Henry and Francis jousted, attended banquets and masses, and protested undying friendship. But it was all playacting; Henry and Wolsey were actually in the process of turning against France, reverting to the earlier pro-Spanish position. In 1523 English forces invaded northern France, anticipating a recurrence of the Battle of the Spurs but not gaining any notable victory. When the pope died in the same year the Spanish promised that they would support Wolsey as a candidate for the papacy, despite the unlikelihood that anyone but an Italian would be chosen. In the end the Spanish cardinals did not vote for Wolsey. Perhaps for this reason, Wolsey shifted his diplomatic position once again, signing a treaty with the French in 1525. Historians have had some difficulty sorting out the motives or general principles that lay behind these diplomatic maneuvers. An appealing but not entirely convincing recent view holds that Wolsey was a consistent advocate of peace and that the war with France was Henry's doing, not his. What seems indisputable is that Wolsey drew great satisfaction from personal involvement in the highest levels of European politics. He probably believed that this enhanced England's prestige, as well as his own.

In the end Wolsey undertook so many different activities that he was seldom able to carry any scheme through to fruition. Perhaps his greatest achievement was actually his own way of life. During the 1520s he supervised the building of Hampton Court, an enormous palace on the River Thames a few miles upstream from London. Here he patronized the finest artists and artisans of the age; here, with the help of five hundred servants, he entertained the king, members of the court, and foreign dignitaries at great feasts and dances. When he fell, Hampton Court was taken over by the royal family, who continued to live there until the eighteenth century. It still stands as the finest example of early Tudor secular architecture.

The King's Great Matter

Aside from his unrealistic attempt to impose peace on sixteenth-century Europe, Wolsey's only significant failure was his inability to solve the king's "Great Matter." This phrase was used at the time to refer to Henry VIII's desire for a divorce from Catherine of Aragon, and it has become common in historical literature.

By 1527 Henry VIII had come to question to validity of his marriage to Catherine. His concern was initially aroused by Catherine's failure to provide him with a male heir. Henry was intent on ensuring the continuity of the Tudor dynasty, and he did not believe that the English people would accept Catherine's only surviving child, a daughter named Mary, as their ruler. Certainly the warfare between Stephen and Matilda in the twelfth century, on the only previous occasion when a woman had claimed the throne, was not an attractive precedent. Catherine had endured a tragic series of miscarriages, stillbirths, and deaths of infants. By 1527 there was no likelihood that she would bear further children, so if Henry were to father a son it would have to be by another wife.

Henry's worry over the succession spilled over into religious introspection. Wondering why God had not given him a son, he turned to the Bible and soon found a verse in Leviticus that forbids marriage to a brother's widow and states that such unions will be childless. Henry became convinced that he should not have married Prince Arthur's wife and, indeed, that the marriage had never been valid because it violated the biblical commandment.

At about the same time, Henry fell in love with Anne Boleyn, the daughter of a minor courtier and sister of an earlier royal mistress. His desire to be free to marry Anne naturally reinforced his eagerness to divorce Catherine. Anne herself was intent on becoming queen, not just one in a series of extramarital consorts.

Because the church regarded marriage as a sacrament that blessed lifelong unions, divorces could be granted only by the church and only if there had

Anne Boleyn, the second wife of Henry VIII.
The portrait is by an unknown artist.
Reproduced by permission of the National
Portrait Gallery.

been impediments that made the original marriage invalid. (Today we would refer to such dissolutions of marriage as annulments.) If a prominent person like a king wished a divorce, only the papacy could render a decision. Henry therefore directed Wolsey to present his case to Pope Clement VII.

There is no reason to believe that Clement had religious or moral scruples about Henry's petition. Most medieval and Renaissance popes were political realists, and Clement's predecessors had granted divorces under somewhat similar circumstances, for instance to Eleanor of Aquitaine's first husband, the king of France. But Clement found himself in a situation where he could not accommodate the English without offending the Spanish: Charles V, the ruler of Spain, was Catherine's nephew and opposed the divorce as vehemently as did Catherine herself. The timing could not have been worse, for Spanish troops invaded central Italy in 1527, sacking the city of Rome and holding the pope virtually prisoner in his own palace. A decision favoring Henry was clearly impossible under the circumstances.

Pope Clement could only play for time, arguing that Henry's circumstances were unusual and that serious study by theologians and legal scholars would have to precede a judgment. In fact he hoped that the case would resolve itself: Henry and Catherine might be reconciled, or Catherine might agree to enter a nunnery and acquiesce in the separation, or she might die, or Henry might die, or the pope himself might die, thus ending the matter.

In fact none of these things happened. In 1529 Wolsey persuaded the pope to set up a special court to meet in London (since Henry had refused to travel to Italy), with Wolsey himself as one of the two judges. Evidence was presented in this trial at Blackfriars, but before a decision could be rendered the pope revoked the case to Rome. Political considerations still made it impossible for the church to grant the divorce.

Thomas Cromwell and the Reformation Parliament, 1529–1536

Disillusioned with Wolsey, Henry VIII stripped him of all his offices except the archbishopric of York and told him to attend to the administration of that diocese, which he had never visited. Wolsey was ordered not to interfere in governmental or diplomatic affairs; when it was discovered that he was corresponding with the French, hoping that they would intervene in the divorce proceedings, he was ordered to return to London, where he would probably have been executed had he not died on the way. Wolsey's place as chancellor was taken by Sir Thomas More, the greatest intellectual of the early Tudor period, but More was opposed to the divorce for reasons of conscience and Henry had agreed that he need not be involved in it.

For help at this crucial juncture, the king turned, not to the chancellor, but to Parliament; he ordered the election of what was to become the famous Reformation Parliament.

This gathering met in November 1529. Obviously the king was eager for advice and assistance in his great affair, but he had not decided on a new policy. Nor were the Lords and Commons prepared to attack the issue of the divorce directly. In several sessions between 1529 and 1532 they passed laws that provided for minor reforms in such areas as the probate of wills and testaments, and they cut away much of the independence of the church by eliminating its power to make canon law without royal assent. Sir Thomas More resigned in 1532 because he felt unable to accept this secular interference in religion. His adherence to traditional Catholic teachings led to his execution three years later. Parliament also gave the king power to cut off

Thomas Cromwell, principal secretary to Henry VIII. The portrait is by court painter Hans Holbein.
Copyright The Frick Collection, New York City.

the payment of annates (a tax on the clergy) to Rome, but this financial threat did not procure the desired results.

Finally, in 1532, a new political direction became possible, largely because of changes in personnel. Archbishop Warham, who had opposed the divorce, died and was replaced by Thomas Cranmer, a Cambridge theologian of reformed views who was willing to assist the king. More's post as chancellor was taken by Sir Thomas Audley, who proved amenable but unimportant. The really significant new minister was Thomas Cromwell.

A brilliant, relatively young administrator who had previously been in Wolsey's service, Cromwell was the son of a blacksmith from Putney, a London suburb. Evidently an undisciplined youth, Cromwell did not have a university education. Indeed, he knocked around the Continent for a time as a mercenary soldier, thus acquiring experience in European languages and politics. He also obtained some knowledge of the law. After Wolsey's fall, Cromwell was taken directly into the king's service.

Like Wolsey, Cromwell acquired a variety of positions that gave him virtually complete control of the government as long as he enjoyed the king's favor. Unlike the cardinal, he was not ordained and did not hold priestly offices in the church. Nor was he ever chancellor. His chief office, one that was to become dominant later in the century, was that of principal secretary to the king. His career, among other things, marks a new secularization of government leadership.

Cromwell realized that traditional diplomacy would never secure Henry's divorce. It could be achieved only if the power to grant it were taken from the pope and assigned to the archbishop of Canterbury. Hence Cromwell drafted the famous Act in Restraint of Appeals, which was passed by Parliament in the spring of 1533. This cut off all appeals to Rome, arguing that the English church was fully competent to settle all matters that arose within the realm. But it went much further: it insisted that papal jurisdiction in England was a usurpation, since in its earliest years the English church had been independent of Rome. So all papal authority was extinguished. The king was recognized as Supreme Head of the Church and its chief governing authority; the pope's spiritual powers were transferred to the archbishop of Canterbury; and the church in England was transformed into the Church *of* England, a separate national entity without allegiance to any external power. Cromwell justified these actions with historical half-truths and with a new political theory that asserted that England was an "empire," that is, a realm ruled, not just by a king, but by an emperor who acknowledged no superior in either secular or religious affairs.

Henry and Anne were secretly married in January 1533. She became pregnant at about the same time. In the spring, Archbishop Cranmer granted Henry's divorce from Catherine and pronounced his marriage to Anne valid. Anne was crowned in June. In September she bore Henry's child—not the son he had hoped for, but a daughter, who was christened Elizabeth. Henry was disappointed but not dismayed, for Anne was still young and a son would surely follow.

The Reformation Parliament continued to meet periodically until 1536. It passed a number of statutes that tidied up the break with Rome, eliminating all financial payments and granting the archbishop of Canterbury power to issue dispensations formerly granted by the pope. It ratified Henry's title of "Supreme Head," gave him the absolute legal right to name bishops and archbishops, and established penalties for any who still advocated papal jurisdiction in England. It is one of the most important Parliaments in English history because it assured a role for Parliament in shaping both religious and social policy.

One may ask why the Reformation Parliament was willing to support such a drastic change as the separation of the English church from the papacy. Some older writers, especially those who were themselves Catholics, held that the king brought improper pressure to bear on the election of members of the Commons, so as to create a house packed with Protestants. Recent research demonstrates that this cannot be true; there was no split between Catholics and Protestants (or, more generally, between conservatives and reformers) as early as 1529, and in any case Henry had no minister capable of applying pressure effectively, since the Parliament was elected during the interim between the fall of Wolsey and the rise of Cromwell.

It seems certain that most members of Parliament sympathized with Henry and thought that the pope was unreasonable in not granting the divorce. The Commons did not care greatly about theological matters; indeed, the chief concern voiced at one stage in the proceedings against the papacy was whether trade would be adversely affected. It is probably true, too, that few people realized how significant and permanent the religious changes were to be. There had been numerous disputes between kings and popes during the Middle Ages, but all of them had blown over eventually. Many thought that Henry VIII's quarrel would follow suit. Religious issues, as opposed to political ones, were to become important later, but they had little influence in the actual break with Rome.

The Dissolution
of the Monasteries

Parliament also initiated the dissolution of the monasteries. Although a few monks were staunch supporters of the pope, the break with Rome need not have been accompanied by an attack on monasticism in England. In fact, Cromwell and Henry were motivated mainly by greed, for the monasteries were wealthy institutions that owned as much as a quarter of all the land in the realm. In order to justify the confiscation of property, commissioners were sent to survey all the religious houses in England and Wales. Their reports alleged specific instances of immorality and misconduct—many of these were probably inaccurate or unjust—as well as a pervasive absence of genuine spirituality. These documents were used to justify an act passed in 1536 that ordered the closure of all religious houses with an income of £200 or less. The larger monasteries and nunneries were suppressed through individual negotiations with their leaders over the next few years,

The ruins of Glastonbury Abbey, one of England's greatest
monasteries, dissolved by Henry VIII.
Reproduced by permission of the Royal Commission on the
Historical Monuments of England.

and their suppression was ratified by Parliament in 1539. Among the greatest houses turned to ruins were Glastonbury, the legendary foundation of Joseph of Arimathea, and Fountains, a beautiful monastery in Yorkshire.

Following the dissolution, all monastic properties were transferred to the king, who proceeded to sell the estates to lay landlords. Monks and nuns were allowed to renounce their religious vows and were given pensions; some monks who were priests received new assignments in parishes or cathedrals. A new financial bureau, the Court of Augmentations, was created to deal with monastic property. Pensions were also paid out of the Augmentations.

Half of the cathedrals in England were organized as monasteries and staffed by monks. In these cases the monasteries were dissolved, but the

Ruins of Fountains Abbey, a large Cistercian monastery in Yorkshire.
Reproduced by permission of the Royal Commission on the Historical Monuments
of England.

cathedrals continued to exist, now served by a dean and secular clergy called
canons. Such cathedrals, including Canterbury and Durham, are called
cathedrals of the new foundation, since they were reorganized and given new
statutes by Henry VIII. At one time Henry's government entertained the
idea of turning quite a large number of the dissolved monasteries into cathedrals, thus reducing the size of dioceses and increasing the efficiency of
administration in the church, but in the end a more modest scheme prevailed. Only six new cathedrals were established, providing a continuing use
for the great monastic churches at such places as Gloucester and Peterbor-
ough. Westminster Abbey was organized as a cathedral for a few years, but in
the later sixteenth century it assumed its present unique position as a "royal
peculiar," a great church used for coronations and other state occasions, but
not the home of a bishop or seat of a diocese. Monasteries that were not
turned into cathedrals were left to fall into ruin or be transformed into
mansions for members of the aristocracy and country gentry.

It is worth pausing to reflect on what was lost when the era of monasticism ended. As we have seen, the monasteries had for centuries provided a refuge for men of spirituality and learning. They fostered the arts of music, architecture, calligraphy, and literature. They offered a continuous round of prayer on behalf of all members of society. They provided alms for the poor and lodging for travelers, and they operated hospitals for the sick. They were large landlords and sometimes treated tenant farmers with understanding and generosity. They offered a community to some persons who in later centuries might have to be cared for in homes for the elderly, infirm, or mentally deficient—the "misfits of society," one might call them. For women, nunneries were the chief alternative to marriage. Many of these functions were less significant in the sixteenth century than they had been earlier, or were being performed less well. Still, the sudden loss of all the religious houses meant a major change in society, not just in religion.

The Reformation in Religion and Society

The break with Rome marked the beginning of the Reformation in England. On the Continent, the Reformation had begun in 1517, when Martin Luther nailed his Ninety-Five Theses to the church door in Wittenberg. In this famous manifesto, Luther denounced the doctrine of the Roman Catholic church on nearly a hundred separate issues. He argued that Christ had instituted only two sacraments (baptism and communion or the Eucharist), not the seven sacraments espoused by Rome. He believed in "the priesthood of all believers" and urged men and women to approach God directly, without invoking the aid of intercessors or saints. His most important doctrine was "justification by faith," which held that God will freely grant salvation to those who have faith: no one is saved by good works, prayers for the dead, or the purchase of special indulgences from the pope or other ecclesiastical authorities. Because Luther protested against many of the doctrines and practices of the Catholic church, he and his followers came to be known as Protestants.

Protestant writings were originally banned in England. Thomas More was given authority to read them, but only so that he could refute their claims, which he did in a number of long, difficult treatises. Henry VIII himself (perhaps with More's scholarly assistance) wrote a book called *The Defense of the Seven Sacraments*, restating the traditional Catholic position on that issue.

But a few young men, especially students at Cambridge, were attracted by Luther's call for reform. One of these was Thomas Cranmer, the first Protestant archbishop of Canterbury.

Foreign ideas, however, were not the only intellectual force behind the English Reformation. The earlier teachings of Wycliffe and the Lollards were in many ways similar to Luther's views, and it may be that the continuing influence of Lollardy was as important as the new inspiration of Lutheranism. Certainly some people were put off, as Wycliffe had been, by the ignorance, laziness, and greed of churchmen, and they were not sorry to see the church lose part of its wealth and power.

The case of Richard Hunne is often cited as proof of such anticlerical sentiment. Hunne was a substantial London merchant who refused to pay the fee required by a churchman for conducting the funeral of his infant son. Indeed, Hunne denounced the covetousness of the church generally. He was arrested, imprisoned in the "Lollards' Tower" attached to St. Paul's Cathedral, and found dead in his cell in 1514. Although the jailer insisted that he had committed suicide, most Londoners were convinced that he had been murdered; the bishop of London alleged that no clergyman could obtain a fair trial, so great was the popular feeling aroused by the affair. But this was an isolated incident, and anticlerical sentiment was probably not as widely diffused as some writers suggest.

Once papal jurisdiction was abolished and Cranmer was installed as archbishop, Protestant ideas were officially sanctioned in England. Cranmer issued injunctions denouncing relics, images, and pilgrimages. Like Luther, he believed that it was acceptable for priests to marry and admitted that he had already taken a wife himself. Like Wycliffe, he supported the publication of an English Bible, so that literate laypersons might read it in their own language, not in Latin. The "Great Bible" was first printed in 1539 and made a significant impact following its publication in a cheap edition the next year. Cranmer also began planning a translation of the services of the church, including the mass, into the English tongue, but this project did not bear fruit until after the death of Henry VIII.

While Cranmer was introducing reformed ideas into the church, Cromwell attempted to bring about a social reformation. Both in the Reformation Parliament and in the Parliaments of 1536 and 1539, he proposed acts for poor relief, legal reform, and even an early form of urban renewal. These were motivated by concern for the social unrest that resulted from the enclosure movement, inflation, and unemployment. While some of Cromwell's measures were so advanced that they did not pass the Lords and Commons, a number did make their way to the statute book. Cromwell's reforms, particularly in the areas of administrative centralization and government finance, were so significant that they have been described as a "revolution in government." He also provided patronage for a number of able young men, some of whom were recruited into government service.

Cranmer and Cromwell may have moved too rapidly, underestimating the extent of conservative opinion. In 1536 opposition was manifested in the Pilgrimage of Grace, a conservative rebellion that began near Lincoln but spread into Yorkshire and other parts of northern England. Partly a protest against the dissolution of the monasteries, it was also a demonstration against reform generally. The Pilgrims believed in traditional Catholic doctrines, and they disapproved of the way in which power had been acquired by Cromwell and Cranmer, neither of whom were members of the old aristocracy. The Pilgrimage indicated the strength of conservatism in many parts of the realm but was harshly suppressed by the government.

The Six Wives of Henry VIII

During the later years of Henry's reign, his marital affairs were closely intertwined with national politics and diplomacy. Each of his six marriages had larger implications than the marital bed.

The king's relationship with Anne Boleyn deteriorated in 1536 when she suffered a miscarriage. It has recently been argued that the aborted fetus was deformed and that this shock led to the charge that Anne was a witch. She was accused of infidelity to Henry and of having had sexual relations with a number of men, both before and after her marriage; she was condemned to death and was executed within the Tower of London. Cranmer found grounds for pronouncing that their marriage had not been valid. Catherine of Aragon died a natural death in the same year.

Almost immediately after Anne's execution, Henry took his third wife, Jane Seymour, the attractive and intelligent daughter of a minor courtier and gentleman. Jane succeeded where Henry's other wives failed, for in 1537 she gave birth to a son, who was christened Edward. Had she lived, Henry might have been happy with Jane for years, but she died within weeks from the complications of childbirth. Edward was to be Henry's last child.

Genuinely grief-stricken, Henry remained a bachelor until 1540. At this time Cromwell and Cranmer were deeply concerned about England's isolation. They feared an alliance of European Catholic powers, mainly Spain and the papacy, which might undertake a campaign to restore the old religion in England. A dynastic marriage appeared to be the best way of gaining an alliance with one of the Lutheran states in Germany or Scandinavia. Henry considered marrying a Danish princess, Christina, but disliked her appearance as represented in a portrait by his great court painter, Hans Holbein. Cromwell then proposed a marriage to Anne of Cleves, the sister of an impoverished Protestant duke in northern Germany. Holbein was sent to Cleves and returned with a portrait that Henry found acceptable. The treaty was signed, and Anne came to England in 1540. When Henry first saw her he realized that he had been deceived, for he found her singularly unappealing. His advisors insisted that the marriage take place, for diplomatic reasons, but Cranmer found an excuse for invalidating it almost immediately. Curiously enough, Anne of Cleves remained in England the rest of her life. Henry granted her a small estate, and she occasionally returned to court, where she dined amicably with her former husband. By this time Henry was no longer very attractive himself; he had grown fat, was often in pain with a persistent sore on one leg, drank too much, and was generally irritable. Anne may well have been happy that the royal marriage did not last.

Soon after his divorce from Anne of Cleves, Henry married his fifth wife, Catherine Howard. Catherine was a cousin of Anne Boleyn and shared many of her characteristics. Like Anne, she was related to the duke of Norfolk, who acquired additional influence as a result of the marriage. Norfolk took advantage of his position, and of Henry's anger over the Cleves affair, to bring down his old rival Cromwell, who was mainly responsible for the Cleves marriage. Cromwell was charged with assuming powers that were rightly the king's own and with adhering to radical Protestant or sectarian religious principles. He was executed in 1540, on the very day that Henry married Catherine Howard. The king never found another capable chief minister; he himself admitted that he did not fully appreciate Cromwell until he was gone.

Catherine Howard's fall was reminiscent of Anne Boleyn's. She too was charged with adultery, found guilty (some of her alleged lovers were probably tortured before giving testimony against her), and executed on Tower Green in 1542.

The king's last wife was Catherine Parr. Already a widow, though still relatively young, she was an intelligent woman, attracted by Protestant ideas. She tried to provide companionship and affection for the king during his last years, and she attempted to give something like a mother's care to Henry's children, especially Elizabeth and Edward, who had never had anything approaching a normal home. Catherine Parr, like Anne of Cleves, outlived the king. After his death she married Jane Seymour's younger brother Thomas and died trying to bear him a son.

Henry VIII's Last Years

Troubles mounted during the last years of Henry VIII's reign. England was increasingly divided into conservative and reforming factions, and their disputes hindered the effective operation of the government. Cranmer's orthodox opponents in the church, men who had joined in rejecting the pope but would not abandon Catholic doctrine, were led by the bishop of Winchester, Stephen Gardiner. The duke of Norfolk provided lay leadership for the conservatives, and relatives of Jane Seymour and Catherine Parr provided support for reform, both religious and social. Only the king seemed able to hold the balance between the rival groups, and his position was unpredictable: he appeared to favor first one side, then the other. Social unrest also mounted.

The conservatives were responsible for the Act of Six Articles, passed in 1539. This measure made it heresy to deny the Catholic doctrine of transubstantiation, which holds that the bread and wine of the communion are transformed into the substance of Christ's body and blood when consecrated by a priest. It became a felony to advocate the marriage of priests, to favor communion in both kinds (the Catholic church gave only the bread to laypeople, reserving the wine for ordained clergy), or to maintain other Protestant doctrines. By these criteria the archbishop of Canterbury was himself a heretic. Henry continued to support Cranmer and he remained in office, but he was forced to send his wife back to Germany. The privilege of reading the Bible in English was restricted by a statute of 1543. Arguing that uneducated laymen and women might misinterpret scripture, the act stated that only men of gentry or aristocratic status might read the Bible, either publicly or privately. Originally women were to have been denied this right altogether, but an amendment proposed while the act was under discussion allowed female members of the nobility to study the Scriptures. A theological compendium issued in 1543 and often called the King's Book because it had been examined and revised by Henry VIII, also reiterated orthodox views.

Diplomacy, military affairs, and government finance presented problems as well. The king and his chief advisors continued to fear a Catholic attack on England, and they spent vast amounts of money constructing new fortifications on the south and east coasts. Some of these still exist; they are magnificent pieces of military architecture, using the most up-to-date methods of ensuring that they could not be besieged successfully. Lacking a shrewd diplomatic consultant after the execution of Cromwell, Henry fell back on the traditional animosity to France and Scotland. A successful but probably unnecessary Scottish campaign culminated in an English victory at Solway

Henry VIII and the pope, by an unknown artist. This allegorical painting shows Henry VIII on his deathbed, passing on authority to his son Edward. Members of the Council appear at the right; the deposed pope is shown at the bottom, with monks fleeing the country. The scene viewed through the window depicts reformers knocking down a statue regarded as being superstitious.
Reproduced by permission of the National Portrait Gallery.

Moss in 1542. It is said that the news of this disastrous Scottish defeat broke James V's heart and caused his death. He was succeeded by his infant daughter, Mary, queen of Scots, who was only a week old. Henry VIII himself again took part in an invasion of northern France in 1545. A treaty signed the next year did make concessions to England, but they were hardly worth the great cost of the campaign.

A number of financial expedients were invoked to pay for these activities. Much of the land confiscated from the monasteries was sold for ready cash rather than being retained as a permanent endowment for the Crown. Parliament was persuaded to grant unprecedentedly large taxes. In addition, the mints were ordered to debase the coinage, putting larger amounts of cheap metal like copper into new shillings in order to produce more coins from the same amount of precious silver. The government thus paid its debts with cheaper coin, but subjects came to realize that the coins had lost much of their value and so they began demanding more of them in exchange for commodities. This pernicious practice was largely responsible for the very serious inflation that began about 1540 and lasted for a century.

At the very end of Henry's reign the conservative faction lost its chief leaders. Bishop Gardiner, always a stubborn man, quarreled with the king over land transactions as well as religion and was dismissed from the Council. The duke of Norfolk and his son, the earl of Surrey, were charged with treason and sentenced to death. Surrey (a distinguished poet though a politically inept hothead) was actually executed; Norfolk's execution was scheduled to take place in 1547 but was postponed and eventually cancelled because of the death of Henry VIII.

Shortly before he died, Henry VIII drafted his will. This provided that his son, Edward, should succeed to the throne. If Edward died without heirs, Henry's older daughter, Mary, was to follow him; should Mary also fail to produce offspring, Elizabeth was to succeed. This was, of course, the normal hereditary pattern of succession, leaving aside the fact that both Mary and Elizabeth had been branded as illegitimate when their mothers fell from favor, and it was recognized by a parliamentary Act of Succession. Henry's will also provided for a council of regency to administer the realm during Edward's minority. A fairly large group, it was evenly divided between conservatives and reformers, but because the chief conservatives (Gardiner and Norfolk) were excluded, the principal leadership was bound to come from councillors who favored Protestantism and social reform. These provisions came into effect when Henry died late in January 1547.

Suggested Reading

Chrimes, S. B., *Henry VII* (Berkeley and Los Angeles: University of California Press, 1972).

Dickens, A. G., *The English Reformation* (New York: Schocken Books, 1964).

Elton, G. R., *England Under the Tudors* (London: Methuen, 1955).

Elton, G. R., *Policy and Police: The Enforcement of the Reformation in the Age of Thomas Cromwell* (Cambridge: Cambridge University Press, 1972).

Elton, G. R., *Reform and Reformation: England 1509–1558* (Cambridge, Mass.: Harvard University Press, 1977).

Elton, G. R., *Reform and Renewal: Thomas Cromwell and the Common Weal* (Cambridge: Cambridge University Press, 1973).

Elton, G. R., *The Tudor Revolution in Government* (Cambridge: Cambridge University Press, 1953).

Guy, John, *Tudor England* (New York: Oxford University Press, 1988).

Haig, Christopher, ed., *The English Reformation Revised* (Cambridge: Cambridge University Press, 1987).

Ives, E. W., *Anne Boleyn* (Oxford: Basil Blackwell, 1986).

Knowles, Dom David, *The Religious Orders in England: III, The Tudor Age* (Cambridge: Cambridge University Press, 1959).

Lehmberg, Stanford E., *The Later Parliaments of Henry VIII, 1536–1547* (Cambridge: Cambridge University Press, 1977).

Lehmberg, Stanford E., *The Reformation Parliament, 1529–1536* (Cambridge: Cambridge University Press, 1970).

Mattingly, Garrett, *Catherine of Aragon* (Boston: Little, Brown, 1941).

Prescott, H.F.M., *The Man on a Donkey* (London: Eyre & Spottiswoode, 1952) (a historical novel about the Pilgrimage of Grace).

Scarisbrick, J. J., *Henry VIII* (Berkeley and Los Angeles: University of California Press, 1968).

Scarisbrick, J. J., *The Reformation and the English People* (Oxford: Basil Blackwell, 1984).

Smith, Lacey Baldwin, *Henry VIII: The Mask of Royalty* (London: Jonathan Cape, 1971).

Warnicke, Retha M., *The Rise and Fall of Anne Boleyn* (Cambridge: Cambridge University Press, 1989).

Williams, Penry, *The Tudor Regime* (Oxford: Clarendon Press, 1979).

CHAPTER EIGHT

The Later Tudors, 1547–1603

Edward VI (1547–1553) and the Triumph of Protestantism

Edward VI was nine years old when he assumed the throne. A precocious child, he was being brought up according to the newest educational theories by distinguished academic tutors, including the grammarian John Cheke and the Protestant theologian Richard Cox. Probably as part of his training, Edward kept a journal that nominally begins with his birth (actually he started writing it about the time of his accession) and runs almost to his death. This remains a primary source for the events of his reign.

Henry VIII's arrangements for a council of regents did not last very long. One of the councillors, Edward VI's uncle Edward Seymour, wished to gain control of the government and soon persuaded his fellow regents to yield their power to him. Created duke of Somerset, he assumed the title "lord protector" of the young king, and thus he is usually referred to as Protector Somerset. Historians disagree about Somerset's character. He was traditionally regarded as "the good duke," liberal, intellectual, and Protestant, but

Edward VI, portrait by a follower of Holbein.
Reproduced by permission of the National
Portrait Gallery.

newer interpretations picture him as an egotistical autocrat who was actually more interested in military activity against Scotland than in religious or social reform. Despite their relationship, he did not get on well with the young king, for he refused to pretend that Edward was already able to be involved in the determination of government policy.

Whether or not he was a sincere Protestant, Somerset was willing to allow the Reformation to proceed. Both Edward VI and Archbishop Cranmer were eager to see the Church of England adopt Protestant doctrines and liturgies; these were not yet in place, for the Reformation under Henry VIII had been essentially political rather than theological. Edward, indeed, came to regard himself as God's chosen instrument to reform the English church, and some Protestants, seeing a biblical parallel, called him the "young Josiah."

The earliest Edwardian measure involved the dissolution of the chantries. Chantries were endowments, held in cathedrals and parish churches, that paid stipends to priests who prayed for the souls of the dead. If Luther's doctrine of justification by faith was indeed correct, prayers for the dead were of no avail. Equally important, as far as the government was concerned, was the wealth of the chantries, which could be confiscated and spent in exactly the same way Henry VIII had expropriated the endowments of the monasteries. More than two thousand chantries were closed under an act passed by Parliament in 1547. Their suppression meant not only the end of prayers for the dead but also the closure of a large number of elementary schools in which chantry priests had taught reading and writing. The impact on education will be considered further in Chapter 12.

By this time Cranmer was busy translating the services of the church from Latin into English. Both he and Edward were convinced, as were the Continental reformers, that it was unjustifiable to expect ordinary men and women to worship in a language they did not understand. Henry VIII read Latin himself and never quite appreciated that his subjects were less learned than he. He loved the Latin mass and refused to abandon it as long as he lived, though he did permit Cranmer to experiment with English versions of the Litany and some Bible readings.

By 1549 Cranmer was ready to publish the first Book of Common Prayer. Intended, as the title indicates, to be used in common by all English men and women, it was brought into operation by a parliamentary Act of Uniformity, which ordered the destruction of all old service manuals as well as the mandatory introduction of the new volume. The Prayer Book contained an English version of the mass, deliberately couched in ambiguous language so as to satisfy both the reformers and the conservatives who still adhered to the doctrine of transubstantiation. It also included the daily offices of Morning and Evening Prayer (called Matins and Evensong), which were derived from the ancient liturgies used in the monasteries. Cranmer attempted to bring everything needed for public worship within the confines of a single volume. He provided services for baptism, confirmation, marriage, burial, ordination of priests, and even the "churching" or purification of women following childbirth. He had a fine sense of literary style, and some of his balanced, flowing phrases may still be found in Anglican books of worship, including those of the Episcopal church in the United States and the Anglican church in Canada.

In most parts of England, the Book of Common Prayer was accepted without much visible opposition, but the inhabitants of Cornwall, arguing that their own tongue was the Cornish dialect and that they understood Latin better than English, took up arms in what came to be known as the Prayer Book Rebellion. (Their rationale was at best a half-truth, and the Cornish should be regarded as religious conservatives who were actually opposed to Protestant reform in general.) After the rebels gained control of the cathedral city of Exeter and held it in siege for several weeks, Somerset sent troops to the Southwest and put down the insurrection.

Unfortunately for him, another rebellion of quite a different sort occurred simultaneously in another part of the country. A leader named Jack Kett drew hundreds of men from East Anglia into an uprising intended to call

Somerset's attention to the economic problems faced by agricultural workers during a time of instability and inflation. Kett's rebels took over the city of Norwich. Possibly because he did sympathize with them, but more likely because he was preoccupied with other matters, Somerset failed to move against the insurgents. Eventually they were routed by forces led by another prominent nobleman, John Dudley, the duke of Northumberland. Kett was hanged from the spire of Norwich Cathedral. More important, Somerset was discredited, and Northumberland was able to displace him as the effective head of the government. Eventually Somerset was executed.

Northumberland's character, like Somerset's, has been subject to reassessment in recent years. He was formerly regarded as a self-seeking, unscrupulous politique, and some still think he was an opportunist in matters of religion. Others have become convinced that he was a sincere supporter of radical Protestant beliefs. His title was "president of the council," not "protector," and he worked with other councillors more effectively than did Somerset. He also got on better with the king.

During the years between 1549 and 1553, while Northumberland dominated the government, Cranmer was able to proceed with further reforms in the church. The archbishop had become dissatisfied with the first Prayer Book soon after its publication: he thought that it was not clear enough in its expression of Protestant beliefs and that it retained too many elements of Catholicism. So a second Book of Common Prayer was published in 1552 and ratified by a second Act of Uniformity. It no longer allowed a belief in transubstantiation, or even the Lutheran doctrine of Christ's "real presence" in the elements of communion, and it ordered that church buildings be modified so that the Eucharist might be celebrated on an "honest wooden table," not a stone altar. Communion tables were to be brought down into the main body of the church. Earlier, altars had stood in isolation at the east end, and priests had celebrated the mass with their backs to the people.

At about this time many elaborate medieval vestments were destroyed (the Prayer Book stated that priests should wear plain linen surplices, not richly colored embroidered copes) and a large quantity of church plate was confiscated. Some of the finest work of medieval silversmiths was lost when these chalices and patens were melted down to yield revenue for the government. Statues of saints and biblical figures were smashed in many churches and cathedrals, during one of several waves of iconoclasm that swept through the English church. Those who destroyed or mutilated these carved figures were convinced that they were superstitious objects prohibited by the biblical commandment against graven images. Some stained glass windows and wall paintings were defaced. Elaborate church music was also criticized by some of the reformers. In any case the Latin masses and anthems formerly sung by cathedral choirs could no longer be performed, since they did not conform to the English texts of the Prayer Book.

Cranmer's final contribution to the Edwardian church was the Forty-Two Articles of Religion, intended to set out Protestant teachings on a number of points of contention with the Catholics. Here Cranmer denounced popes, who had erred and would doubtless continue to do so; rejected Catholic doctrines, like transubstantiation and adoration of the sacrament; and affirmed the English church's acceptance of such Protestant beliefs as justification by faith and predestination. These Articles, together with the second Prayer Book, represent the high point of radical Protestantism within the Church of England.

By the time the Forty-Two Articles were published in 1553, Edward VI was seriously ill. Never robust, he appears to have contracted several diseases, probably including smallpox, measles, and tuberculosis, simultaneously. When it became clear that he could not live long, Northumberland and Cranmer began to dread the accession of his half-sister Mary, who had been brought up in the Catholic faith and was certain to restore it if she gained the throne. Wishing his Protestant settlement to endure, Edward was persuaded to sign the Device for the Succession, which excluded both Mary and Elizabeth and gave the throne to an obscure member of the royal family, Lady Jane Grey. Lady Jane, who had married Northumberland's son, was a descendant of Henry VII's younger daughter Mary and her second husband, the duke of Suffolk. Most English men and women had never heard of Lady Jane, and they did not support the attempt to set aside both heredity and Henry VIII's will. Jane was indeed proclaimed queen following Edward's death, but her reign lasted only nine days. Even Northumberland had to admit that the attempt to divert the succession was a failure. Despite the Device, Mary came to the throne.

Mary Tudor (1553–1558):
Catholicism, Exiles, and Martyrs

L oyalty to the Catholic faith was the one overriding trait in Mary's mind. With single-minded clarity she regarded Catholics as right and Protestants as wrong. She was convinced that salvation was not possible outside the Catholic church, and she was intent on returning her realm to the papal fold as rapidly and completely as possible.

Mary Tudor, portrait by an unknown artist.
Reproduced by permission of the National
Portrait Gallery.

There were several stages in the Marian Counter-Reformation. In 1553 the queen's first Parliament passed the first Act of Repeal, which wiped away all the religious legislation of Edward VI's reign, thus turning the clock back to 1547. Prayer Books were destroyed; the Latin mass, transubstantiation, and associated Catholic theology returned. Priests who had married under Edward VI were forced to put away their wives or leave the church.

The first Act of Repeal did not, however, undo Henry VIII's break with Rome. Mary seems to have thought that she needed a husband's support before she undertook the revival of papal supremacy, and in 1554 she married Philip II, heir to the Spanish throne. Mary was always conscious of her own descent from the Spanish royal family, through her mother Catherine of Aragon, and she rejoiced in the renewed bond with Spain. Many subjects were less enthusiastic; indeed, it was necessary to suppress a rebellion, led by Sir Thomas Wyatt, which protested the marriage treaty.

With Philip at her side, Mary persuaded Parliament to pass a second Act of Repeal. This expunged Henry VIII's religious legislation, thus reestablishing the position of the pope as it had existed before 1529. Cardinal Pole, an Englishman who had lived abroad under Henry and Edward, now returned from Rome as Mary's archbishop of Canterbury, and he formally absolved the entire realm from the sins of heresy and schism.

Although many men and women welcomed the restoration of the old faith, there were staunch Protestants who thought that they could not, in good conscience, abandon the reformed teachings they had accepted. When Mary made it clear that there could be no toleration for Protestant beliefs, about eight hundred English men and women fled to the Continent so that they could worship as they wished, mainly in such Protestant cities as Frankfurt, Strassburg, Geneva, and Zurich. Many of these exiles experienced financial distress, for those who were artisans were often denied the opportunity to practice their crafts in other countries. An underground Protestant church continued to exist in London, and its members sometimes sent money to their friends abroad. Although some of the exiles were content to worship according to the 1552 Prayer Book, others became even more radical and experimented with freer liturgies. The congregation at Frankfurt split over such issues, the more conservative faction being led by Edward VI's former tutor Richard Cox and the radicals accepting the teachings of John Knox, a disciple of John Calvin. The more extreme exiles can be regarded as forerunners of the Elizabethan Puritans, whose activities will concern us shortly.

The Marian exiles suffered great hardship, but their lot was better than that of the Marian martyrs. About three hundred Protestants were burned at the stake during the last three years of Mary's reign. (Burning had been the traditional manner of executing heretics for several centuries.) It was these executions that caused the queen to be known as "Bloody Mary." Although most of the victims were simple men and women, a few were high-ranking clergymen, like Bishops Ridley and Latimer, who were burned together at Oxford. Another of the Oxford martyrs was Thomas Cranmer. Deprived of the archbishopric at Mary's accession, Cranmer had been imprisoned and asked to renounce his Protestant beliefs. He did sign several recantation documents, but when he came to meet his death he denied their validity, insisted that his Protestant teachings were true, and said that he would thrust his right hand, with which he had signed the recantations, first into the flames, so that it could be punished while he was fully conscious.

The sufferings of these men and women were described, sometimes in lurid detail, in the famous *Book of Martyrs* compiled by John Foxe. Himself a Marian exile, Foxe collected information about the martyrs and brought out several editions of his work, which became one of the most popular publications of the sixteenth and seventeenth centuries. Only the Bible was reprinted more frequently. During the reign of Elizabeth all parish churches were required to have a copy of the *Book of Martyrs* available for parishioners to read. Even those who were not literate could study the woodcuts with which early editions were illustrated. These showed (among other things)

The burning of Archbishop Cranmer. This illustration is from John Foxe, Acts and Monuments of the Christian Martyrs.
Courtesy of the Special Collections, University of Minnesota Libraries.

Cranmer's hand being consumed. The influence of Foxe's work remained strong until the eighteenth century and helps account for the almost irrational anti-Catholic attitude of many English people.

Mary's last years were filled with tragedy. The executions, which she regarded as a sad necessity, were unpopular. Philip, who might have given her support or advised a more lenient policy, became king of Spain and spent little time in England. Mary suffered from the delusion that she was about to bear a child, only to learn that her physical condition was caused by illness rather than pregnancy. The French took advantage of Mary's poverty and lack of interest in military affairs to besiege the town of Calais. This last toehold on the Continent was lost early in 1558, to the great distress of the queen and many subjects. Even the pope turned against Mary in her final years, as the result of a quarrel with Spain over the possession of Naples and Sicily. Alone, ill, and despondent, Mary died on November 17, 1558. Cardinal Pole died later the same day.

Elizabeth I (1558–1603) and the Settlement of Religion

There was no attempt to alter the succession at the time of Mary's death. Henry VIII's only surviving descendant, Elizabeth, was crowned without incident. Indeed, her accession was widely acclaimed. A chronicler contrasted the "intolerable misery and dashing showers of persecution" experienced under Mary with the "clear and lovely sunshine" and "world of blessings" expected under Elizabeth, and one of the tableaux presented during Elizabeth's coronation procession through the streets of London depicted the former "Ruinous Republic" and the coming "Well-Instituted Republic." Elizabeth's Accession Day was celebrated as a holiday during her lifetime, with services of thanksgiving, bonfires, and peals of church bells; unofficial commemorations persisted into the eighteenth century.

It was fortunate that the new queen enjoyed wide support, for she faced a large number of problems. Most urgent among these was religion. It seemed clear that Elizabeth would not countenance the continuation of Catholicism, for the Catholic church had never recognized the validity of Henry VIII's marriage to her mother, Anne Boleyn, and thus regarded her as illegitimate. But no one knew exactly what Elizabeth's personal beliefs were or how Protestant a church she would erect.

Historical hindsight suggests that "comprehension" was her overriding goal: she was intent on including all her subjects, regardless of their individual convictions, within a single comprehensive state church. If this was to be achieved, the Elizabethan church would have to be middle-of-the-road, adopting a position somewhere between Rome and Geneva (where Calvin had established himself as the leader of the Continental Reformation), and it would have to be tolerant of private views as long as they did not subvert the queen's policy or endanger her security.

The Elizabethan Religious Settlement, based on these premises, was enacted in 1559 by the queen's first Parliament. A new Act of Supremacy gave Elizabeth the title "Supreme Governor of the Church"—she was not to be

Elizabeth I. Marc Gheeraerts the Younger painted this portrait late in the queen's reign, probably in 1592. She is depicted standing on a map of England, her feet on the county of Oxfordshire.
Reproduced by permission of the National Portrait Gallery.

called "Supreme Head," as Henry VIII and Edward VI had been, but she still intended to determine religious affairs. By implication this act once again eliminated papal supremacy and jurisdiction in England. A second measure, the Act of Uniformity, mandated the use of a new Book of Common Prayer. It used to be thought that the queen herself would have liked to bring back the ambiguous Prayer Book of 1549, even though radical reformers such as the Marian exiles pressed for new liturgies that would be reformed even more drastically than Cranmer's revision of 1552. We now realize that there is no evidence to support this interesting hypothesis. Virtually everyone expected the return of the 1552 Book of Common Prayer, which would have remained in use had Mary's reign not intervened. But—perhaps at the insistence of the queen—modifications were introduced to permit varying theological interpretations of the communion, and the traditional arrangement of the altar was reinstated. Ministers were also directed to wear the vestments that had been in use at the beginning of Edward VI's reign: copes were once again permissible, and the surplice was the least elaborate vestment allowed. The basic structure and moderate tone of the 1559 Book of Common Prayer have remained influential into our own time. They, rather than the extreme position of the original 1552 Book of Common Prayer, have shaped the development of the Anglican communion throughout the world.

In order to enforce these changes, all clergy were required to swear an oath recognizing the royal supremacy. More than three-fourths of the parish priests did so, but virtually all the bishops remained loyal to Rome and refused the oath. They were then ejected from the church. Elizabeth experienced severe problems in replacing them. She did find an archbishop of Canterbury who shared her views—this was Matthew Parker, formerly a scholar at Cambridge University whose chief interest was the history of the Anglo-Saxon church. But some of the other positions had to be filled with more radical Protestants, many of whom had been Marian exiles.

The Elizabethan Religious Settlement was completed by the adoption of the Thirty-Nine Articles of Religion. These were based on Cranmer's Forty-Two Articles; minor modifications made them a bit more moderate, but they remained strongly Protestant. They were printed in the Prayer Book so that subjects could easily read them, and all persons ordained to the ministry of the church were required to declare their belief in them.

Although the queen herself would have preferred celibate clergy, priests were once again allowed to marry. Most of them did so. A married priesthood has remained characteristic of Anglican churches throughout the world; clerical celibacy has been one of the principal issues separating Anglicans and Catholics.

Puritanism and Recusancy

Many of the queen's subjects, both clergy and lay, were dissatisfied with the Religious Settlement of 1559. Some of them supported it originally in the belief that it was the first step toward a more fully reformed Protestant church, but they grew disillusioned when it became clear that Elizabeth regarded the Settlement as permanent and opposed further religious change.

Those who sought a more complete Reformation are often referred to as Puritans. The term reflects their desire to purify the English church by eliminating anything that smacked of Catholicism, or what the reformers called "popery and superstition." Some Puritans were moderate reformers, but others were staunch Calvinists who disapproved of religious art, elaborate church music, the fixed Prayer Book, and even the institution of bishops. Puritans drew their beliefs almost exclusively from the Bible and tended to reject the tradition of the church as an adequate reason for current practices. They emphasized sermons rather than sacraments—they viewed preaching as extremely important in converting hearers to more virtuous lives. Some of them were chiefly concerned with morality or an individual relationship with God. Bills calling for Puritan reforms were introduced in virtually all the parliamentary sessions of the 1560s and 1570s. Several passed the House of Commons, but Elizabeth found ways to prevent them from becoming law.

The earliest serious conflict between the queen and the Puritans involved the issue of vestments worn by the clergy while officiating at services. As we have seen, royal policy required the use of surplices—white linen garments worn over a long black cassock—but Puritans objected on the grounds that Catholic priests wore surplices, hence Protestants should not. The Puritans favored a simple black "preaching gown" such as that worn by Calvin himself at Geneva. When Elizabeth refused to give ground, a number of adamant reformers were forced out of the church. They established the earliest nonconformist congregation at Plumbers' Hall, London, in 1571.

Virtually all the Elizabethan Puritans hoped that the state church would eventually become sufficiently reformed that they could be at home in it. Until the coming of that happy day, most of them remained within the church, changing what they could and tolerating some practices that could not yet be altered. For a time this faction found a leader in Elizabeth's second archbishop of Canterbury, Edmund Grindal. A Marian exile, Grindal sympathized with the Puritans and hoped to accommodate them as far as possible. Unfortunately he fell out with the queen over the issue of what were called "prophesyings." These were regional gatherings of clergy at which unlearned ministers could practice preaching and have their sermons discussed by better-educated colleagues. Elizabeth feared that the prophesyings would be used for the dissemination of Puritan views and the criticism of her government (a concern that was in fact unfounded), and she ordered Grindal to suppress them. Believing that in conscience he could not do so, Grindal offered to resign. His resignation was not accepted, and he remained in office until he died, but he was stripped of his power and the queen's policies were implemented by more conservative bishops.

Elizabeth's last archbishop of Canterbury, who outlived her by a year, was John Whitgift. He had the reputation of being a stern disciplinarian, for while he was at Cambridge University he had silenced several radical preachers who he thought were spreading dissension and discontent. As archbishop he demanded conformity to the legal position of the state church. A few persons who refused to comply were imprisoned or even executed for their beliefs.

Two groups of Puritan nonconformists who separated themselves from the state church are especially interesting. The "Brownists," followers of the radical minister Robert Browne, established an independent congregation at Norwich in 1581. Faced with persecution if they remained within England, they went as religious exiles to the Netherlands and then to Scotland, but eventually they decided to return to England and accept the requirements of the state church. The followers of Henry Barrow formed another important separatist congregation; Barrow himself was executed for nonconformity in 1593. The Congregational church in England and America (where it is now part of the United Church of Christ) sometimes traces its ancestry back to these groups.

Elizabeth's desire to comprehend all her subjects within a single church thus failed to be realized as far as the Puritans were concerned. Some Catholics, too, remained outside the Church of England, continuing to have private masses whenever they could find a priest. Because they refused to attend services of the state church, these persons are called "recusants." Although it was illegal for Catholic priests to minister in England, a number of them risked martyrdom by doing so. The Jesuits were especially active in this work, and some, like Edmund Campion, gave their lives for it. The recusants included a number of aristocratic families, and Catholic priests were often harbored or hidden away in their country houses, sometimes in secret rooms called "priests' holes." The preservation of the Catholic faith in England owed much to William Allen, an Englishman who helped found a seminary at Douai in the Netherlands for the training of English priests. He was the first to have the Vulgate Bible (the Latin text accepted by Catholics) translated into English—it is called the Douai Bible—and was named a cardinal by the pope.

Recent studies suggest more and more strongly that the moderate state church that Elizabeth erected failed to win the hearts of numerous subjects. Nonconformity, dissent, separatism, and recusancy began their growth during her reign. Most subjects remained obedient to the commands of the government, and belief in Catholic doctrines and ceremonies collapsed, largely under Henry VIII and Edward VI. But enthusiasm for Protestantism did not always take the place of Catholicism; many subjects simply adopted a more secular outlook. By 1570 only a minority of the population could be characterized as being truly committed to either Catholic or Protestant teachings.

Domestic Politics and
Foreign Policy

Queen Elizabeth was exceptionally intelligent and well educated. Her skill in foreign languages enabled her to answer European ambassadors in their own tongues and to deliver brilliant extemporaneous Latin orations when she visited the universities of Oxford and Cambridge. Her speeches in Parliament were elegant pieces of oratory in English. Sometimes the queen denied parliamentary requests, but in such conciliatory and opaque language that members praised her nonetheless. She had a shrewd sense of politics and was gifted in choosing wise councillors who generally shared her own cautious, conservative views. She delighted in music, understood theology and diplomacy, and is characterized by one biographer as the most intellectual monarch in all English history.

Throughout most of her reign her chief minister was Sir William Cecil, whom she ennobled as Lord Burghley. Educated at Cambridge, Cecil had been the principal secretary to Protector Somerset. He held the same office under Elizabeth and, like Thomas Cromwell, used it as a vehicle for dominating virtually every aspect of governmental activity. Other prominent members of Elizabeth's Privy Council were Sir Francis Walsingham, another principal secretary whose various activities included the collection of intelligence from the chief cities of Europe, and Sir Walter Mildmay, chancellor of the Exchequer and an expert in government finance.

During the earlier decades of her reign, Elizabeth met great pressures for her to marry. Concerned about the succession, Parliament petitioned her to take a husband (she was irritated by this intrusion into her personal life), and several foreign princes sought her hand. Philip II, king of Spain, proposed to her but was summarily rejected, as was Erik XIV, king of Sweden. The suits of two members of the French royal family (the dukes of Anjou and Alençon) were more protracted, for Elizabeth appreciated the diplomatic advantages that might be secured by dangling the prospect of a French connection. But the French dukes too went home empty-handed. Elizabeth enjoyed close personal relationships with several of her subjects, including Robert Dudley, earl of Leicester (Northumberland's son) and (late in her reign) Robert Devereux, earl of Essex. She probably came closer to marrying Leicester than any other man. The fact that she did not do so probably indicates that she was unwilling to share power with a husband. As she told the House of Commons early in her reign, it was enough for her that her tombstone declare that she lived and died a virgin.

The great fear shared by Elizabeth and her advisors during the early years of her reign was that the Catholic powers would join forces to overthrow her and restore the old religion. Spain under Philip II was if anything more zealous than the papacy itself. France was officially Catholic, although there was a substantial minority of Protestants (called the Huguenots). At the time of Elizabeth's accession, Scotland remained Catholic and was firmly attached to the old French alliance. A joint attack was in fact unlikely—France and Spain disliked each other more than they disliked Elizabeth—but the mere possibility was an awesome specter.

Elizabeth and her councillors were fortunate in being able to face these adversaries singly. French diplomatic problems came to a head first, for Elizabeth inherited Mary's war in which Calais had been lost. Although neither power wished to continue the hostilities, it was not easy to negotiate a suitable treaty. Finally it was agreed that the French would retain Calais for eight years, after which time it would revert to England unless the English in the meantime committed a hostile act. Because the French could surely find some sign of unfriendly behavior, the treaty in fact abandoned Calais, but with face-saving clauses for England.

In the 1560s Elizabeth was persuaded to send aid to the Huguenots, a group of French Protestants whose privileges were being threatened by the French monarchy. Elizabeth was flattered by their insistence that she was the leader of the Protestant cause and their sole hope of survival, but she later came to regret that she had been dragged into an expensive conflict that did not advance England's own interests. In later years she assured French neutrality by flirting with Anjou and Alençon and by renouncing an interest in internal French affairs.

Scotland and Mary,
Queen of Scots

The political and religious situation in Scotland changed dramatically soon after Elizabeth's accession. In 1558 James V's daughter Mary, queen of Scots, was legally the sovereign, but she had been wed to a member of the French royal family and was living in Paris. Her mother, the French noblewoman Mary of Guise, remained in Edinburgh as regent, and Catholicism remained the state religion.

Mary, queen of Scots. The portrait is by an
unknown artist.
Reproduced by permission of the National
Portrait Gallery.

In 1559 the husband of Mary, queen of Scots, succeeded to the French
throne as Francis II, but he died the next year, as did Mary of Guise. The
queen of Scots then returned to rule Scotland, only to find the Scottish
Reformation in progress. Led by John Knox, Scottish Protestants had gained
control of the church and ushered in a Reformation that was in many ways
more radical than the one that had taken place in England.

The ideas that Knox disseminated in Scotland were essentially those of
John Calvin. Like the Anglicans, Calvin believed in a single state church
encompassing all who lived in a geographical area. Unlike the Anglicans
(and the Catholics), he rejected the institution of bishops, since he could
find no biblical justification for their existence. The Calvinistic church that
Knox established in Scotland is generally called the Presbyterian church, a
reference to its form of government with power rising from local churches to
national conferences or synods rather than flowing down from the top,
through bishops and priests. In fact, Knox was willing to compromise, and
the Scottish Presbyterian church actually retained bishops, although they
had little authority in the new structure. The Scottish church adopted a
service manual considerably more advanced than the English Prayer Book.

Although Mary continued to adhere to Catholicism herself, she was un-able to reverse the Reformation, and she sometimes attended services in which Knox attacked both her faith and her sex: he did not believe that women were qualified to be rulers.

It was not religion but rather her own rashness coupled with the unsettled state of Scottish politics that brought about Mary's fall. Soon after her return to Edinburgh she married a distant relative, Lord Darnley, and in 1566 she bore him a son, the infant who was destined to be crowned James VI of Scotland and James I of England. Queen Elizabeth was gravely distressed at this turn of events, for Darnley was descended from the English royal family, and both Mary and her child might be considered rival candidates for the English throne. But Mary herself turned against Darnley, whom she found stupid and egotistical. She also blamed him for the murder of her secretary and favorite, David Rizzio. Mary's attention was now seized by the dashing Scottish nobleman James Hepburn, Lord Bothwell. Bothwell divorced his wife, masterminded a plot to murder Darnley, abducted the Scottish queen, and induced her to marry him.

All of this was more than Mary's subjects were prepared to stomach, and they took up arms against her. Bothwell surrendered and was exiled to Den-mark, where he died insane a decade later. Mary was forced to abdicate in favor of her infant son, who became king of Scotland a few weeks after his first birthday. Mary was imprisoned, but in 1568 she made her way to freedom and crossed the border to England, throwing herself on Elizabeth's mercy.

Mary's situation presented Elizabeth with one of the most difficult dilem-mas of her reign. Elizabeth herself was inclined to treat Mary favorably: the two queens were cousins, and Elizabeth believed that Mary was a lawful ruler who had been improperly treated by rebellious subjects. Elizabeth's council-lors, on the other hand, warned her that Mary was a threat to her own security, since Mary was the leading Catholic claimant for the English throne. Elizabeth compromised by treating Mary honorably but keeping her confined in one or another country house, where loyal subjects could watch her movements and censor her correspondence.

Even so, the councillors warned, Catholic plots were bound to occur, and indeed they did. The year 1569 saw the Northern Rebellion or Rising of the Earls, in which a group of subjects from northern England threatened to overthrow the government. They were led by the earls of Northumberland and Westmoreland, who demanded a return to the old religion and to a government dominated by the old noblemen rather than new, nonaristocratic professional administrators. The insurrection was harshly suppressed but served as a warning that Elizabeth's policies were not universally popular.

The situation became still more menacing after 1570, when the pope excommunicated Elizabeth and indicated that it would be a meritorious deed for a Catholic to displace or assassinate her. The Ridolfi Plot of 1571 was intended to place Mary on the English throne. After it was quashed, Parliament urged Elizabeth to kill Mary, but she refused to do so, agreeing instead to execute the duke of Norfolk, whose marriage to Mary had been proposed as part of the conspiracy. Further plots were discovered in 1583 and 1586. Councillors once again tried to persuade Elizabeth to order Mary's execution, and in 1587 Elizabeth finally signed a death warrant. Mary was then beheaded in the great hall of Fotheringhay Castle, protesting that she died as a martyr for her Catholic faith. When Elizabeth learned of the execution she became distraught and insisted that she had not ordered the warrant to be put into effect. Her distress may have been prompted by fear of diplomatic reprisals from France and Scotland (which did not take place), but it was probably also genuine.

In later years the English government worked at maintaining good relations with James VI, who had been raised a Protestant and was a willing ally, and the focus of English diplomatic concern shifted to Spain.

The Netherlands and the Armada

The greatest of the challenges to Elizabeth came from Spain. Religion was of course the underlying issue separating the two realms; Philip retained a special interest in England because of his time as joint ruler with Mary.

England and Spain initially came into conflict as a result of the Revolt of the Netherlands. Philip had inherited the rule of the Low Countries, just as he had inherited the Spanish throne. But many of those who lived in the Netherlands came to hate Spanish domination for two reasons. One was simply nationalism: they wished to determine their own affairs without the intervention of a distant monarch. The religious issue was perhaps even more important. Many of the Dutch had accepted Protestant teachings and were no longer willing to have Catholicism forced on them by Spain.

The Dutch revolt against Spanish rule began soon after Elizabeth came to the English throne. Initially Elizabeth declined to become enmeshed in it. She had learned a lesson from her involvement with the Huguenots, and her advisors made it clear that she lacked the financial resources necessary for vigorous intervention. But the Dutch continued to plead for help. After a few years Elizabeth agreed to give them secret financial aid and to allow Englishmen to volunteer for service in the rebel armies. When this level of support failed to produce victory, she finally made an open commitment, signing a treaty with the Dutch in 1585 and promising to send a large army to the Netherlands. An English victory was achieved in the Battle of Zut-phen, but it was not decisive. Indeed, the combat is remembered primarily because of the death of Sir Philip Sidney, the "perfect" Elizabethan courtier and poet.

At about the time of the execution of Mary, queen of Scots, Philip II conceived a grand scheme to end the Dutch Revolt and restore England to the Catholic church. His plan called for the gathering of a large Spanish fleet, or Armada. The ships were to transport fighting men to the Nether-lands, where they would make short work of the rebels, and then to England, where (with the assistance of those Englishmen who remained loyal to Ca-tholicism) they would assassinate or imprison Elizabeth and proclaim Philip as king.

English agents monitored Philip's activities, and Elizabeth attempted to destroy the Armada before it could sail by sending the great sea dog Sir Francis Drake with an English fleet to Spain in 1587. But the Spanish knew that he was coming. Their vessels dispersed, and Drake inflicted little dam-age. In the summer of 1588 Philip directed his admiral, the duke of Medina Sidonia, to proceed with the voyage to England and the Netherlands, even though preparations were inadequate. Philip believed that the Armada was invincible because he was convinced that God was on his side and would remedy any human deficiencies.

England prepared for the coming of the Spanish, organizing a large fleet that included private trading vessels as well as ships of the Royal Navy, all commanded by Lord Howard of Effingham. Watchmen were placed at the entrance to the English channel, and on July 19 they saw the Armada approach. Inconclusive fighting between English and Spanish ships in the Channel followed. It was not until the Armada sailed past Dover that the English took advantage of an unusual opportunity. When a windstorm arose, the Spanish ships dropped anchor, intending to remain stationary until the gale abated. The English then took a number of old hulks, loaded their cannons, and set them on fire, so that they would drift, unmanned, into the Spanish vessels.

The approach of these fire-ships, or "hell-burners," so dismayed the Span-ish that they cut their cables, leaving their anchors on the Channel floor, and sailed away in disarray. An invasion of the Netherlands or England was now impossible, and it was unthinkable to return to Spain via the Channel, which had become an English lake, full of English ships. Medina Sidonia ordered his followers to sail around the north of Scotland and the west of Ireland, but a number of Spanish vessels were wrecked on these coasts, and only a pathetic remnant of the Armada returned to Spain. The English, naturally, gloried in the defeat of the Spanish force. They proclaimed that it was God's doing as well as their own, for the "Protestant wind" had aided the valiant English sailors.

In 1589 and again in 1596, England attempted to retaliate by sending counter-Armadas to Spain, but neither campaign met with success. In fact, the two sides were evenly matched; neither could defeat the other, and they could only settle into a state of protracted hostility, sometimes likened to a modern "cold war." English merchant vessels continued to prey on Spanish shipping—this legalized piracy was called privateering—and fruitless fighting continued in the Netherlands, on a smaller scale than before, until a peace treaty was finally concluded in 1604, shortly after Elizabeth's death.

Essex's Rebellion and Execution

The situation in Ireland under the Tudors will be given fuller consideration in Chapter 9. Here it is necessary only to note the last of several Irish rebellions and its effect on England.

In 1594, not long after the defeat of the Armada, Hugh O'Neill, earl of Tyrone, turned against the English, whom he had previously supported. He thought that his role as an arbiter between the two cultures was insufficiently appreciated. In addition, he expected the arrival of a second Armada, bringing Catholicism to Ireland if not to England. It did not come, but once armed hostilities began in Ireland they lasted for the rest of Elizabeth's reign.

In 1599 the queen's young favorite, the earl of Essex, cajoled her into naming him commander of the English forces dispatched to defeat Tyrone. Essex was specifically ordered to fight, not parley. Nevertheless, he opened negotiations with the Irish earl. When Elizabeth reprimanded him he concluded that his motives were misunderstood at court; he abandoned his troops and returned to England so that he could confront the queen personally. Despite their earlier relationship, Elizabeth was angry at Essex's behavior. He was sent to the Tower and was later placed under house arrest in his own London mansion. A professional soldier, Lord Mountjoy, took his place in

Ireland and eventually secured Tyrone's surrender. This occurred while Elizabeth lay on her deathbed. Tyrone signed his capitulation six days after her death.

Meanwhile Essex chafed in confinement. As he brooded on his fate, he became more and more paranoid, convinced that his enemies at court had poisoned the queen's mind against him. So in 1601 Essex took to the streets of London, attempting to raise an army that would "free" the queen from the clutches of her advisors. Few understood Essex's position or agreed with it; he was easily captured, charged with treason, and sent again to the Tower.

Essex begged for his life and, according to a romantic legend, sent back a ring that Elizabeth had earlier given him as a token of her affection. The queen was moved to tears but refused to countermand the execution. Once again reason of state took precedence over affairs of the heart.

The Virgin Queen's Last Years

The years after Essex's death were lonely ones for the aging queen. By the end of the century Elizabeth had outlived all of her original companions and counsellors. Those who followed Burghley, Walsingham, and Mildmay were less able than they. Elizabeth can be faulted for not ensuring a continuing intake of bright young men into her government. With both Leicester and Essex gone, Elizabeth had few close personal friends. Her great achievements lay in the past: she had shepherded her realm through a religious upheaval and had seen it survive military threats unscathed.

The last great scene in the Elizabethan drama was played out in the Parliament of 1601. At its closing ceremony the queen delivered her "Golden Speech," a valedictory summarizing the achievements of her reign. Among these, Elizabeth cherished most the fact that she had loved her people and had won their love in return. Never wed to any man, Elizabeth had been married to the realm of England in an exceptional union unique in English history. She had her faults—she could be evasive, uncommunicative, dilatory, stubborn, and dictatorial. But she was an excellent judge of people and had a fine sense of popular sentiment. As her last Parliament ended, its members thronged forward to kiss the aged queen's hand. According to one chronicler there was not a dry eye in the house.

Elizabeth died in March 1603, a few months before her seventieth birthday. She was the last Tudor, and her dynasty died with her.

Suggested Reading

Bossy, John, *The English Catholic Community, 1570–1850* (New York: Oxford University Press, 1976).

Collinson, Patrick, *The Birthpangs of Protestant England* (New York: St. Martin's Press, 1988).

Collinson, Patrick, *The Elizabethan Puritan Movement* (London: Jonathan Cape, 1967).

Fraser, Antonia, *Mary Queen of Scots* (London: Weidenfeld & Nicolson, 1969).

Johnson, Paul, *Elizabeth: A Study in Power and Intellect* (London: Weidenfeld & Nicolson, 1974).

Jordan, W. K., *Edward VI: The Threshold of Power* (Cambridge, Mass.: Harvard University Press, 1970).

Jordan, W. K., *Edward VI: The Young King* (Cambridge, Mass.: Harvard University Press, 1968).

Lehmberg, Stanford E., *The Reformation of Cathedrals: Cathedrals in English Society, 1485–1603* (Princeton: Princeton University Press, 1988).

Loades, D. M., *The Reign of Mary Tudor* (New York: St. Martin's Press, 1979).

MacCaffrey, Wallace T., *Queen Elizabeth and the Making of Policy, 1572–1588* (Princeton: Princeton University Press, 1981).

MacCaffrey, Wallace T., *The Shaping of the Elizabethan Regime* (Princeton: Princeton University Press, 1968).

Martin, Colin, and Geoffrey Parker, *The Spanish Armada* (London: Hamilton, 1988).

Mattingly, Garrett, *The Armada* (Boston: Houghton Mifflin, 1959).

Neale, J. E., *Queen Elizabeth I* (London: Jonathan Cape, 1934).

Ridley, Jasper, *Thomas Cranmer* (Oxford: Clarendon Press, 1962).

Tittler, Robert, *The Reign of Mary I* (London: Longman, 1983).

Whiting, Robert, *The Blind Devotion of the People: Popular Religion and the English Reformation* (Cambridge: Cambridge University Press, 1989).

Wormald, Jenny, *Mary Queen of Scots: A Study in Failure* (London: George Philip, 1988).

CHAPTER NINE

The Celtic Lands and the Tudors

The Celtic Peoples

The lands that ringed England to the west and north—Wales, Ireland, and Scotland—remained ethnically different from England itself. Their populations were descended from the Celtic peoples who had lived there in prehistoric times. Except in the Lowlands of Scotland, there were no major settlements of Germanic invaders and no admixture of Norman or Viking blood.

In the sixteenth century, as today, the Welsh, Irish, and Scots were very much aware of their own unique cultures and eager to maintain their own ways of life, despite continuing pressures from England. Their responses to England's attempts to dominate the British Isles followed separate, divergent patterns.

Wales

Geographically closest to England, Wales also came closest to being integrated into the English system of government. The fact that the Tudor monarchs could claim Welsh ancestry made it easier for them

to extend their control. Henry VII had landed in Wales, had recruited follow-
ers there, and had marched to victory under the Welsh banner of Cadwaladr.
Many of the Welsh went so far as to believe that Henry's defeat of Richard
III represented a Welsh triumph over the English. Some also realized that
Henry's wife, Elizabeth of York, was descended from the great Welsh hero
Llywelyn.

A number of ambitious young Welshmen found profitable employment in
London after 1485. One of these was Dafydd Seissyllt, whose grandson,
having Anglicized his name, became Elizabeth's great councillor William
Cecil. Henry VII's uncle Jasper Tudor, who had helped plan the Tudor invasion, was ennobled as duke of Bedford and was named justiciar of South
Wales. The Council in the Marches of Wales, established by the Yorkists,
was given additional power by Henry VII and worked effectively in maintaining order and justice. Prince Arthur, Henry VII's older son whose very name
honored his Welsh blood, was installed as Prince of Wales when he was
fifteen. After his death, his brother Henry held that title before succeeding
to the throne. The concord between England and Wales was demonstrated
symbolically in a tournament held at Carew Castle in 1507. At its end the
champions representing the patron saints of the two realms, St. George and
St. David, embraced.

When Henry VII came to the throne, Wales was still divided into two
separate administrative units. The so-called principality of Wales encom-
passed the North and West; it was already organized into counties and governed on the English model. Southeast Wales, which in the later Middle
Ages had been ruled by Anglo-Norman noblemen, was divided into Marcher
lordships and retained a greater independence. Late in his reign Henry VII
issued charters to the principality and to some other lordships. These charters
conferred the right to hold land and office in England and to inherit property
according to English law, thus in effect repealing the restrictive acts of 1401.
In 1525 Wolsey moved to strengthen the Council in the Marches, so that the
English government could attain firmer control there.

It was the decade of the 1530s, however, that became the great turning
point in Welsh history. One of the overriding policies of Thomas Cromwell,
Henry VIII's chief minister during this period, was to extend the direct
control of the central government over all of England and Wales. Cromwell
wiped away some of the independent jurisdictions, called palatinates, that
remained in England, and he was responsible for several acts that assimilated
Wales into the fabric of English government. The most important of these,
the Act of Union passed by Parliament in 1536, "shired" all of Wales
by creating new counties in the South and mandating the appointment of

sheriffs and justices of the peace in Wales, as in England. It is important to note that the justices of the peace were chosen from among the local gentry, thus ensuring some degree of self-government for the Welsh. Those who lived in Wales were subject to laws made at Westminster, but after 1536 they had a say in making those laws, for they were granted representation in the House of Commons, as were their English counterparts. Welsh boroughs, however, were given a single member rather than two, as in England, on the grounds that they could not afford to pay the costs of more than one burgess. Considering the small size of the Welsh population the limitation was not unreasonable. Many of the Welsh gentry supported Henry VIII's policies.

The church in Wales operated under the jurisdiction of the archbishop of Canterbury and thus was affected by the Reformation just as the church in England was; the Act of Union ensured that Parliament's ecclesiastical legislation applied in Wales. Thus, Henry VIII terminated papal authority, and the Welsh monasteries, including such great houses as Tintern Abbey, were dissolved during his reign. The progress of the Reformation was hindered by the fact that a number of the bishops and lower clergy did not speak Welsh, and many of the natives knew little English. The language of Cranmer's Book of Common Prayer was hardly more comprehensible than the old Latin, and Protestant preaching was not very effective. Some elementary religious texts, like the Lord's Prayer, were translated in 1546—they became the first book to be printed in Welsh—but the Prayer Book was not published in Welsh until 1563, and a Welsh translation of the Bible did not appear until 1588. The publication of these texts served as a major impetus for the development of Welsh as a literary language. The Tudors made no attempt to suppress the native tongue, as they were to do in Ireland, and there was a flowering of Welsh poetry during the sixteenth century.

Under Elizabeth the effects of the Act of Union became more and more apparent. Her rule was generally popular, and few Welsh men and women were attracted by the Catholic church. The Tudor dynasty lost some of its symbolic association with Wales after 1547, however; because the later Tudors had no offspring, there were no more Princes of Wales until the seventeenth century.

Ireland and Henry VIII

In some respects the relationship between England and Ireland was surprisingly similar to the situation in Wales. Ireland also was inhabited by two groups of people, the native Celtic or Gaelic population and the English settlers or colonists, who spoke different languages and were governed according to different systems. Here too the decade of the 1530s formed a watershed, as Cromwell and Henry VIII attempted to gain fuller direct control than their predecessors had enjoyed.

At the beginning of the Tudor period the Northwest of Ireland remained in the hands of Gaelic natives. The Southeast was more or less subject to English rule. A deputy of the English king controlled Dublin and the Pale, and outlying areas were left in the hands of Irish lords who had adopted English ways and held English titles of nobility.

The earl of Kildare, head of the Fitzgerald family, was the most important of these Anglo-Irish lords. Generally accepted by both the English and the Irish, he was able to maintain a semblance of order. But Kildare foolishly supported Perkin Warbeck's rebellion against Henry VII. In 1492 he was deprived of his position, charged with treason, and imprisoned. Henry VII then sent an Englishman, Sir Edward Poynings, to rule Ireland as his lord deputy. The famous statute called Poynings' Law was passed in 1494. It ended the independence of the Irish Parliament by requiring the king's prior approval before the Irish assembly could meet and limiting the bills that could be considered to those already drafted and accepted by the King's Council in London. The statute has often been misinterpreted as an attempt to take away powers previously enjoyed by the Irish. In fact only the richer Englishmen who had settled in Ireland were represented in the Irish Parliament, either before or after Poynings' Law, and the act was primarily intended to prevent disloyal royal deputies from using the Parliament for their own purposes.

Government by English officers like Poynings soon proved to be expensive, however, and Kildare was restored to his position. Henry VII remained concerned about the concentration of power in Kildare's hands and once considered a personal expedition to repress what he called the "wild Irish." But the cost appeared to be too high, and Kildare was left in charge. Henry VIII, like his father, tried replacing Kildare with an English deputy, in this case the earl of Surrey (1520–1522), but once again the experiment proved a costly failure. The English kings could not obtain real control of Ireland unless they were willing to spend money on it.

Events came to a head in 1534. By this time Thomas Cromwell had consolidated his position as Henry VIII's chief minister and had formulated his policy of ruling both Wales and Ireland directly. He dismissed Kildare, who was now old and infirm, only to be confronted with a serious rebellion led by Kildare's son, known as "Silken Thomas." Thomas believed, incorrectly, that his father had been executed. During his uprising the rebels besieged the city of Dublin and murdered the archbishop, John Alen. The English finally reasserted their control; the old earl of Kildare died in the

Tower of London, and his son, who succeeded as earl, surrendered in 1535. But the events probably confirmed Cromwell's belief that there would be no peace without direct rule.

A major aspect of Thomas Cromwell's policy in Ireland was the procedure known as surrender and regrant. Under this system, native chieftains were required to surrender their existing rights and titles and to swear loyalty to the English Crown. They were then regranted their lands, to be held from the king of England, and they were given English titles of nobility as a means of tying them to the English government. They were required to adopt English laws and customs, and they were often expected to send their sons to England to be educated. The policy was not carried out effectively following Cromwell's fall; it was his hope that it would bring about cultural assimilation, as similar measures had begun to do in Wales.

After the death of Henry VIII, the attempt to rule all of Ireland directly was abandoned for a time, since it imposed demands that seemed beyond England's resources. Instead, the mid-Tudor governments concentrated on the lands immediately adjacent to the Pale. Intending to create a buffer zone of reliable loyalty, they confiscated territory from Gaelic landowners and gave it to Englishmen who were willing to settle in Ireland. Such areas were called plantations; the areas resettled in this way under Mary Tudor and her husband, Philip, were called Queen's County and King's County.

Queen Elizabeth and the Irish

Elizabeth and her advisors returned to a program of direct rule, achieved if necessary by conquest and plantation. During the 1580s they tried to force Protestantism on the Irish who lived in the area known as Munster, south of Dublin and extending to the west coast. Persecution of the native Catholics led Gerald, earl of Munster, to rebel. After they defeated him the English devastated the countryside, burned the harvest, and massacred herds of cattle. They then confiscated the land from the natives and turned it into another English plantation.

As many as twenty-two thousand English men, women, and children eventually settled in Munster. They founded new towns and stimulated the economy by introducing new breeds of cattle and sheep as well as building new iron mills and woolen works. By the standards of the time this was a major movement of population, and it can be regarded as one of England's earliest efforts at colonization. Some Gaelic natives were assimilated and integrated in the plantation, but most lost their means of livelihood and sank deeper into poverty.

Elizabeth was well served by a succession of able deputies in Ireland, the most important of whom were the earl of Sussex, Sir Henry Sidney, and Sir William Fitzwilliam. None of them found his work easy. They were faced with continuing disorder and disobedience, and the costs of English rule always exceeded the queen's estimates.

The last and greatest rebellion of the sixteenth century was led by Hugh O'Neill, the earl of Tyrone, who dominated the county of Ulster in north-eastern Ireland. Tyrone gathered a large army, estimated at six thousand men. Elizabeth initially sent the earl of Essex to deal with Tyrone. Essex had a personal interest in northern Ireland, since he had been licensed to establish a plantation there. As we have seen, he opened negotiations with Tyrone instead of fighting him, and he returned to England when the queen criticized his actions. His successor, Lord Mountjoy, finally defeated Tyrone in 1603. The English were also able to defeat a large force of Spanish soldiers who had been sent to fight alongside the Irish.

The English victories that came during the last years of Elizabeth's reign completed the conquest of Ireland, and James I inherited a country that had been reduced to obedience, at least on the surface. But the cost had been high. Millions of pounds had been spent on warfare, and the toll in human lives, among the English and the Irish alike, had been great. What appears a military success was in fact a failure, for the Tudors were unable to gain the support of the Irish. The policy of plantation and colonization sowed the seeds of strife that persists today.

Religion in Ireland

The coming of the Reformation interjected religious issues into the Irish situation. An Irish Reformation Parliament met in 1536 and passed measures that paralleled the statutes of the Reformation Parliament in England. Papal jurisdiction was terminated, the king was declared "Supreme Head of the Church," and the monasteries were dissolved. Henry VIII's control over the Irish church was further strengthened in 1541, when he assumed the title "king of Ireland." An act passed by the Irish Parliament asserted that his ancestors had enjoyed "kingly jurisdiction" even though they had called themselves lords of Ireland rather than kings. The new title was intended to emphasize the obedience due to the king, and it gave him more precise legal rights.

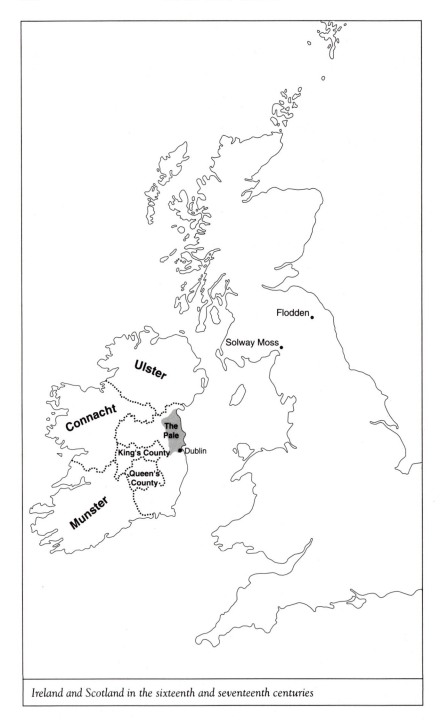

Ireland and Scotland in the sixteenth and seventeenth centuries

In the long run, attempts to impose Protestantism on Ireland were unsuccessful. But it was not immediately clear, and perhaps not inevitable, that this would be the case. The Irish church, especially in Gaelic areas, was acknowledged to be corrupt and badly in need of reform, and the monasteries no longer provided the spiritual and intellectual leadership of earlier centuries. Indeed, few Irishmen were drawn to monastic life in the sixteenth century. Most monasteries had fewer than six inhabitants, and married monks were not uncommon. It is also true that relations between Ireland and the papacy had not been especially close or cordial.

In the later sixteenth century, while Elizabeth was queen, serious efforts were made to extend the Anglican church to Ireland. English bishops were named to the Irish dioceses, and a new university, Trinity College, was founded in Dublin to provide the teaching of Protestant beliefs. But the English church served mainly the English settlers. Few of the natives were won over. Most of them could not understand sermons preached in English, and the Prayer Book was not translated into Gaelic. By the end of the century it seemed clear that most natives would remain Catholic. Those who were able began to send their sons to Catholic universities on the Continent rather than to Dublin or Oxford, and Catholic missionaries, mainly Jesuits, began risking their lives to bring Catholic services to the Irish people. The religious policy of the Tudors failed, as had their governmental policy, and Ireland was not assimilated to English rule or religion.

Scotland in the Sixteenth Century

Scotland is often described as being lawless and backward in the sixteenth century. Such a picture, however, is partial and misleading. In fact the period was chiefly characterized by peace, intellectual progress, and growing self-confidence. The Stewart monarchs James IV (1488–1513) and James V (1513–1542) were able, popular kings. Realizing their country's limited resources, they demanded little from their subjects and attempted to increase their international prestige through diplomacy rather than warfare. James IV, for instance, tried to galvanize the European powers into undertaking a crusade against the Turks during the opening years of the century.

As we have seen, Henry VII followed similar policies in England and sought to foster good relations' between the English and the Scots through the dynastic marriage between James IV and Henry's daughter Margaret. It was unfortunate for the people of both realms that friendship was not achieved. England remained Scotland's only enemy throughout the first half

James IV of Scotland. The portrait is by an unknown artist.
Reproduced by permission of the National Galleries of Scotland.

of the sixteenth century, and the Scots were badly defeated in two senseless battles. In 1513 James IV died in the mud of Flodden Field, along with most of the leaders of the Scottish church and state. The Scots' losses were estimated at 10,000, English fatalities at only 1,500. There were few casualties at the Battle of Solway Moss in 1542, but it was another humiliation for the Scots and for James V, who died within weeks after hearing of the debacle.

James V was succeeded by his infant daughter, Mary, queen of Scots. Her story has already been told, since it affected Elizabethan England so directly. Here we need only note that Scotland remained without a mature, resident monarch between 1542 and 1560. During this period the English used diplomacy, bribery, and "rough wooing"—campaigns that ravaged the borders—as a means of assuring peace and increasing their influence.

Mary's abdication in 1567 placed another infant on the throne: her son became James VI. During his minority there was a confusing succession of councils of regency. Elizabeth's advisors took advantage of the situation to bring Scotland more and more into England's orbit. The coming of Protestantism to Scotland meant that there were religious reasons for alliance between the two realms, and James VI, after he achieved maturity, perceived the advantages of friendship. Not least of these was the possibility that he

*James V of Scotland. The portrait is by an
unknown artist.
Reproduced by permission of the National
Galleries of Scotland.*

might succeed to the English throne, since Elizabeth had no heirs and he
could trace his ancestry (on both sides) back through Margaret Tudor to
Henry VII. An intelligent and highly educated man, James established a
brilliant and sophisticated court in Scotland, but he was hopelessly extravagant and had little understanding of the plight of his poorer subjects. His
quirks of mind were to become even more apparent following his accession
to the English throne in 1603.

The Reformation in Scotland

The Reformation did not reach Scotland officially until 1560. Before
that time the established church remained Catholic. During the regency of Mary of Guise there were French troops in Scotland, helping
her ensure that Protestant heresies did not gain the upper hand.

Lutheran views and writings, however, had been seeping into Scotland
since the 1520s. Many were brought by merchants trading with England or

Germany. Following the Scottish defeat at Solway Moss, the English tried to export Protestantism to Scotland. By the 1550s many Scottish leaders had accepted reform and were awaiting a propitious time for action.

This came in 1560. The death of Mary of Guise removed French influence as well as her own resolute opposition. At about the same time, the great religious leader John Knox returned to Scotland after years of exile in Geneva. More than a hundred lords and gentry attended the Scottish Reformation Parliament, which ended papal jurisdiction, outlawed the mass, and brought in a Calvinist confession of faith. The Reformation thus came later to Scotland than to England, but when it arrived it produced a church that was more radically reformed than the Church of England. Protestant ideas and organization, however, did not affect all of Scotland. The Reformation made little impact in isolated areas of the Highlands and offshore islands, where many people continued to adhere to Catholic beliefs.

Mary, queen of Scots, disliked these changes—she remained loyally, perhaps fanatically, Catholic to the day of her death—but she realized that she was powerless to prevent them. James VI was brought up as a Protestant and had no desire to restore the old faith, but he was intent on demonstrating royal supremacy over the church. He also wished to have the Scottish church governed by bishops, as in England. Such episcopal organization was basically incompatible with the Presbyterian form of church government that had been adopted in 1560, and it was opposed by most Calvinists, but in the end James succeeded. The Scottish kirk thus became a peculiar anomaly, a Presbyterian church with bishops.

The Scottish Reformation had important economic consequences. Scottish monasteries were dissolved and their property was confiscated, as in England. (They had already fallen on hard times, and few people were sorry to see them go.) Cathedrals were also closed—this is a specific way in which the Scottish Reformation was more drastic than the English—and most cathedral buildings were torn down or allowed to fall into ruin, as at St. Andrew's. Occasionally, part of a cathedral was preserved as a parish church. About a third of the men who had been tenants on church lands were able to buy their freeholds and become independent owners, but another third found their land sold out from under them, to landowners ("lairds") who had no need for their services. Much of the income from tithes (called "teinds" in Scots) found its way into the pockets of laymen. There was thus a vested interest in the preservation of the reformed church; economic advantage ran hand in hand with Protestant theology.

The services of the Scottish church were also different from those in England, for the Scots actually put into effect many of the reforms that the

Puritans advocated fruitlessly in England. Elaborate church music was prohibited, and organs were removed or smashed. Services were less formal than
those prescribed by the Book of Common Prayer. There was greater interest
in the regulation of private morality in Scotland than in England; only those
whose lives were approved could obtain tickets to attend communion. The
celebration of Christmas and Easter was forbidden, as were all frivolous
activities on Sundays. As one contemporary writer commented, there was
"no merriness" left in Scotland after the stern morality of the Calvinists
triumphed.

The End of an Era

When Elizabeth died in 1603, it appeared that Wales had been
successfully integrated into the English governmental system
and church. Ireland had been reduced through military conquest
and colonization to a state of submission, and for the time being it was quiet.
Ties with Scotland were closer than ever before. James VI could look forward
with confidence to the day when he would rule all the British Isles. He would
be the first king to do so.

Suggested Reading

Cowan, Ian B., *The Scottish Reformation: Church and Society in Sixteenth Century Scotland* (New York: St. Martin's Press, 1982).

Ellis, Steven G., *Tudor Ireland* (New York: Longman, 1985).

Moody, T. W., F. X. Martin, and F. J. Byrne, eds., *A New History of Ireland, Vol. III: Early Modern Ireland, 1534–1691* (Oxford: Clarendon Press, 1976).

Ridley, Jasper, *John Knox* (Oxford: Clarendon Press, 1968).

Williams, Glanmor, *Recovery, Reorientation, and Reformation: Wales, c. 1415–1642* (Oxford: Clarendon Press, 1987).

Wormald, Jenny, *Court, Kirk, and Community: Scotland 1470–1625* (London: Edward Arnold, 1981).

The Early Stuarts and the Civil War, 1603–1649

The Seventeenth Century

Perhaps more than any other period in British history, the seventeenth century can be regarded as a drama, continually unfolding its complex plot. Unity results from the ongoing theme of conflict between king and Parliament. Diversity is provided by shifting subplots. Dramatic scenes and fascinating characters abound. The first act ends with a horrifying spectacle, the only public execution of a monarch in the history of the British Isles. A revolution terminates Act II.

Among the problems that came to a head in the earlier seventeenth century, one can identify differences of opinion about the role of monarchy and Parliament, inadequate government revenue, economic and social change, and religion.

King James VI and I

After ruling England for nearly half a century, Elizabeth died in March 1603. She was followed on the throne by her "cousin of Scotland," King James VI. As king of England he became James I, since no earlier English monarch had borne that name. He also adopted the English spelling *Stuart,* although his dynasty in Scotland was generally referred to as the Stewarts.

The casual observer would not have predicted trouble. Elizabeth had been a popular sovereign, and she left her realms in peace. The succession was not seriously disputed. Earlier, there had been fear that rival claimants would emerge if the queen died without heirs. There were no more descendants of Henry VIII, and the throne would have to pass to a different branch of the royal family. But by the end of the sixteenth century it was generally accepted that James would follow Elizabeth. Through both his father and his mother he was descended from the first Tudor, Henry VII. At the age of thirty-seven he was a mature man with considerable experience in governing the Scots. Although she had stubbornly refused to designate her successor, Elizabeth had tacitly acknowledged the inevitability of James's accession, and during the last years of her life a number of English courtiers and ministers were busy ingratiating themselves with the man who was to become their master. One even sent James a lantern inscribed with the appallingly apt biblical text, "Lord, remember me when thou comest into thy kingdom." (The words were originally spoken by one of the thieves crucified with Christ.)

More acute analysts might have foreseen difficult days. James was a strange man, gifted with high intelligence but little common sense. He never made much effort to understand the needs of his people, either in England or in Scotland. He knew little English history and did not fully appreciate the working of English politics. He was dependent on personal favorites. He had a high view of his own position. Indeed, he had written a treatise on political theory, published just before his accession to the English throne, which set out the classic statement of the doctrine of divine right of kings. According to this theory God rules the universe but has chosen to delegate reponsibility for earthly territories to their kings. Thus the monarchs are deputies of God; they are to be obeyed without criticism just as God is, and they can claim absolute power, as God does. Should they falter, God will punish them hereafter. Subjects have no right to resist them now.

James's attitude toward Parliament was quite different from that of most members of the House of Commons. God does not share jurisdiction with a heavenly Parliament, and James did not quite appreciate why he should be forced to do so on earth. He spoke often of royal prerogative—those matters that belonged solely to the king. He believed that these included religion, foreign policy, his private income, and his private life. He did not understand the way in which the English Parliament had come to work with the king in governing the country. Parliamentary leaders remembered the history of

James I. This portrait is by Daniel Mytens.
Reproduced by permission of the National
Portrait Gallery.

the Tudor period, when Parliament had frequently legislated about religious matters. They were concerned about the maintenance of their parliamentary privileges, especially the right to free speech, not about the king's prerogative.

James's views might not have mattered so much had he not inherited several serious problems that Elizabeth and her advisors had sidestepped. The most important of these involved government finance and religion.

In the Middle Ages and throughout the Tudor period it was generally believed that the English monarch should be able to "live of his own" except in times of crisis. Parliament had never granted taxes on a continuing basis, but only as a temporary response to specific emergencies. Feudal revenues and income from royal estates, it was argued, ought to be adequate for the maintenance of the court and, indeed, the entire government unless there were rebellions or wars that might justify tax grants. By Elizabeth's reign this doctrine was hopelessly out of date. Ordinary royal revenues were quite inadequate to meet the growing needs of the realm and were actually declining year by year, as the ruler was forced to sell properties in order to meet immediate charges. But because England was at war during the later years of the queen's life, Parliament was easily persuaded to make large grants of taxes. So the theoretical issue was never tackled, and a king who sought peace would find it hard to obtain sufficient money.

The position of the Church of England was also less stable than it appeared. It had not won over all the queen's subjects, and many of those who accepted it were lukewarm in their belief. Catholic recusants and Puritan separatists were more zealous. Under pressure from the queen and Archbishop Whitgift, the Puritans had given up their attempts to alter the Elizabethan Religious Settlement. Elizabeth probably thought that the movement was dead. In fact, the Puritans had merely gone underground, biding their time until the demise of the obtuse queen. They knew that James had grown up in Scotland, where the established Presbyterian church had adopted many of the reforms they sought in England, and they hoped that he would support their demands.

James I and the Puritans

As James was journeying from Edinburgh to London in 1603 he was met by a group of Puritans who presented him with the document known as the Millenary Petition. (The title refers to the fact that its signers supposedly numbered a thousand—*mille* in Latin. There were actually fewer.) The petitioners looked to the new king for help. They wanted shorter services, simpler music and vestments, more preaching, stricter observance of the Sabbath, and the abolition of such popish symbols as the sign of the cross and even wedding rings. James expressed his willingness to talk about these matters, and early in 1604 he summoned Puritan leaders to meet with clergy from the established church at Hampton Court Palace.

The Hampton Court Conference began well. James made a lengthy oration on church history, and some issues, like the revision of the Prayer Book, were discussed calmly. Then one of the Puritan leaders touched on the question of bishops and their powers. The Puritans probably believed that James, who had lived with a Presbyterian church in Scotland, would favor introducing its more democratic form of government in England. But the king was incensed. He had actually hated Presbyterianism and had eagerly awaited the time when he could be supreme governor of an episcopal church. "No bishop, no king," he broke out. A Presbyterian church, he continued, agreed as well with monarchy as God agreed with the Devil. He would hear no more of the Puritan proposals. Indeed, he would force the Puritans to conform to the established church or he would harry them out of the realm. Later events were to show the Stuarts doing just that.

The breakdown of the Hampton Court Conference was probably caused as much by the Anglican bishops' intransigence as by the king's outburst. Before the gathering broke up, some committees were established to consider proposals for reform, but they achieved nothing. The one positive result of the meeting was the new biblical translation often known as the King James Bible. There was general agreement that existing translations were flawed. Anglicans and Puritans worked together to produce the new English text, which was published in 1611. James applauded their work but had little to do with it, beyond perhaps insisting on one or two specific English equivalents of Greek and Latin words: he preferred the collective term *church* rather than the separatist-sounding *congregation* as a translation of the Latin term *eccelsia*. The translators deliberately chose to use an elevated literary style, not the ordinary conversational language of the day. The elegance of their phraseology and the beauty of their rendering of poetic texts, especially the Psalms, ensured a long life for their work. Even today many persons prefer it to modern translations.

In appointing bishops, James gave positions to men who favored reform as well as to those who supported the existing establishment. By such temporizing he merely postponed a crisis.

James's First Parliament

By the end of the Tudor period Parliament had become an important part of the English government. Its legislation regulated religion, taxation, economic and social issues, and some aspects of the legal system. What were called private bills also sanctioned special privileges for certain localities, professions, and individuals who faced problems not easily solved in the law courts. It has recently become fashionable for some historians to play down the importance of the Stuart Parliaments and to minimize their conflict with the king. Although it is true that Parliament was not the actual center of power, it provided the chief point of contact between the court and the country. If the policies of the king and Council differed from those of politically conscious persons throughout the realm, Parliament was the stage on which the clashes occurred.

James's first Parliament convened in 1604, shortly after his coronation, and continued to meet for several months each year until 1611. Many issues that were to prove common themes for decades arose before its dissolution.

The first matter to be discussed in the House of Commons was a disputed election case. Earlier, the Chancery had certified those duly elected to the House, but the Commons now sought the right to adjudicate such disputes themselves. James finally agreed that they might do so, thus giving the Commons an additional privilege that they have exercised ever since.

Much of Parliament's time was spent discussing James's proposal for a union between England and Scotland. The king wished to bring his two realms into complete fusion, with common citizenship, a single church, one legal system, and a merged Parliament. Despite his reiterated pleas, Parliament refused to accept his scheme. Many of the English looked down on the Scots, whom they considered beggarly and uncivilized, and were not eager to extend privileges to them. The law courts eventually ruled that James's Scottish subjects could not be considered aliens in England. Other aspects of the union had to wait for a century, until an Act of Union was passed in 1707. Even then the religious and legal institutions were allowed to remain separate, as they still are today.

The most exciting event in this Parliament was the Gunpowder Plot. In this fanatical scheme a small group of Catholic zealots, led by Guy Fawkes, attempted to kill the king and members of both houses of Parliament by blowing up the Parliament building during the ceremonial opening of the 1605 session. They imagined that a new Catholic government could easily be installed once all the existing leaders were dead. The plotters had actually filled the basement of the Lords' chamber with explosives before the conspiracy was uncovered. Fawkes was apprehended at the last moment, as he was about to ignite the fuses. He was executed as a traitor and his name became infamous: Guy Fawkes Day is still celebrated in England on November 5, the anniversary of his arrest. For centuries it was a focus for anti-Catholic sentiment. Now it has become the occasion for pranks, like Halloween in America, and for bonfires, on which children burn effigies of "the Guy."

The most serious difficulties in Parliament arose over the question of finance. Members of the Commons were particularly critical of several sorts of revenue that the king collected without parliamentary approval. These included purveyance, wardship, and impositions. Purveyance was the king's right to commandeer food and other supplies from those who lived near the various royal residences, paying whatever he chose rather than the usual market price. Wardship was his power to act as guardian of minor heirs to estates held from the Crown and to collect the profits from their lands until they came of age. Both were aspects of the outmoded feudal system that had not been abandoned when feudalism ceased to be functional. Impositions were duties levied on imports and exports, theoretically for the purpose of regulating trade rather than for taxation. They differed from tunnage and poundage, a customs duty that was admittedly a tax and that had been granted to James by Parliament.

James believed that purveyance and wardship were part of his royal prerogative, and he ordered the Commons to cease discussing the issue.

The Somerset House Conference, 1604. This painting by an unknown artist depicts members of James I's Council. The figure at the right front, prepared to act as secretary, is Sir Robert Cecil.
Reproduced by permission of the National Portrait Gallery.

Parliamentary leaders, on the other hand, were convinced that their right of free speech included the privilege of dealing with all matters that were legitimate concerns of subjects. This was the position taken in the Apology of the Commons, the earliest of several strong statements of parliamentary privilege to be presented by the early Stuart Parliaments. The king also regarded impositions as part of the prerogative, on the grounds that the regulation of trade was an aspect of foreign policy and diplomacy. The matter became increasingly urgent because imposition rates were increased early in his reign as part of an attempt to reduce the government's annual deficit. Some merchants refused to pay, even though a court decision in Bate's Case confirmed that impositions were lawful, and some members of the Commons objected to them as being essentially taxes that had never been granted by Parliament. James's attempt to dissuade Parliament from discussing impositions led to the Commons' Petition of 1610, in which they reiterated their "ancient and undoubted right" to debate "all matters which do properly concern the subject."

Throughout this period the king's chief minister was Sir Robert Cecil, Burghley's son, now ennobled as the earl of Salisbury. A famous painting shows him acting as secretary at an international peace conference held at Somerset House in 1604. In 1610 Salisbury attempted to settle a number of outstanding problems through a compromise called the Great Contract. This would have abolished purveyance and wardship, limited impositions and acknowledged that they were a tax, and granted the king, in lieu of these sources of income, an annual subsidy of £200,000. For a time it appeared that the compromise would be enacted, but early in 1611 it fell apart and Parliament was dissolved. The king, after seeing some calculations, decided that the proposed tax was insufficient, whereas members of Parliament feared that they would lose control of government policy if they granted continuing revenues. Salisbury, distressed at his failure, resigned his offices and died in 1612.

Royal Favorites

Salisbury was the most able minister of the early seventeenth century. He had done much to ensure the calm transition from the Tudors to the Stuarts. After his death James was dominated by men who were far less competent. Unlike Elizabeth, who chose officials on the basis of their abilities, James tended to rely on those whom he found personally attractive. The result was a deterioration in the honesty and efficiency of government leaders. When this was perceived by members of Parliament and ordinary subjects, it led to a loss of trust in the administration.

The earlier of James's two great favorites was Robert Carr, a young Scotsman who had come to England in 1603 as part of the king's entourage. Although he was virtually illiterate and knew nothing of English government, he became the king's confidant. James gave him lands, revenues, and a title of nobility and facilitated his marriage to Lady Frances Howard by virtually ordering the courts to grant her a divorce. Carr might have retained his position at court for some years had there not been a great scandal in which Lady Frances was convicted of hiring accomplices to poison Carr's servant, Sir Thomas Overbury. Carr, too, was found guilty of conspiring in the crime. James ultimately pardoned the couple, but they lost their influence.

By 1617 James had found his second favorite, George Villiers, to whom he gave the title duke of Buckingham. A native Englishman, Buckingham was far more intelligent than Carr, but he grew increasingly unpopular as people heard of the king's fawning affection for him, and it did not help when James excused himself by saying that even Christ had had his beloved disciple. Buckingham was made lord admiral and lord treasurer, and he regulated access to the king like a modern appointments secretary.

During the later years of his life, James saw little of his wife, Anne of Denmark, whom he found boring. His older son, Prince Henry, had died in 1612, leaving Prince Charles as heir to the throne. Charles and Buckingham became friends, and by the 1620s they managed to manipulate the king so that they could control the government, leaving him an impotent observer.

James's Later Parliaments

Most of James's later Parliaments were no more cooperative than his first gathering. Many of the same issues remained, since they had not been resolved. A Parliament summoned in 1614 lasted only two months and passed no legislation at all; for that reason it came to be known as the Addled Parliament. When he dissolved it, James threatened to have no more Parliaments, and he told the Spanish ambassador he could not understand why his predecessors had established the institution. The comment, of course, displayed his lack of understanding of English history.

James did make do without Parliament for seven years, but financial necessity forced him to call elections in 1621. The chief issue was now the question of English involvement in the Thirty Years' War on the Continent. This struggle between Catholics and Protestants had begun in Bohemia, a country in eastern Europe, in 1618. It appeared that England could hardly remain neutral, since one of the chief figures in the conflict was James's daughter Elizabeth. She had married Frederick the elector palatine, a Protestant nobleman from Germany. The Bohemian Parliament (called the Diet) wished to designate a Protestant king and offered the Bohemian crown to Frederick. He accepted; he and Elizabeth went to Prague and were crowned. But the kingship of Bohemia was traditionally held by a Catholic member of the Hapsburg family, which also ruled Spain and the Holy Roman Empire, and the Hapsburgs were not willing to abandon it without a fight. The Bohemians insisted that their monarchy was elective and that they could choose a Protestant king if they wished. They too were prepared to go to war if necessary. The result was a bloody military conflict, perhaps the most devastating so far experienced in Europe.

James's original intention was to avoid involvement. He hated war—his personal motto was one of the Beatitudes, "Blessed are the peacemakers"—and he knew that England lacked the financial resources necessary for effective intervention. But many of his subjects thought that England had an obligation to fight for the Protestant cause, which was losing ground, and James finally agreed to undertake a campaign if Parliament would pay for it.

The Commons would gladly have voted money for such a war but wished to debate foreign policy and to criticize James's friendly relations with Spain. They could not understand the logic of fighting the Catholics on the one hand while remaining friendly to the Catholic Hapsburg rulers of Spain on the other. James predictably told them that foreign policy was part of the prerogative, not a fit subject for parliamentary discussion, and the Commons predictably retorted by adopting the Great Protestation, another statement of their right to free speech. When this was presented to James, the irate king ripped it out of the Commons' Journal and dashed it to the floor. Some money was voted, but not enough for effective intervention.

The 1621 Parliament is also notable for its revival of impeachment. As we have seen, medieval Parliaments impeached corrupt government officers on several occasions, but there had been no impeachments during the Tudor period. The procedure was revived, first to impeach several men who had been granted objectionable monopolies by the king and then to disgrace the lord chancellor, the great philosopher and jurist Sir Francis Bacon. (The witty king once said that Bacon's philosophical writings were like the peace of God, which "passeth all human understanding.") Bacon admitted that he had accepted gifts from suitors in cases where he sat as judge, but he said that the practice was common and that his judgment had remained impartial. Perhaps that was part of the problem—those who had given bribes were irate when they did not receive favorable decisions. In any case Bacon was fined and declared unfit to hold public office.

Despite parliamentary criticism, James continued his policy of friendship with Spain. His position was actually not as odd as it appeared. He knew that England lacked the resources to fight all the Continental Catholic powers, and he sought to detach the Spanish from the Catholic alliance and neutralize them through diplomacy. As part of his program he had proposed a marriage treaty between his son, Prince Charles, and the Spanish Infanta. When negotiations bogged down, Charles and Buckingham conceived the idea of going personally to Spain. James was fearful of what might happen to them, but their repeated attempts at persuasion wore him down. Their personal diplomacy, however, was fruitless. They were not well treated, and at last it became clear that the Infanta was unwilling to marry a Protestant, whom she regarded as a heretic. Charles and Buckingham returned to England empty-handed and angry.

The last Parliament of James's reign, held in 1624, was managed by Charles and Buckingham, not by the king himself. It was more friendly than earlier Parliaments of the seventeenth century, primarily because there was now unanimity in foreign policy. Everyone (except James, who was disregarded) now opposed the Spanish, and Parliament willingly voted substantial taxes, going so far as to add an unusual provision that they be used specifically for a naval war with Spain. This Parliament continued the use of impeachment, now condemning the lord treasurer, the earl of Middlesex, who was unpopular because he had tried to eliminate tax evasion and reduce expenditures at court. James objected but was ignored.

Already ill by the time of the Parliament, James suffered a stroke and died in March 1625. His throne and his problems passed to Charles.

Scotland: "Government by Pen"

Although he visited his native land only once after his accession to the English throne, James bragged that he was able to govern it with his pen, by writing dispatches telling his deputies how to implement his policies. To a considerable extent he was successful.

James managed the Scottish Parliament through a committee, called the Lords of the Articles. He built up a group of new noblemen loyal to him by granting titles freely and by endowing these "lords of erection" with lands that had earlier been confiscated from the church. Justices of the peace were first appointed in Scotland in 1609. James hoped that they would provide a new avenue for the extension of royal authority, but they were generally unwelcome and ineffective. Still, the central government did begin to penetrate the localities. Even the Highland chieftains, who had earlier been allowed to go their own way with little government control, were increasingly brought within a unified national system.

The king was particularly interested in the church, but he seems to have understood the stubbornness of Scottish Presbyterians sufficiently that he resisted the urge to initiate major changes. In 1621 he did issue a statement requiring kneeling for the communion. This was a foretaste of the attempt to make the church in Scotland more like that in England, which was destined to create a great furor during the reign of Charles I.

Ireland: The Plantation of Ulster

In Ireland, the aftermath of Tyrone's rebellion spawned a major upheaval soon after James's accession. The attention of the English government focused on Ulster, in northern Ireland. Dominated by Tyrone and other members of the O'Neill family, Ulster had remained essentially Gaelic, while southern parts of Ireland were more heavily influenced by Anglo-Norman settlers. The disloyalty of Tyrone and some other Irish earls led to a government survey of Ulster, which determined that virtually all the land should be forfeited to the king. In 1608 James and his advisors decided to extend the old Tudor policy of planting Protestant subjects in Ireland, creating the very large Ulster plantation. They were convinced that the resistance of the native Irish could be overcome only by persuading or forcing them to conform to English institutions and that this goal could best be accomplished by surrounding them with English colonists.

Under James the land ownership in five counties of northern Ireland (Armagh, Cavan, Donegal, Fermanagh, and Tyrone) was completely reorganized. Protestants called "undertakers," who came from both England and Lowland Scotland, were offered grants ranging from 1,000 to 2,000 acres in size. They were required to come to Ireland by 1610 and complete building homes there within three years. A few chief undertakers were given even larger tracts of land and were expected to resettle at least twenty-four able-bodied males, representing at least ten different families. About one hundred undertakers (together with their families and followers) actually migrated, with the Scots in a slight majority. In all, more than ten thousand Scots eventually came to Ulster. The county of Coleraine was set aside for development by the City of London, which arranged for its colonization under the new name Londonderry.

A few Irish who had been loyal to the English government were granted land in Ulster, and some Irish laborers were permitted to remain as tenants, despite the original intention to expel them. Land was also set aside for the Anglican bishops in Ireland and for the endowment of Trinity College in Dublin as well as free schools in each county. A few years later James's government established similar, smaller plantations in Wexford and the Irish Midlands. In all of these areas King James, who was always generous when making gifts that cost him nothing, gave special grants to personal favorites. He never visited Ireland and had little sympathy for the natives whom he dispossessed.

In order to provide money for the defense of Ulster, James created a new honorary order, the baronets. A baronetcy was in essence a hereditary knighthood. Each man who received this distinction was required to pay just over £1,000, which was calculated to be enough to maintain thirty foot soliders in Ireland for three years. Originally only two hundred baronets were to be named, but James found that this was an easy way to raise money and later increased the number. He also began creating baronets of Ireland and Scotland. Like knights, baronets used the title "sir," but added "bart." following their surname. Their wives were called "lady." Baronets were not automatically summoned to either house of Parliament. The title remains in existence; it was particularly popular with Victorian industrialists, who were able in this way to buy prestige and respectability.

The long-term results of James's Irish policy, coupled with the English refusal to allow toleration to Irish Catholics, were enormous. One effect was to drive two opposing groups together: both the Irish natives and the Old English settlers, some of whom had ancestries going back to the twelfth century, were Catholics, and they now found that they had a common interest in opposing England and resisting the expropriation of their land. James's reign had begun with the hope of constructive reform in Ireland but ended in comprehensive economic, social, and administrative failure.

Charles I (1625–1649)

It has been said that James steered the ship of state straight for the rocks but left it for his son to wreck. Charles's failure to deal with the accumulated problems of the sixteenth and seventeenth centuries led to civil war and ultimately his own death.

Charles's troubles are all the more tragic because he had many good qualities. His morals were above reproach; he was a faithful husband and good father. He cared deeply about religion. He had a regal bearing that seems especially impressive in the portraits left by his great court painter, Sir Anthony Van Dyke. (See the illustration on page 325.) He was a discriminating connoisseur and patron of the arts. His tragic flaw, much like that in ancient Greek drama, was pride (the Greek *hybris*), coupled with isolation. He did not make an effort to learn how ordinary people lived or what they thought. He was convinced that his own opinions were superior, and he was surrounded by flattering courtiers who encouraged him in that view.

Charles was not unpopular at the time of his accession, but several dismal omens followed it almost immediately. There was a serious visitation of the plague in 1625, the worst since 1603, leading some observers to note that epidemics seemed to coincide with the coronation of Stuart monarchs. Many

Charles I. This portrait is by Daniel Mytens. Reproduced by permission of the National Portrait Gallery.

of Charles's subjects also regarded his marriage as a disaster. After the breakdown of the Spanish courtship, Charles had engaged in negotiations with France, and he was married to the French princess Henrietta Maria shortly after his accession. The marriage ceremony was a peculiar one, for the groom did not attend, being represented by proxy, and the vows were exchanged outside the closed doors of Nôtre Dame in Paris, since the French religious authorities did not approve of marriage to a Protestant. After Henrietta Maria came to England she was allowed to have Catholic masses in her private chapel, and Charles promised her that he would extend toleration to his Catholic subjects. Such liberal religious views were unpopular, as was the foreign marriage itself.

Military and parliamentary problems were intertwined during the earlier years of Charles's reign. He summoned a Parliament soon after his accession, counting on a continuation of the good feeling that was evident in 1624 and on further grants of money for the Spanish war. But the 1625 session did not go well. Members of the Commons criticized the king's marriage and his continued reliance on Buckingham as his chief minister. Only minimal revenues were voted, since Parliament had no confidence that larger sums would be spent wisely. There was even a wrangle over tunnage and poundage, the principal tax on foreign trade. It was customary for the first Parliament of each new king's reign to give him the right to collect these customs duties for life, but the Commons refused to do so. They offered a grant for one year only, with possible renewals; the Lords rejected this as a novelty. In the end, tunnage and poundage was not granted at all. The government continued to collect it, arguing that Parliament was guilty of an oversight.

Because virtually everyone agreed that a campaign against Spain should be mounted as part of the Thirty Years' War, Buckingham (as lord admiral) undertook a naval expedition in 1625. His goal was to occupy the port city of Cadiz and if possible intercept a Spanish treasure fleet bearing gold and silver from mines in the New World. Nothing was accomplished. The Spanish had learned of the English campaign and had evacuated Cadiz, removing all articles of value as well as supplies of food that Buckingham needed to reprovision his ships. Hundreds of English sailors died of malnutrition on the return voyage, and many of those who reached home were seriously ill.

Because the money voted in 1625 had been spent on this fiasco, Charles had to call another Parliament in 1626. The session was notable for the emergence of Sir John Eliot as a leader in the House of Commons. In a series of speeches Eliot argued that all England's evils could be traced to Buckingham, and he urged that the duke be impeached. Rather than allow this, Charles terminated the session.

Left without parliamentary taxes, the king and his financial advisors decided to resort to a forced loan. His richer subjects were asked to lend money to the government, without any real prospect of repayment. When a number of them (including Eliot) refused to do so on the grounds that this was actually a tax that had not been granted by Parliament, they were imprisoned. Some of the judges were unhappy with the proceedings, and the lord chief justice, Sir Randolph Crew, was dismissed for refusing to acknowledge the loan's legality. In the Five Knights' Case, brought by men who had been jailed without charges against them being specified, the remaining judges ruled that the plaintiffs were not entitled to bail. This was widely interpreted as legalizing the forced loan and as a sign that the law courts had lost their traditional independence and their zeal to protect the rights of subjects from infringement by the king.

Buckingham spent some of the money raised by the forced loan on an expedition to La Rochelle, a port on the French coast. The object was to aid the beleaguered French Protestants (the Huguenots) and if possible to demonstrate that Buckingham was capable of undertaking a successful campaign. It was not the disaster that Cadiz had been, but it was expensive and produced no positive result.

For a moment it looked as if good relations might be restored in 1628, when Charles agreed to accept the Petition of Right presented to him by the two houses of Parliament. The Petition reacted to recent events by declaring forced loans and imprisonment without specified charges illegal. It also prohibited the quartering of troops in private homes and the use of martial law in peacetime, practices in which Buckingham had engaged. After the king's concession, Parliament did vote substantial tax revenues, but when Eliot reiterated his charges against Buckingham the session was curtailed.

During the summer of 1628 Buckingham was assassinated by a disgruntled naval officer, Lieutenant Felton, who became something of a popular hero. This might have cleared the way for improved relations between the king and Parliament, but in fact the 1629 session revealed new grounds for dissension, mainly religious. Charles was criticized (indirectly, for there was a parliamentary custom that the king himself could not be attacked) for favoring Catholicism and for appointing bishops who supported Arminianism. This was a movement that sought to restore a number of traditional beliefs and practices that had been jettisoned at the time of the Reformation because they smacked of Catholicism. It was to grow in importance, and it will be described in greater detail shortly.

Sir John Eliot introduced resolutions branding as enemies of the realm those who favored Arminianism and popery, as well as those who paid the forced loan or advocated its collection. When Charles heard of this he sent a ceremonial messenger to bring the session to an end before a vote could be taken. The Speaker of the Commons attempted to comply with the king's order but was forcibly held in his chair while the resolutions were adopted by acclamation. The Parliament was then dissolved.

Charles's Personal Rule, 1629–1640

After this breakdown in relations between the king and the Commons, Charles resolved never to summon another Parliament. For eleven years he adhered to this policy. The period is sometimes referred to as the Eleven Years' Tyranny, but one ought to avoid that loaded term. Charles's rule was not necessarily tyrannical, since nothing in the English constitution required him to summon Parliament. Certainly he attempted to rule personally, not in partnership with Parliament. Certainly his decision was unwise and a sign of his indifference to public opinion.

Charles began by imprisoning nine members of Parliament who had been critical of his regime. All but Eliot were soon released; Eliot was kept in the Tower, under unhealthy conditions, until he died in 1632. He was even buried there, although his relatives sought to have his remains interred in the family cemetery in Cornwall. He is sometimes regarded as a martyr for the cause of free speech and parliamentary government.

Next the king attempted to introduce retrenchments that would enable him to survive financially without parliamentary taxes. In order to avoid further military expenditures he made peace with France and Spain, thus abandoning the Protestant cause in the Thirty Years' War and denying aid to his own sister Elizabeth. He also tried, without much success, to control the extravagance of his court.

His financial advisors, the attorney general and the lord treasurer, proved adept at finding sources of income that did not, according to their understanding of the constitution, require parliamentary consent. Although tunnage and poundage had not been granted, they continued to collect it. They revived several medieval customs, including distraint of knighthood, which required all landowners with incomes larger than £40 a year to become knights or pay fines. (Many subjects were eager to avoid this honor because they were not sure what financial obligations they would have to assume as knights.) They found ancient maps delineating the boundaries of the royal forests and fined those who had encroached on them. They revived early Tudor laws against enclosures and also Queen Elizabeth's proclamation prohibiting new construction in London, not because they cared about the issues but because they could penalize violators. They rewarded the king's friends with monopolies rather than money—these monopolistic rights, for instance that on the production and sale of soap, raised the price for consumers. (Some of the monopolists were Catholic, and there was a great outcry against what was called "popish soap," which, it was said, would corrupt both body and soul.)

Finally, they collected Ship Money. This assessment was based on the old idea that port cities and shipowners might be requested to lend vessels to serve in the Royal Navy during times of crisis. Although no crisis was evident, ships were demanded, but the government was willing to accept money in lieu of the actual vessels. After a few years in which Ship Money was collected successfully from the ports, the levy was extended to inland towns, which could not possibly have provided vessels, and it became clear that it was really a form of taxation.

In the short run these clever measures proved quite successful. They did bring in substantial sums of money, and the money seems to have been spent more responsibly than usual, some of it even funding improved poor relief. But a number of the measures did not yield continuing income—it was not possible, for instance, to fine enclosers on an annual basis—and some of them, especially Ship Money, attracted increasing opposition simply because they were successful. Advocates of parliamentary government became more and more unwilling to make any sort of financial payment that had not been approved by Parliament.

Charles's personal rule might have broken down eventually because it could not continue to generate adequate funding, but that was not the reason it ended in 1640. To understand why Parliament was finally summoned, one must turn to the issue of religion in both England and Scotland.

Religion During the Personal Rule

Policies designed to alter the basic condition of the Church of England had begun to attract attention in Parliament before 1629. They were implemented more fully during the years without parliamentary sessions.

The king himself had two goals. He wished to provide toleration for Roman Catholics, and he sought to reform the state church by restoring practices that many of his subjects regarded as popish. As we have seen, many aspects of medieval theology and worship had been dropped at the time of the Reformation, and the Puritans had argued for the abolition of such "dregs of popery" as remained. Despite the unwillingness of Elizabeth and James to grant the more radical Puritan demands, the established church had become essentially Calvinistic in outlook. Charles wished to return it to what is sometimes called a "high church" tradition, closer to that of the Catholics. Those who agreed with his views came to be referred to as Arminians—the name of a Dutch theologian, Arminius, was borrowed as a label for their beliefs. One difference between Arminius and the Calvinists was that Arminius believed in grace and free will (each individual's opportunity to control personal actions and achieve personal salvation), whereas Calvin taught the doctrine of predestination, which held that one's whole life was predetermined by God, from the time of birth or even before. But other issues were more important. The Arminians reemphasized the sacraments, sought to restore solemnity and "the beauty of holiness" to Anglican worship, and cherished elaborate church music and art that did not appeal to Puritan minds.

Charles had the authority to appoint the leaders of the Anglican church, and he proceeded to place Arminians in office. Some of these, including John Donne and Lancelot Andrewes, were distinguished literary figures. The king's chief advisor in religious matters, even before 1629, had been William Laud, an outspoken advocate of Arminian policies. Laud was named arch-bishop of Canterbury in 1633, when the position became vacant, and he proceeded to force his views on the English people.

Laud did not have an attractive personality. Aside from the king, he had few friends. He had risen from the lower middle classes through his own intellectual abilities, sharpened by his education at Oxford. He himself cher-ished elaborate ceremonies, which he thought could lead to a heightened inward spiritual life, and he valued sacraments more than sermons. Like Charles, he had little understanding of the views of ordinary people, and he did not care much about them. He believed that he had the power to reshape the church, and he set about using it in the face of general opposition. Clergymen who were not willing to conform were suspended or ejected, and censorship of religious writings was enforced. Some Puritans even fled the realm. One such group founded the Massachusetts Bay Colony in 1628. The number of Puritans who migrated to the New World increased during Charles's personal rule. Had Parliament been in session there might have been a forum for discussion of religious disagreements. As it was, Charles and Laud went forward without appreciating the extent of opposition to their beliefs.

An attempt to alter the character of the Scottish church proved even more disastrous. Unlike James I, Charles had no firsthand knowledge of Scotland, and he understood its people less well than his father had. In an attempt to increase the powers and revenues of his chosen leaders of the Scottish church, he took some ancient church revenues away from laymen who had acquired them following the Reformation (partly under James) and restored them to the bishops. In so doing he alienated many landowners. Still worse, he ordered the introduction of a new Service Book in 1637. Similar to the Prayer Book used in England, it had been drafted by Laud, even though Laud had no jurisdiction in Scotland. At this point thousands of Scots swore an oath that they would resist this attempt to establish what they called popish religion and tyranny. These "Covenanters" took up arms and prepared to fight for their convictions.

It was for these reasons that the so-called First Bishops' War broke out in 1639. The name is unfortunate, for the role of bishops was only one of the issues at stake. Charles realized that military action would be necessary if he was to maintain his royal authority in Scotland, but without Parliament he did not have access to adequate funds for a substantial army. He bought time through a truce with the Scots, promising to reconsider religious policy. Meanwhile he consulted with his councillors to see if they could suggest a way out of the crisis.

At this point Thomas Wentworth, the earl of Strafford, emerged as the king's chief minister. Although Strafford was an opponent of the duke of Buckingham earlier in Charles's reign, he had been won over to the king's side, partly because he shared the religious views of Charles and Laud. In 1633 Charles had sent him to govern Ireland, and he appeared to have been exceptionally successful there, maintaining order by ruling firmly. Strafford's motto was "Thorough," and it encapsulated his attitude to government. His greatest project in Ireland was the plantation of Connacht, in western Ireland, along the same lines as Ulster. Here there was less justification for the confiscation of land, for the existing inhabitants were loyal, and many of them were Old English.

The plantation of Connacht was never completed because Strafford was summoned back to London to become the king's chief advisor. He soon convinced the king to swallow his pride and call Parliament into session. Strafford believed that Parliament would understand the seriousness of the Scottish threat and would vote taxes for a military campaign against the Convenanters.

The Short Parliament, 1640

Charles I's personal rule ended in April 1640. The newly elected Parliament was asked for a vast sum of money, twice as much as it had ever granted Elizabeth at one time. The king and his councillors expected that Parliament would be hostile to the Scots, as it had been when James had proposed a union of realms, and would gladly support a campaign against the rebels. But some parliamentary leaders reasoned otherwise. John Pym, who assumed the role of leadership in the Commons left vacant by the death of Sir John Eliot, argued that the Scots were protesting against Arminianism and arbitrary government, precisely the same things that were causing distress in England. Charles interpreted their debate as a discussion of foreign policy, which he believed to be part of the prerogative. Against the advice of Strafford, he dissolved the Parliament when it had been in session less than three weeks. The gathering, which passed no legislation, has always been known as the Short Parliament.

Instead of attempting conciliation with the Scots, Charles and Laud stubbornly proceeded to draw up new Arminian regulations for the Scottish church. One of these, to be read publicly by all ministers, promulgated the doctrine of divine right of kings. Not convinced by this rhetoric, the Scots reopened the fighting. Charles borrowed money to finance an army, and Strafford talked of bringing his Irish troops to fight in England. But their activities were ineffectual; the Scots invaded northern England and routed the English forces in a battle near Newcastle upon Tyne. Once again a truce was negotiated, but on the Scots' terms. The Scots were to remain in occupation of two counties in northern England until the religious issue was resolved, and the English were to pay the expenses of the Scottish army, calculated at £850 a day. It was a historical novelty for one side in a conflict to agree to pay its enemy's costs.

In the autumn of 1640 it was even clearer than it had been in the spring that Charles could not survive without parliamentary taxation. He was forced to call Parliament once again, and he realized that he would have to bow to its demands.

The Long Parliament, 1640–1660

The new Parliament convened on November 3. Because it was not finally dissolved until 1660, it is always known as the Long Parliament.

Pym and his fellow leaders in the House of Commons now proposed a three-pronged policy. They began by insisting on the release of those who had been unjustly imprisoned during Charles's personal rule. These were mainly outspoken Puritans, like John Bastwick, who daily prayed, "From bishops, priests, and deacons, good Lord, deliver us." Next Parliament sought to rid the country of those who had assisted the king in his arbitrary rule. Several Royalist advisors fled to France. Others were arrested and eventually executed. After difficult parliamentary proceedings Strafford was finally attainted of treason, partly on the grounds that he had proposed to turn his Irish army loose against all the king's opponents, English as well as Scots. (Strafford denied the charge.) The king felt unable to resist parliamentary demands, and he allowed Strafford to be executed in 1641, with as many as 200,000 spectators looking on. Laud was sent to the Tower in 1641 but survived a bit longer; he was not beheaded until 1645.

More constructively, Parliament passed several acts that would make a repetition of the personal rule impossible. A triennial act said that no more than three years could elapse between sessions of Parliament; if the king did not summon Parliament, the members of the previous assembly were still to gather. Another act prevented the king from dissolving the Long Parliament without its own consent—this had proved necessary because the government needed to borrow money, but lenders would not provide it without assurances that Parliament would be in existence to underwrite repayment. Some of the financial measures of the personal rule, like Ship Money and distraint of knighthood, were declared illegal. Tunnage and poundage was finally granted, but only for two months at a time. Parliament also abolished several prerogative courts, including the Star Chamber, which was accused of arbitrarily enforcing the king's will. (Under the Tudors the Star Chamber had been popular, since it was able to provide speedy justice without the delays and costs of the Common Law courts, but many people came to believe that it was used tyrannically by the Stuarts because it did not employ either the Common Law or the principles of equity in settling cases. The term *Star Chamber procedure* is still used occasionally in American politics as a way of denouncing arbitrary actions.) The High Commission, a church court that Laud had used to punish those who disregarded his religious orders, was eliminated as well.

These reforms passed the Lords and Commons with little dissent. But in 1641 affairs became more tangled, as Parliament proceeded to debate the issue of religion. The more radical members of the Commons wished to abolish bishops altogether, thus reforming the church "root and branch." Moderates agreed that the bishops had become too haughty and intolerant but sought merely to clip their wings by limiting their powers and revenues. Proposals for reform did not pass in the House of Lords, where the bishops still had seats and votes.

The Irish Massacre, 1641

Debate over religion was interrupted when news of an Irish Massacre reached London. The uprising had begun in October 1641: it was motivated by religious differences; by continuing animosity against the English government and English plantations, especially Ulster; and, specifically, by the fact that the wages of the soldiers stationed in Ireland had fallen months into arrears. Rebellion was relatively easy because Strafford's restraining hand had been removed and no effective successor had been provided. Pamphlets that circulated in England contained shocking woodcuts showing the Irish actually roasting English children and preparing to eat them. This was an exaggeration. The Irish were not cannibals, but they were responsible for the deaths of several thousand settlers. In Ulster, Catholic priests do appear to have blessed the massacre of women and children who had settled in the new Protestant plantation.

There was general agreement that the Irish had to be punished, but talk of raising an army revealed a new dilemma. Some members of Parliament did not trust military commanders appointed by the king, for they feared that a royal army might take action against opposition groups within England as well as in Ireland and Scotland. They wanted to gain control of military appointments, which had always been in the hands of the king and which Charles was not likely to relinquish. An effort to compromise resulted in the appointment of several men who were trusted by both the king and Parliament, but the basic issue remained.

The Attempt on the Five Members, 1642

A climactic scene took place on January 3, 1642, when the king and four hundred armed men forced their way into the Commons' chamber in an attempt to arrest five members whom Charles blamed for provoking opposition. Word of this intervention had been received in advance, and Charles was forced to admit that (in his own phrase) "the birds had flown." They were in fact safe in the City of London, several miles away from Westminster.

Charles's policies during this critical period were unstable and contradictory; he vacillated between conciliation and a display of force. His more arbitrary actions may have been counseled by Henrietta Maria, who was used to the greater power of the French monarchy and who often told her husband, "Charles, be king." There is some reason to think that the queen actually feared that Parliament would attempt to impeach her in 1642. Charles was unwise to listen to her. Once he attempted to use force against the Commons, an action unparalleled in the history of Parliament, conciliation became virtually impossible. It can be argued that the Attempt on the Five Members made the Civil War inevitable.

A week later the king, now concerned for his own safety, left London and set up a temporary court at York. A few members of Parliament who supported him joined him in the North. He sent his wife and some of his children to France. A final attempt at reconciliation, called the Nineteen Propositions, was presented to the king in June. In reality it was a parliamentary ultimatum; if the king had accepted it, he would have become a mere figurehead, with less real power than a twentieth-century monarch. It is not surprising that he refused.

Throughout the spring both the king and Parliament were busy raising armies. The rejection of the Nineteen Propositions confirmed that both sides expected military action. The Civil War actually began on August 22, 1642, when the king ordered that the royal battle standard be raised over his camp at Nottingham.

Causes of the Civil War

N o issue has been more hotly debated among historians than the question of the causes of the English Civil War. In one sense, simply to narrate the events that preceded the outbreak of hostilities explains them. It is also worthwhile, however, to back off from events, to take a longer view, and to identify underlying issues and problems.

The English Civil War is a peculiarly complex phenomenon, and it is particularly interesting to see how historians writing at different periods have identified different sorts of fundamental causes. During the seventeenth century itself, a number of persons who participated in the events believed that they were fighting for their religious beliefs. Oliver Cromwell was one of these. He once wrote that he did not originally think that religion was the chief issue, but by the time the war was over, he had concluded that "religion was all." He believed that differences between the Puritans and Arminians could be settled only on the battlefield. Some of the newest writing about the war reverts to this position and views the English conflict as one of the seventeenth-century wars of religion, like the Thirty Years' War on the Continent.

In contrast, many nineteenth-century historians, especially those interested in the rise of democracy and parliamentary government, viewed the war as a constitutional conflict between king and Parliament. Some of these writers, often called the "Whig" historians, believed that victory of the parliamentary forces was inevitable because in the long run, royal power declined and parliamentary control of politics became dominant. Their attempt to impose Victorian standards on the Stuart period was basically unhistorical and is now generally rejected, but the notion of a constitutional conflict retains a certain validity.

The twentieth century has seen still different interpretations. Partly under the influence of Marxism, some historians have argued that social and economic troubles accounted for the conflict; war was necessary in order to transfer some powers from the king and members of the nobility, who were declining in wealth, into the hands of the merchants and members of the urban middle classes, who were rising. Others have noted the connections between religion and society, for Puritanism was strongest among urban artisans and merchants, and have pointed out the intellectual influence of the Scientific Revolution, which helped destroy easy acceptance of established authority. It has always been clear that geography was a factor: most of the Northwest was Royalist, as was Wales, while most of the Southeast (including London and other urban centers) supported Parliament and Puritanism. Local or regional issues, sometimes nothing more than petty jealousies between rival families of magnates, have recently been identified as well. One or two prominent writers have argued that none of these causes can explain the war adequately, that there were in fact no issues that were sufficiently divisive to make war necessary. These writers account for the outbreak of war by emphasizing the king's rash decision to resort to force in the expectation that he could easily defeat his opponents and reaffirm the strength of his rule. The difficulty of ruling three realms, especially given the different religious views of the Scots and the Irish, is another point emphasized in the newest study.

A further point to be noted is that not all English men and women were enthusiastic about being forced to choose sides. A substantial number remained neutral throughout the conflict. Some families were split between Royalists and Parliamentarians. In particular, some younger sons supported Parliament, hoping to gain control of their family estates if the old order and the law of primogeniture were upset. War resistance was also to become evident, for residents of certain areas organized themselves as "clubmen" to resist the entry of troops, whether Royalist or Parliamentarian, into their lands. They did not wish to see their crops burned or their property destroyed.

It is unlikely that agreement will emerge. Historians enjoy debates, and their discussions continue to throw new light on old situations. Still, one may suggest a simplified synthesis. It can be argued that the English Civil War did have underlying causes, the origins of which can be traced back to the sixteenth century. These included religious differences, problems over theories of monarchy and taxation, divergent views of the relative importance of the king and Parliament, changing intellectual and social conditions, and the differing conditions of the three British realms. No one of these was great enough, in itself, to bring about a war, but when they came together at the same time they produced sufficient tinder for a conflagration. A single act of intransigence and stupidity, like the Attempt on the Five Members, was enough to ignite the fire.

The Civil War, 1642–1646

As the war began it was evident that the king had a small professional army, relatively well trained and equipped. He had immediate access to some financial reserves, both his own and those of his aristocratic supporters who might be persuaded to sell some of their costly possessions. His forces enjoyed a clear chain of command, for the king was obviously in overall control of affairs himself. He established his headquarters at Oxford, where a number of university buildings were put at his disposal. During the fighting he himself developed a certain amount of knowledge and skill in military matters. One of his generals, his nephew Prince Rupert, was also an expert commander with considerable experience from the Thirty Years' War.

Parliament was eventually able to field a larger army, or rather group of armies, since at the beginning of the war there were several uncoordinated forces fighting against the king. Originally Parliament had fewer experienced leaders, but it found great generals by the end of the conflict. It was more difficult for parliamentary committees to direct the fighting than it was for the king. Parliament's supporters were, as individuals, less wealthy than Charles's, but Parliament acquired control of the machinery of taxation and thus was able to raise continuing revenue better than was the king. The fact that the capital city of London was dominated by Parliamentarians was of major importance, although not all of London's civic leaders had joined in the opposition to Charles. Parliament also secured the navy and so could prevent French aid from reaching the Royalists. The Royalist soldiers, some of whom dressed elegantly and wore their hair long, were sometimes called Cavaliers; the short-haired Parliamentary fighters were nicknamed Roundheads.

Under these circumstances it was likely that the king would have the upper hand for the first year or two of the fighting. If the war lasted longer, Parliament's greater staying power was bound to make itself felt.

Campaigns in the fall of 1642 were a draw. The Royalists stood off their opponents in the first major battle, fought at Edgehill, near Warwick, but failed to follow up an advantage that could have been theirs. They then tried marching up the Thames valley to London, hoping that they could capture the capital and bring the war to a speedy conclusion, but they were repulsed by Parliamentary troops at the outskirts of London and forced to retreat to winter quarters. Fighting in the summer of 1643 was also inconclusive, with a series of minor skirmishes rather than great set battles.

In September 1643 the leaders of Parliament concluded a treaty with the Scots, called the Solemn League and Covenant. The Scottish army was thus

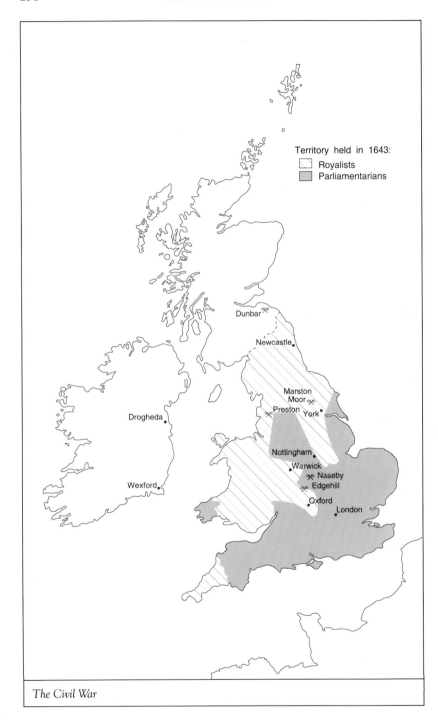

Territory held in 1643:
☐ Royalists
▨ Parliamentarians

Dunbar

Newcastle

Drogheda

Marston
Moor
Preston York

Nottingham
Warwick
Naseby
Edgehill
Oxford
London

Wexford

The Civil War

drawn into the war against the king. In return for this military alliance, Parliament promised to establish Presbyterianism as the official religion in England. Nearly two thousand Anglican clergy were subsequently deprived of their positions, some of which were given to Presbyterian ministers or friendly Puritans. At about the same time Charles entered into an alliance with Ireland. This proved to be a blunder. No Irish troops reached England, but some wavering Englishmen turned against the king because of their dislike of the Irish Catholics.

The first major battle in which the Scots participated was fought at Marston Moor, near York, during the summer of 1644. It proved a decisive defeat for the king, who lost control of northern England as a result. But the Scots do not deserve credit for the victory; it was chiefly the size of Parliament's army, about twenty-six thousand to the king's ten thousand, and the valor of the "Ironsides" from the Eastern Association of English counties that turned the tide.

Charles's forces did well, however, in southwestern England during 1644. Parliamentary troops fighting in Cornwall had to surrender or flee. When the leaders of Parliament realized that divided leadership was impeding their effort, they enacted legislation establishing the New Model Army, a smaller but more professional, better led group than earlier Parliamentary forces. The New Model proved its worth in June 1645, at the Battle of Naseby in the English Midlands. The most decisive engagement of the war, this was a disaster for the king. The Royalists lost the bulk of their supplies and weapons, and many of their soldiers had to surrender to the Parliamentary army. A few later engagements were merely the last gasp of the Royalists. The king himself surrended in 1646. He chose to give himself up to the Scots at Newark rather than to Parliament or the English army. In Ireland, Dublin surrendered to Parliamentary forces in 1647.

The Search for Peace

Parliament and the Scots won the war, but it was harder for them to find an acceptable peace.

Shortly after the end of the fighting the leaders of Parliament negotiated a treaty with the Scots. The Scottish army was given half of the back pay due to it, and they agreed to return home. They transferred the king to parliamentary custody.

A rift then opened between Parliament and the English army. Leaders of the House of Commons attempted to disband most of the army, seemingly a reasonable proposition since the fighting had ended, but army leaders insisted that the troops remain as a political force until they had obtained full payment of their arrears and guarantees of religious toleration. The religious issue now surfaced again as a matter of great importance. Many members of the New Model Army were Independents who did not believe in any established state church; for them Presbyterianism was little better than Anglicanism. They thought it was essential for the army to stay together, since no other group would lobby effectively for religious toleration. Some members of the army also held radical views regarding economics and social organization. They were eager to reshape English society by "turning the world upside down" and leveling the distinction between the rich and the poor.

Parliament now seemed closer to the Scots than to what had been its own army. In 1648 Parliament actually concluded an alliance with the Scottish leaders, and the Second Civil War was fought. The new alignment of forces pitted Parliament and the Scots against the English army. The New Model was again victorious, badly defeating the Scots in the Battle of Preston. Oliver Cromwell, who now led the English troops, was convinced that God's favor lay with his men, for they had easily defeated a rival force more than twice their own size. "God made them stubble to our swords," he wrote.

The Trial and Execution of Charles I

The army, no longer under the control of Parliament, thus became the strongest force in England, able to dictate government policy. Its views had become increasingly radical during the later years of the fighting. In addition to desiring religious toleration, the army leaders now demanded the death of the king. "I tell you, we will cut off his head with the crown on it," Cromwell said.

When the House of Commons displayed reluctance to consider executing the king, troops were sent to Westminster to prevent the more moderate members from taking any further part in deliberations. This coup was called Pride's Purge, since an officer named Pride had led it. Those who remained—hardly more than fifty out of the five hundred who had originally been elected—were given the unflattering nickname "the Rump Parliament."

Early in January 1649 the Rump ordered the creation of a special court to try Charles Stuart for treason and high crimes against his people. The Lords refused to cooperate but were declared to be unrepresentative and were ignored. When the tribunal, a group of 150 jurors, convened, Charles appeared and summoned up dignity and oratorical skill that he had not displayed earlier in his reign. He insisted that no court on earth could try him, a crowned king and annointed representative of God; he pointed out that the legal definition of treason was making war on the king, and that there was no precedent for turning the tables; and he insisted that the special court convened for the occasion was not a proper part of the English constitution and thus had no jurisdiction to try anyone.

These compelling arguments were ignored, and the king was found guilty. Some jurors who did not want his blood on their hands were reluctant to sign the death warrant, but Puritan preachers whipped up religious zeal and fifty-nine signatures were finally obtained. Those who signed are known as the regicides, a word derived from the Latin "to kill the king."

On January 30 Charles was led out an open window of the Banqueting House in Whitehall, a beautiful building that James I had built to house court festivities. A scaffold had been erected level with its upper story. Charles had prepared a farewell oration, in which he would have said that he had devoted his life to serving his subjects and would continue to do so by dying. But the throng was so large and noisy that he could not be heard. He spoke quietly to those around him, saying that he forgave them and would die as a good Christian. He laid his head on the block, and there was a stunned silence as the ax descended. According to a persistent legend, Cromwell was heard to mutter, "cruel necessity."

Suggested Reading

Ashton, Robert, *The English Civil War: Conservatism and Revolution, 1603-1649* (London: Weidenfeld & Nicolson, 1978).

Carlton, Charles, *Archbishop William Laud* (London: Routledge & Kegan Paul, 1987).

Fletcher, Anthony, *The Outbreak of the English Civil War* (London: E. Allen, 1981).

Hibbert, Christopher, *Charles I* (New York: Harper & Row, 1968).

Hill, Christopher, *The Century of Revolution, 1603-1714* (Edinburgh: Nelson, 1961).

Hill, Christopher, *Intellectual Origins of the English Revolution* (Oxford: Clarendon Press, 1965).

Hill, Christopher, *Society and Puritanism in Pre-Revolutionary England* (London: Secker & Warburg, 1964).

Kenyon, J. P., *The Civil Wars of England* (New York: Knopf, 1988).

Kishlansky, Mark, *The Rise of the New Model Army* (Cambridge: Cambridge University Press, 1979).

Lee, Maurice, Jr., *Government by Pen: Scotland Under James VI and I* (Urbana: University of Illinois Press, 1980).

Morrill, John, *The Revolt of the Provinces* (New York: Barnes & Noble, 1976).

Notestein, Wallace, *The House of Commons, 1604-1610* (New Haven: Yale University Press, 1971).

Russell, Conrad, *The Causes of the English Civil War* (Oxford: Clarendon Press, 1990).

Russell, Conrad, *Parliaments and English Politics, 1621-1629* (Oxford: Oxford University Press, 1979).

Stone, Lawrence, *Causes of the English Revolution, 1529-1642* (New York: Harper & Row, 1972).

Wedgwood, C. V., *The King's Peace, 1637-1641* (London: Collins, 1955).

Wedgwood, C. V., *The King's War, 1641-1647* (London: Collins, 1958).

Wedgwood, C. V., *Thomas Wentworth, First Earl of Strafford, 1593-1641* (London: Jonathan Cape, 1961).

Wedgwood, C. V., *The Trial of Charles I* (London: Collins, 1964).

Willson, David Harris, *King James VI & I* (London: Jonathan Cape, 1956).

CHAPTER ELEVEN

The Interregnum, Restoration, and Glorious Revolution, 1649–1688

The Interregnum, 1649–1660

After the execution of Charles I in 1649, England had no king until 1660. It was almost as if eleven years without Parliament had to be balanced by a similar span of time without a monarch before the traditional partnership between king and Parliament could be restored.

The period between reigns is known as the Interregnum. Several different forms of government were experimented with during these years. England was a Commonwealth from 1649 to 1653, then was organized as a Protectorate between 1653 and 1660.

The Commonwealth

Soon after the execution of Charles I, the House of Commons declared that it represented the English people and thus possessed all political power. It resolved never to have another king, or any single person in charge of the government. It also abolished the House of Lords, on the grounds that the upper chamber was useless and dangerous. England now became a Commonwealth and Free State. Rule rested in the hands of the Rump House of Commons and a new Council of State, a smaller committee that was to handle affairs whenever Parliament was not in session. The new constitution gained a symbol when the statue of Charles I, outside the houses of Parliament, was thrown down; on its empty pedestal were carved the Latin words *Exit Tyrannus, Regum Ultimus* ("Farewell, O tyrant, the last of our kings").

The Commonwealth was immediately beset with problems in Ireland and Scotland. Ireland had been left alone during the time of the Civil War, and vengeance for the Irish Massacre had never been exacted. But the horror of that event stuck in the minds of the English leaders, who decided to send Oliver Cromwell and most of the English army to Ireland in 1649. When the Irish garrison at Drogheda, north of Dublin, refused to surrender to him, he ordered them slaughtered. A number of Catholic priests also suffered, but there was no general massacre of the inhabitants. Cromwell's men also killed a large number of Irish at Wexford, on the southeast coast. Here the slaughter was indiscriminate, and about two thousand men and women died. Cromwell justified his action on the grounds that it was "a righteous judgment of God upon these barbarous wretches who have imbrued their hands with so much innocent blood"—a reference to the Irish Massacre—but in fact the residents of Drogheda and Wexford had not been involved in that rebellion, so if they were guilty it was only by association. After these atrocities, which remain fresh in the folk memory of the Irish people, Cromwell secured control of the isle.

Having subdued the Irish, Cromwell turned his attention to Scotland, which had fought against the army in the Second Civil War and had recognized Charles II as king immediately on the execution of Charles I. Once again military victory came easily; the Scots were defeated ignominiously at Dunbar in September 1650. It was said that Scottish fatalities were three thousand to England's thirty. Charles II, who had been in Scotland, escaped; spent a short time in England, mainly near Worcester; and finally made his way to France, where he remained throughout most of the Interregnum.

The Commonwealth found it much harder to deal with internal problems, which could not be solved by military action. The new government was unpopular with both conservatives and radicals. The Royalists had lost the war, but they had not disappeared. They continued to embarrass the government by issuing satirical tracts, like the mock will of Oliver Cromwell that suggested that he was descended from Pluto, Cain, Judas, and Machiavelli. Committed Presbyterians were also hostile to the government, which favored

Independency rather than any established state church, and many Presbyterians openly prayed for Charles II.

The radical groups that presented left-wing opposition were smaller but in some ways even more difficult to deal with, since Cromwell and some other leaders of the Commonwealth sympathized with some of their beliefs. The most important such group, the Levellers, argued that all adult males (not just property owners) should have the right to vote and that the government should adopt financial policies that would distribute wealth more evenly among the social classes. A protocommunist group, the Diggers, practiced communal cultivation of a small piece of land near London. A flock of religious zealots (the Fifth Monarchists) believed that the world would soon end and that they—the true believers—should take control of government in order to prepare England for the Last Judgment. Censorship was used as a means of trying to block the publication of antigovernment tracts, and a few opponents of the Commonwealth were imprisoned.

The most serious fundamental difficulty facing the Commonwealth involved the House of Commons itself. It was clearly no longer representative, for there had not been a general election since 1640. Royalist members had left in 1642, and moderates had been purged in 1648. Many constituencies were left without representation. But the leaders of the Rump realized that genuinely free elections would almost certainly return an unfriendly House of Commons, perhaps one dominated by Royalists. In 1653 the leaders attempted to solve the dilemma by suggesting that vacant seats be filled in a new election (the Royalists being disenfranchised) and that all existing members would retain their seats without having to face the voters. Cromwell and his fellow army officers could not stomach this proposal, which they termed a perpetuation bill. So they came down to the Parliament house and turned out the Commons, disregarding the fact that neither they nor, indeed, anyone had legal authority to do so.

The army, and Cromwell as its commander-in-chief, now held political power, but they were eager to disguise their military rule with a thin veneer of parliamentary government. Borrowing an idea from the Fifth Monarchists, who believed that the godly had a special right to rule, the army proposed that a new House of Commons should be chosen according to an unusual system: Independent congregations were asked to nominate suitable men, from whom leaders of the army made a final selection. The resulting gathering is known as the Nominated Parliament, the Parliament of Saints, or Barebone's Parliament. The last of these titles is derived from the picturesque name of one of the members, Praise-God Barbon, or Barebone.

Oliver Cromwell, lord protector of
England, Ireland, and Scotland. This
statue stands outside Westminster Hall.
Reproduced by permission of the Royal
Commission on the Historical Monuments
of England.

The Parliament of Saints met throughout the second half of 1653. Its members were well meaning but inexperienced, and they cherished false hopes of simplifying the government. When they heard complaints that the Court of Chancery was thirty years behind schedule in hearing cases, they simply abolished the court, leaving more than twenty thousand suitors without legal recourse. They hoped, vainly, to reduce the entire legal system to a slim pocket compendium so that every man could be his own lawyer, thus eliminating any need for a legal profession. By December even the more sensible members of Parliament themselves had grown disillusioned. They voted against any further continuation of the session, and the experiment at rule by the elect ended in failure. Once again power reverted to the army and to Oliver Cromwell.

Because Cromwell was in fact running the country, and because no system of rule by Parliament seemed workable, the obvious solution was to give constitutional status to Cromwell's position. So he was recognized as lord protector of England, Ireland, and Scotland—a single person with executive powers, despite the Rump's earlier determination not to concentrate authority in this way.

The Protectorate

Those who placed Cromwell in office, mainly army officers, also drew up a written constitution, the first such document in the history of England. Known as the Instrument of Government, it was declared to be in effect in December 1653. In addition to recognizing Cromwell as protector, it provided for elections to a new Parliament, still to be composed only of the House of Commons. Seats were redistributed so as to give some additional recognition to the rising merchants and artisans; Scotland and Ireland were granted representation; a triennial clause ordered new elections every three years, to prevent any Parliament from growing old and unrepresentative. Royalists were disenfranchised, ensuring that Parliament would not vote to restore the monarchy. There remained a Council of State, dominated by army officers and members of the Commons, which was authorized to pass ordinances when Parliament was not in session.

Oliver Cromwell now came to rule England, virtually as a king though without the title, for the rest of his life. He is a fascinating figure, alternately attractive and repellant. Born into a family of minor gentry in eastern England, he attended Cambridge University, where he came under the influence of Puritan ministers but had an undistinguished academic career. He was elected to the House of Commons in the Long Parliament and was an army officer from the beginning of the war, but his position was not notable until its last years. He was not one of the five members whom Charles tried to exclude, and he was not placed in full command of an army until the Second Civil War. By 1648 he had emerged as a military genius, and by 1653 he was recognized as the soundest and most politically acceptable head of the civil government. Himself an Independent in religion, he favored toleration within England, although he was not prepared to countenance Irish Catholicism. He was devout and headstrong, always convinced of his own righteousness. His rise to power reminds one of the passage in which Shakespeare has one of his characters observe that some men are born great, others achieve greatness, and still others have greatness thrust on them. Cromwell belongs in the third of these categories; circumstances catapulted him into office at a time when no one else could control a deeply troubled situation.

When the First Parliament of the Protectorate met in 1654, its members immediately questioned the validity of the Instrument of Government, which had never been adopted by Parliament or by any vote of the people. Some made it clear that they could not accept the power given to Cromwell; ninety of these extreme republicans were excluded from the House of Commons. When dissent persisted, Cromwell dissolved Parliament, just as his Stuart predecessors had done. According to the Instrument of Government no session of Parliament could be terminated by the protector until it had lasted five months. Cromwell kept the letter but not the spirit of the constitution by waiting until the end of five lunar months, counting each as having only twenty-eight days.

Shortly after the dissolution of Parliament, Cromwell had to face a Royalist revolt in southern England, known as Penruddock's Rising. He had no difficulty in repressing the rebellion, but the episode marked a change in his attitude toward the Royalists and the country generally. Earlier, he had hoped to win over those who were not supporters of his regime simply by gentleness and good rule. In 1655 he decided that harsher control was needed. He divided England into military districts, each under the rule of a major general, and he ordered the introduction of severe Puritan social policies that included the suppression of plays, gambling, racing, and alehouses.

The cost of maintaining the army, coupled with the expense of naval wars with Spain and the Netherlands that were fought during the Interregnum, necessitated the gathering of another Parliament to vote taxes. (It is fascinating to see the leaders of the Interregnum facing the same problems as the earlier Stuarts and reacting to them in similar ways.) The Second Parliament of the Protectorate, elected in 1656, contained even more opponents of the existing regime than had the First, but on this occasion Cromwell decided to exclude some of his critics on the basis of a clause in the Instrument of Government that directed voters to choose "persons of known integrity, fearing God and of good conversation." About a hundred men who opposed the policies of the government, especially in religion, were declared not to meet these requirements and were prevented from taking their seats.

Those who did attend the session expressed dissatisfaction with the structure of the government. Some thought that there should be a second house in Parliament, to prevent the Commons from making rash decisions without an opportunity for reconsideration. Concern was also expressed about the position of the lord protector. The Instrument of Government included no provision for succession to this office, either by heredity or by election, once Cromwell himself died. The matter appeared especially urgent when a plot to assassinate him was discovered. If it had been successful, England might have been plunged into anarchy and chaos.

An appealing possibility was that Cromwell might become king and thus found a new dynasty of monarchs. Restoration of the old constitution, including the two houses of Parliament, might finally end the unsuccessful search for a workable governing system. Members of the Commons did in fact vote to offer Cromwell the Crown. He was sorely tempted to accept—not, he said, out of ambition, but as a means of stabilizing the country and ensuring that the Stuarts would not be brought back—but after several months of prayer and introspection he declined. Word that the army would not countenance the revival of the monarchy, even if he were the monarch, probably determined his decision.

But if Oliver Cromwell would not accept the title, he could still be given the powers of a king. Those who favored this course (again mainly conservative army officers) drafted a new constitution to supersede the Instrument of Government. Called the Humble Petition and Advice, this was declared to be in effect in May 1657. It gave Cromwell the authority to designate his own successor. He immediately named his oldest son and said he would favor heredity as the basis for succession. The Petition also erected a second chamber in Parliament, which was composed of some army officers, some members of the Commons who were promoted, and a few old noblemen. They were to hold office for life, without election, but their places were not to be inherited. There was some problem about what to call the new chamber. Most of its members were not noblemen, so the old term *House of Lords* was inappropriate, and members of the Commons disliked the term *Upper House*, since it implied a lower status for them. The new body was generally known simply as the "Other House," a sign of its ambiguous situation. Cromwell was reinstalled as protector, now wearing purple and ermine rather than a military uniform and carrying a scepter instead of a sword. There could not have been a clearer symbol that England was moving ever closer to a restoration of the system of government that it had rejected in 1649.

Cromwell's relations with the Commons after the adoption of the new document were strained. A number of his supporters had been named to the Other House, and those who had originally been kept out were now brought back, since the new constitution prohibited such exclusion. Some of the more radical members of the army were also unhappy. Rather than tolerate dissent, Cromwell dissolved his last Parliament in February 1658. Although not an old man, he was worn out by the cares of war and office. His health declined during the summer, and he died on September 3, the anniversary of his victories at Dunbar and Worcester. He had not been able to establish a satisfactory constitution, and he had not won the support of a majority of those who lived in England, Ireland, and Scotland, but he had averted anarchy as no other contemporary leader could have done.

. After lying in state, Cromwell's body was buried in Westminster Abbey, at the east end of Henry VII's chapel. At the time of the Restoration it was disinterred and dragged through the streets of London to Tyburn Gallows, where it was hanged. Cromwell's head was then cut off and displayed on a pike outside Westminster Hall until at least 1684. It remained in the possession of Cromwell's descendants until 1960, when it was finally accorded decent lasting burial in the chapel of Cromwell's old college, Sidney Sussex at Cambridge.

Cromwellian Ireland and Scotland

In ruling Ireland, Oliver Cromwell extended the policy of confiscation and colonization, so often regarded as a panacea for Irish troubles. The cost of Cromwell's conquest of Ireland was calculated to be about £3,500,000, and the expense of maintaining an army in Ireland continued throughout the Interregnum. English leaders hoped to recover much of this by selling Irish land to English "adventurers." A series of acts passed by English Parliaments ordered the confiscation of more than 2 million acres. Indeed, the Act of Settlement of 1652 mandated an almost universal seizure of land held by Catholics.

About a thousand adventurers acquired property in Ireland. Most of them had connections with the London merchant community. A few received large estates, ranging up to as much as 32,000 acres, but most acquired much smaller properties, only 60 or 70 acres. English soldiers were also allowed to claim Irish land. As many as thirty-five thousand had the right to do so, although fewer actually chose to settle. Irish Catholics were cleared from large areas. Those who had served in the army were allowed to seek military employment abroad. Some others were forcibly transported to work on plantations in the West Indies and in Virginia. (The New England colonies refused to accept Irish Catholics.) Those who remained were supposed to be resettled, mainly in Connacht, where they received much smaller allotments than they had previously held. In practice a number remained in their old homes, reduced to the status of landless tenants. Throughout the Irish Midlands the proportion of land confiscated ranged from 60 percent to 75 percent. In 1641 Irish Catholics owned more than half of the land in Ireland, but by 1660 this had declined to substantially less than a quarter.

The severity of this settlement and the human misery it caused can hardly be exaggerated. Much of Ireland's nineteenth- and twentieth-century distress and anger has Cromwellian roots. In other ways Ireland was well governed during the Interregnum. Oliver Cromwell's son Henry served for a time as major general, a post that made him the effective ruler of Ireland. He tried to introduce reforms and to maintain peace with as little harshness as possible. Catholics were not required to attend Protestant services. Attempts were made to improve education and to foster trade and economic development. Under the Instrument of Government, Ireland was allotted thirty seats in the English House of Commons. This provision was not as generous as it sounds, however, since only Protestant landowners could vote.

In 1653 Scotland, like Ireland, was given representation in the English Parliament. This was more genuine than in Ireland, but even in Scotland many political activists were disenfranchised because they had been opposed to the Cromwellian forces, and many of the members were in fact chosen by the government. A serious Royalist uprising took place in the Highlands but was suppressed by General George Monck, whom Cromwell left behind to govern Scotland after his conquest. The union between England and Scotland that James I had envisioned was temporarily achieved during the Interregnum. No attempt was made to interfere with the established Presbyterian church, but penalties for nonattendance were removed and coercive powers were taken away from it. Monck's rule was effective and not unnecessarily stringent. The Scots naturally disliked the alien military government, but most of them had to admit that it was benevolent. One Scotsman wrote, with delicious ambivalence, "We always reckon those years of usurpation a time of great peace and prosperity."

Religion During the Interregnum

The diversity of religious views held by English men and women became increasingly evident during the middle years of the seventeenth century. As we have seen, the fundamental dichotomy was between Anglicans and Puritans, but each of these groups manifested internal divisions. Those who supported the Church of England were split between Arminians and Calvinists, and those who sought further purification and reform fragmented into a still wider variety of sects and factions.

Anglican worship according to the Book of Common Prayer was illegal during the Interregnum. Most Anglican clergy were ejected from their positions. The office of bishop was abolished, and the endowments of bishoprics and cathedrals were confiscated by the government. Some Anglican clergy did succeed in remaining in their old homes, acting as schoolmasters and sometimes conducting illicit services for those who shared their faith. Parish churches were converted into Presbyterian or, occasionally, Independent places of worship. Some cathedrals were closed, their organs and windows having been smashed during the war. Others were used by Presbyterians. In at least one case (Exeter), a new internal wall was erected, so that the Presbyterians might use the east end and the Independents the western portion of the building.

The views of the Scottish Presbyterians had become important in England following the Solemn League and Covenant, in which the Long Parliament promised to establish Presbyterianism as the state religion in England. A large gathering of clergy and laymen, called the Westminster Assembly, met in the later 1640s to draw up a Presbyterian religious settlement. This group framed the Westminster Confession as well as the so-called Directory, which was intended to replace the Book of Common Prayer.

Within the army, however, Independent beliefs were far more prevalent than Presbyterian teachings. The Independents objected to any state church, whether Anglican or Presbyterian, arguing instead that local congregations of like-minded believers, gathered voluntarily, should operate independently, without any coercion or superior authority. Because they separated themselves from the state church, they are also known as the Separatists. They sought general religious toleration and freedom, though (as Cromwell once remarked) they were not in fact very tolerant of those who did not agree with them.

Because of their belief in the independence of individual congregations, the Independents or Separatists are often regarded as the intellectual ancestors of modern Congregationalists. (In the United States, the Congregational church has become merged into the United Church of Christ.) Another group of Independents, the Baptists, also grew in strength during the Interregnum. The Baptists were distinguished by their disapproval of the Anglican custom of infant baptism. They held that only adults, who could understand the meaning of their baptismal vows, should receive the sacrament, and some of them believed that candidates for baptism should be fully immersed in water, as Christ had been, not merely sprinkled with it.

The Quakers, too, gained a considerable number of followers during the 1650s. Emphasizing the value of the "inner light" that could be found in all persons, Quakers denounced the formality of "Prayer Book religion" and the authority of ordained priests and ministers. One of their early leaders, James Nayler, was condemned by the Second Parliament of the Protectorate, the grounds being in part that he had impersonated Jesus by riding on a donkey into the city of Bristol on Palm Sunday. He was not executed, but Parliament did invoke severe punishment, with physical mutilation that included piercing the preacher's tongue. George Fox, who lived until 1691, is a more significant figure than Nayler and is often regarded as the founder of the Society of Friends. Despite intermittent imprisonment, both during the Interregnum and following the Restoration of the monarchy, Fox conducted missionary trips to Scotland, North America, and the West Indies, and he converted many to his democratic, introspective views. Industriousness and pacifism came to be hallmarks of the Quakers, or Friends.

Smaller sects, but still interesting groups, were the Muggletonians, whose leader claimed almost divine powers, and the Ranters, who were accused of sexual license and blasphemy. Some of these radical groups wished to "turn the world upside down," so that the rich and powerful would have less influence than the poor and downtrodden.

Two of England's greatest writers, John Milton and Paul Bunyan, are associated with the Independent sects. Milton, a notable scholar as well as poet, was the Latin secretary to Cromwell's government and would have remained in office longer had he not begun to go blind. Best known for his epic poem *Paradise Lost*, Milton also wrote tracts arguing against bishops and in favor of civil divorce, as well as *Areopagitica*, the most eloquent plea for free speech ever written in the English language. Bunyan did not publish his great allegory *Pilgrim's Progress* until 1678, but he began preaching during the Interregnum, attracting the opposition of both Presbyterians and Anglicans. His writings, unlike Milton's, were readily accessible to uneducated readers, and he gained a wide following.

Richard Cromwell, 1658–1659

After the death of Oliver Cromwell, his only surviving son, Richard, succeeded as lord protector without incident. (Two older brothers had died, one of them from smallpox contracted during the war.) Richard was very different from his father: he was not interested in military or governmental affairs and was not personally ambitious. He tried his hand at ruling only briefly and was relieved when he was able to return to his small country estate.

Richard did call a Parliament, which met in 1659. A breach between Parliament and the army erupted. At the army's insistence Richard dissolved

Parliament in April and abdicated in May. In theory the Commonwealth was then reestablished; in practice England was left with no civil government, and the power of the army was unmasked. As a last resort the Rump was brought back, but it too quarreled with the army and was expelled.

Because no one in England seemed able to find a way out of the country's difficulties, it was left for General Monck to assume the initiative. Without any real authority, and without saying exactly what his plans were, Monck marched from Edinburgh to London at the head of a substantial army. He was well received wherever he stopped on the way. In January 1660 he entered the English capital.

Monck reconvened the Rump and then brought back as much of the Long Parliament as could be reconstituted twenty years after its election. After naming Monck commander-in-chief, the Long Parliament agreed to its own dissolution and ordered fresh elections, according to the system in use before the war. This produced the Convention Parliament of 1660, so called because some strict constitutional theorists said it was not a lawful Parliament, since it had not been summoned by a king, and so should be regarded merely as a convention.

The Convention Parliament was dominated by Royalists, who at last had an opportunity to make their views heard. Its leaders, cooperating with Monck, opened negotiations with Charles Stuart, the older son of Charles I. In a declaration issued at Breda in the Netherlands, Charles said that he was willing to assume the throne. He promised "amnesty and oblivion" to those who had fought against his father, religious toleration and liberty of conscience to all, and payment of arrears owed the army. He sidestepped the question of ownership of properties that had been confiscated from Royalists and the church by saying that he would allow Parliament to determine such matters.

His statement was shrewdly calculated to win support, even from groups like the army, which might have been hostile. Parliament voted to restore the monarchy with Charles II as king. On May 25, 1660, he landed at Dover and the Interregnum came to an end.

Charles II and the Restoration

A few days later, on his thirtieth birthday, Charles II made his triumphal entry into London. John Evelyn, a contemporary diarist, tells us that members of the army were present, "brandishing their swords and shouting with inexpressible joy; the ways strewed with flowers, the bells

Charles II. This portrait is from the studio of
John Michael Wright.
Reproduced by permission of the National
Portrait Gallery.

ringing, the streets hung with tapestry, fountains running with wine." Evelyn could only believe that it was "God's doing," for many of the same people had fought against Charles I.

The new king was in robust health and cut a fine figure. Years of exile had made him a shrewd observer of politics. Unlike his father, he knew when to compromise and dissemble. He often said different things to different people and could be unreliable and two-faced. This trait eventually led to a peculiar situation in which English troops were fighting on both sides of a European war simultaneously. He was lazy and irresolute. He enjoyed the company of a succession of mistresses, and a distinct air of lax morality hovered over his court. But few of his subjects objected. After the stark Puritanism of the Interregnum, the looseness of the Restoration was generally welcome. It is true that one of Charles's mistresses was unpopular, but that was because she was French and Catholic, not because she was his mistress. The situation was made clear in an amusing episode that occurred early in the reign: when Nell Gwynn, an English actress to whom Charles was attracted, was booed by a London mob as she rode through the streets in a royal coach, she had her driver stop so that she could say, "Be quiet, good people, for I am the Protestant whore." They then applauded.

The period beginning in 1660 is often referred to as the Restoration. The term is also used to describe styles in art, architecture, furniture, interior decoration, and literature. "Restoration comedies" were popular on the stage, once the theaters were reopened.

The Restoration Settlement

It was generally understood that traditional forms of government and society would be restored along with the monarchy. But it was not easy to undo what had happened during the preceding years, and it took Parliament some years to complete the legislation known collectively as the Restoration Settlement.

The most pressing matters were dealt with in 1660 by the Convention Parliament, which Charles accepted as being a legitimate assembly. Amnesty was granted to all former opponents of the Stuart monarchy except the regicides; the surviving twenty-six men who had sent Charles I to the scaffold were executed in 1660.

The land settlement was more difficult. During the Interregnum, property that had belonged to the royal family, together with land confiscated from the church, had been sold by the government in order to pay the army. Some Royalists had also suffered from confiscation, but it was more common for Royalist families themselves to sell land in order to pay the special taxes that were laid on them. Now that the monarchy was restored, those who had lost property hoped that it too would be returned to the original owners, but those who had paid good money for land were unwilling to give it up without compensation. It would have been impossibly expensive for the government to buy back the lands from the purchasers, so there was really no hope of a truly equitable settlement. In the end, Parliament restored the former properties of the king and church, without compensation, but it did nothing for individual Royalists. Some of them sued for their land in the courts, which finally ruled that confiscations should be restored but sales should be confirmed. Thus many Royalists failed to regain their estates. Some complained that the king had forgotten them and that he was following a policy of amnesty for his enemies, oblivion for his friends.

Government finance was placed on a new footing in the 1660s. The idea that the king should live of his own was finally abandoned in favor of a continuing annual income. Parliament acknowledged that a substantial sum (more than a million pounds) was required, but it never provided taxes that actually yielded that amount. Feudal dues, purveyance and wardship, and impositions were abandoned—the whole feudal system had finally died in the 1640s and was not resurrected. Excise taxes were now placed on coffee, tea, and chocolate, beverages that were newly popular during the Restoration, as well as on wine and beer. A new property tax, based on the number of fireplaces or hearths in each house, was also introduced. Clergymen were no longer exempt from parliamentary taxation, but they were now permitted to vote for Members of Parliament (M.P.s).

Although the Anglican church was reestablished in many places immediately following the Restoration, religious legislation was deferred until the election of a new Parliament. This assembly, which met in 1661, was so strongly Royalist and Anglican that it was dubbed the Cavalier Parliament. Because it was not dissolved until 1679, it is also sometimes called the Long Parliament of the Restoration.

The Clarendon Code

The religious settlement enacted by the Cavalier Parliament between 1661 and 1665 is known as the Clarendon Code. The name honors the earl of Clarendon, a staunch Anglican and advisor to the king. In fact, Clarendon did not write the Code, which was less tolerant of nonconformists than either Charles or Clarendon wished. It would have been more appropriate to call it the Sheldonian Code, for it reflects the stiffer views of Gilbert Sheldon, the archbishop of Canterbury.

The Code includes four statutes. The Corporation Act imposed religious tests on those holding office in municipal corporations, so that only Anglicans could qualify. The Act of Uniformity brought back the Book of Common Prayer, now slightly modified but with no concessions to the Puritans. (The 1662 Prayer Book remained in official use in England until the late twentieth century.) Clergy were required to swear that they would conduct services according to the Prayer Book. Some two thousand refused and were deprived of their offices, to become the nucleus of nonconforming congregations. Worship and preaching outside the state church were regulated by the Conventicle Act and Five Mile Act. The first of these statutes outlawed conventicles, a term for nonconformist places of worship, while the second made it unlawful for unlicensed ministers to preach within five miles of any incorporated city or town.

In the Clarendon Code the government acknowledged, for the first time, the permanent existence of dissenting or nonconformist churches. Previously it had hoped to persuade or force all subjects to worship in the state church. After 1660 it was not illegal to be a dissenter, but such persons were placed in a severely disadvantaged position and not accorded the full toleration that Charles had promised. The Quakers and the Unitarians (a relatively new sect whose adherents did not believe in the divinity of Christ or the Holy Spirit as a member of the Trinity) were persecuted with special severity under the Clarendon Code. The king attempted to issue a Declaration of Indulgence, which would have granted automatic pardons to both Catholic recusants and Protestant nonconformists who violated the religious statutes, but Parliament objected and he was forced to yield.

In summary, the Restoration Settlement began with the goal of reestablishing traditional monarchical government as it had existed before the Civil War, but in practice it introduced a number of changes. Not all property that had changed hands was restored to its original owners. Feudal structures were not resuscitated. Prerogative courts like the Star Chamber were gone forever, and government finance was altered in significant ways. The Church of England was restored, but the existence of nonconformist sects and the continued presence of Catholicism were acknowledged.

The Settlement in Wales, Ireland, and Scotland

The Restoration presented few problems in Wales. Charles's return was celebrated with bonfires and loyal toasts. Royalists succeeded in regaining their offices and their prominence in local affairs. There was some residue of bitterness, but most Welsh men and women were glad to be rid of Cromwell's rule. Perhaps more than the English themselves, the Welsh continued to celebrate the anniversary of Charles I's execution, January 30, as an occasion to honor the memory of the blessed royal martyr.

Because so much land in Ireland had changed hands during the Interregnum, the property settlement there presented difficult problems. The English Parliament ratified Cromwell's confiscations, but with a clause that said that lands formerly belonging to the Anglican church, colleges, and "innocents" were to be restored. In the end a few Catholics did recover their property, to the anger of Protestant settlers who were dispossessed, but most of the Irish did not benefit from the Restoration.

The hope of religious toleration in Ireland was dashed as well. A promise that all penalties that hindered the practice of the Catholic religion would be removed was disregarded. Jesuit schools in Drogheda were forcibly closed. The power of Anglican bishops was strengthened by an Irish Act of Uniformity, modeled on that passed by the English Parliament, which required the use of the Book of Common Prayer.

Land was not a serious problem in Scotland, but religion was. Here the Restoration Settlement brought back the religious establishment as it had existed in 1633, so that bishops and presbytery were once again combined. Ministers who refused to accept this arrangement or swear loyalty to Charles

II were expelled, leaving about a third of the parishes vacant. In some areas, most notably Galloway (the territory nearest to Ulster in Ireland), whole congregations followed their ministers. Their worship services gradually degenerated into gatherings of armed bands, their sermons into political diatribes against the government. Thus, peace was not restored to either of these outlying kingdoms as easily as to England and Wales.

Clarendon's Ministry, 1660–1667

One of Charles's companions in exile had been Edward Hyde, the first earl of Clarendon. In 1660 Clarendon became the king's chief minister, responsible for managing both domestic matters and foreign policy. General Monck, created duke of Albemarle, remained in command of the army, and the king's younger brother, James, duke of York, was made head of the navy.

Clarendon was blamed for a number of unfortunate events, over some of which he had no control. He did arrange the marriage between Charles II and a Portuguese princess, Catherine of Braganza: the king was perfectly happy with his mistresses, who bore him numerous illegitimate children, but he acknowledged a responsibility to marry and sire a lawful heir to the throne. Clarendon was attracted by the Portuguese offer of a large dowry, which included both cash and the outposts of Bombay (in India) and Tangier (in the eastern Mediterranean). Charles's marriage to a foreign Catholic was generally unpopular; the marriage failed in its aim of producing children; the new territories were expensive to maintain and, in the short run at least, unprofitable. Indeed, Tangier was abandoned before the end of Charles's reign.

Clarendon was also accused of mismanaging the Second Dutch War (1665–1667). This was a commercial naval conflict with the Netherlands, resulting from trade rivalry. It closely resembled the First Dutch War, which Oliver Cromwell had undertaken in the early 1650s. In both wars the Dutch protested the English Navigation Acts, which attempted to ensure that goods bound to or from England would be carried in English ships or vessels of the country of origin, thus barring the Dutch from the profitable carrying trade. English military efforts were badly hampered by two natural disasters, the Great Plague of 1665 and the Great Fire of London, 1666.

The Great Plague, a new visitation of the dread Black Death, proved to be the last such epidemic in England. It was not unique—there had been several outbreaks earlier in the seventeenth century—but it was probably the most severe since the fourteenth century. At its peak the mortality rate in London exceeded seven thousand a week. The Great Fire, which spread from the ovens of a baker in Pudding Lane, burned out of control for several days and destroyed two-thirds of the City of London, including civic buildings and St. Paul's Cathedral as well as dozens of churches, hundreds of shops, and thousands of houses. Samuel Pepys, the greatest of the English diarists, left vivid accounts of both disasters. He was secretary of the navy and was fortunate that the navy office, in which he lived as well as worked, was one of the few buildings to be spared by the fire. As a precaution Pepys had sent his wife and choice furniture up the Thames to safety and had buried his wine in the garden.

Taking advantage of these crises, the Dutch humiliated the English, even sailing up the River Medway, burning English ships in the harbor at Chatham, and towing away the Royal Charles, the largest vessel in the English navy, to become part of the Dutch fleet. When peace was made the English were in a weak bargaining position. The Treaty of Breda, signed in 1667, granted the Dutch the trading concessions they desired. It did transfer New Netherlands to England, but no one imagined that this Dutch settlement in North America, now renamed New York in honor of Charles's brother, would prove particularly valuable. Clarendon was blamed, unfairly, for bungling the war and mismanaging the money that Parliament had voted for its prosecution. In addition, he had grown unpopular because of his religious and moral principles, which others thought inflexible and stuffy. In 1667 he was dismissed as lord chancellor, and the Commons began impeachment proceedings against him. Although the Lords refused to convict him, he fled into exile in France, where he lived out the rest of his life writing a history of the Civil War or, as he called it, the Great Rebellion. After his death his remains were brought back to England and interred in Westminster Abbey.

The Cabal and
the Third Dutch War

Charles did not appoint a single minister to replace Clarendon. Instead, he kept foreign affairs in his own hands and relied in other matters on the assistance of a group of five prominent men: Sir Thomas Clifford; Henry Bennett, lord Arlington; the second duke of

Buckingham; Anthony Ashley Cooper, lord Ashley; and the Scottish earl of Lauderdale. Observers noted that the initials of these surnames or titles, if arranged properly, spelled the word *cabal*, a term suggesting an alliance of unscrupulous men to advance their own interests.

Charles's diplomacy became of critical importance during the period of the Cabal (1667–1674). The king had always admired Louis XIV, the great "Sun King" of France, and tried to emulate his court as far as England's more limited resources permitted. Charles's beloved sister Minette had married Louis' brother, generally known as "Monsieur," and in 1670 Louis and Charles went further, signing the Secret Treaty of Dover. In fact only part of the treaty was kept secret. Public clauses pledged England to join in a French war against the Netherlands, where Louis was trying to nibble away at Dutch territory and add it to his own empire; France in return promised to give Charles an annual subsidy. The secret clause said that Charles would publicly declare his own conversion to Catholicism and would return all of England to the old faith as soon as it was politically expedient. Should this result in rebellion, France would assist by sending money and troops. Historians remain undecided whether Charles was serious about these religious provisions of the treaty. Certainly he found Catholicism attractive, but he may have been playing diplomatic games.

For two years the treaty produced no tangible results. Then, in 1672, Charles issued a new Declaration of Indulgence, granting toleration to Catholic and Protestant nonconformists, and he announced the opening of the Third Dutch War. This conflict was quite different from the first two Dutch Wars. They had been limited to naval operations, and they were motivated by the genuinely English desire to limit Dutch shipping. The new war had to be fought primarily on land, and it represented English involvement in a campaign intended basically to benefit France. Expenses far exceeded Louis' subsidy and Parliament's willingness to levy taxes. The English government became virtually bankrupt, even locking the doors of the Exchequer office for a time because there was no money for government creditors. Several businesses failed as a result of this "stop of the Exchequer."

In 1673 word of the treaty's secret clauses leaked out. Parliament was irate. It forced Charles to cancel the Indulgence. It then passed the Test Act, which was meant to exclude Catholics from government office and military command. Similar to the earlier Corporation Act, it required officeholders to receive communion in the Church of England and renounce the Catholic doctrine of transubstantiation. The act broke up the Cabal: some of its members refused the tests, and those who supported the act were dismissed by the king. Charles's brother James resigned as lord admiral, for he made no attempt to hide his adherence to the Catholic church. Charles was forced to withdraw, at least for the time being, from a war that had been costly and useless.

Danby and the Rise of Political Parties

Charles now ennobled a leading politician, Sir Thomas Osborne, as the earl of Danby and made him chief minister in the government. Danby had few scruples and was prepared to do the king's bidding, whatever it might be. He was thought to be a shrewd manipulator of parliamentary politics, dangling bribes and lucrative offices before the faces of wavering members.

During Danby's ministry (1674–1679), England followed contradictory foreign policies, eventually arriving at one of the most absurd situations in the realm's history. The king continued to connive with Louis, sending troops to fight for France in the Netherlands in exchange for French subsidies. Parliament insisted on going to the aid of the Dutch: it sympathized with them because they were Protestants and because they were defending their land from invasion by a foreign autocrat. A new marriage alliance linked William of Orange, the chief Dutch leader, with a member of the English royal family, Mary, the daughter of the duke of York and his first wife, Anne Hyde (Clarendon's daughter). There were thus personal ties with both sides in the struggle between France and the Netherlands, and when Parliament sent troops to fight alongside the Dutch there were English soldiers on both sides as well.

It is not surprising that this ludicrous situation mobilized opposition. Few members of the once-Royalist Cavalier Parliament were now willing to support the king and Danby. Public opinion turned against them even more on the discovery of a supposed "popish plot" in 1678. This was a scheme to murder Charles II and place his Catholic brother, James, on the throne, thus restoring Catholicism as the official religion of England. In fact the affair appears to have been a hoax, very likely invented by Protestants as a means of discrediting their enemies. The king was never convinced of its truth, but the vindictive Parliament instituted a virtual reign of terror, sending five Catholic noblemen to the Tower and more than thirty other persons to the scaffold. Charles retaliated by dissolving the Cavalier Parliament (now no longer very "cavalier"), which had sat intermittently for eighteen years.

The elections of 1679 were the first ones to be fought along party lines. Those few who still adhered to the king and Danby formed the Court party; critics of the regime were referred to as members of the Country party. Anthony Ashley Cooper, who was now the earl of Shaftesbury, became the Country party's leader. He and his friends announced that they supported the policy of excluding Roman Catholics like James from the succession, and they promised to introduce an exclusion bill into the next Parliament. Rival candidates faced each other at the polls more frequently than had been common earlier. When the new Parliament met it became obvious that almost all members adhered to the Country faction. Danby had to resign, and he was sent to spend several years in the Tower.

The Exclusion Parliaments

Because an exclusion bill was introduced in 1679, the Parliament is called the First Exclusion Parliament. It did not last long. Because Charles continued to favor heredity and the succession of his Catholic brother, he dissolved the session before it could embarrass him by enacting the bill.

The king ordered fresh elections in the fall, hoping for a more cooperative assembly. It was in this contest that the terms *Whig* and *Tory* became common party names. Both words were used scornfully by those who disliked the group in question, and there was some relevance: Whigs were originally Scottish cattle thieves (hence staunchly Protestant, like the Country party), whereas Tories were Irish bandits (and thus Catholic sympathizers, like members of the Court party). The analogies were far from perfect. Although many Whigs favored toleration for nonconformists, relatively few of them were Presbyterian. Most Tories were noted for their loyalty to the Anglican church, and many of them opposed freedom for either recusants or Protestant dissenters.

In this campaign Shaftesbury announced that if Catholics were indeed excluded from the throne he would favor naming the duke of Monmouth as Charles's heir. Monmouth was the king's illegitimate son, acknowledged by Charles as his offspring. But Charles remained adamant about adhering to the normal succession; he preferred a legitimate Catholic to a bastard Protestant. The Second Exclusion Parliament was speedily dissolved, as the first had been. Trying still again for a favorable gathering, Charles called elections in 1681 and had the Parliament meet in Oxford, where he hoped members would imbibe Royalism by osmosis. It did not work; the session lasted only a week.

Charles never summoned another Parliament. By 1684 he was technically violating the Triennial Act, but no one seemed to care. The Whigs lost ground, partly because Monmouth was not generally popular and partly because some of the leaders went too far, attempting to assassinate Charles in the so-called Rye House Plot so that Monmouth could be installed immediately. This was too much for many people who had earlier supported exclusion.

The last year of Charles's life seemed a happy one. The "merry monarch" was surrounded by his frolicking court, untroubled by Parliament and unfriendly politicians, confident that his brother would succeed him. Early in 1685 he had a stroke. When it became evident that he was dying, a Catholic priest was summoned to administer the last rites of the church. Whatever he may have meant when he signed the Treaty of Dover, Charles II appeared to die a Catholic.

James II (1685–1688)

Despite earlier efforts at exclusion, James II succeeded without incident in 1685. He was the first avowed Catholic ruler of England since Bloody Mary. As might be expected, his accession was received with joy in Ireland. As King James VII of Scotland he was warmly welcomed by many people in the Scottish Highlands, whose friendship he had cultivated during several long visits while he was duke of York. The idea of a Catholic monarch went down less well in the Scottish Lowlands and in Wales.

His reign began surprisingly well. James announced that he would not hide his own religious convictions but would abide by the existing laws that established the Anglican church. His coronation was almost normal: the archbishop of Canterbury placed the crown on his head, as usual, but James did not receive communion from the archbishop's hands, preferring instead a private Catholic mass that followed the public ceremony. A Parliament held shortly after the coronation was quite cooperative, granting the king generous revenues and refusing to adopt a resolution calling on him to enforce anti-Catholic acts.

*James II. This portrait is by Sir
Godfrey Kneller.
Reproduced by permission of the
National Portrait Gallery.*

Very unwisely, the duke of Monmouth picked the moment of James's greatest popularity for a revolt intended to unseat him. Charles's illegitimate son had been in exile in Holland. In June 1685 he landed in southwest England with a pathetic invading force numbering not more than 150. His followers were easily defeated by a royal army that was hastily gathered and included some Oxford undergraduates. Monmouth was found asleep in a ditch. He surrendered and begged for mercy but was promptly executed. His Scottish friend, the duke of Argyll, was unsuccessful in rallying the Covenanters to Monmouth's banner. Argyll too was captured and killed. The Battle of Sedgemoor, in which Monmouth was defeated, was the last actual fighting on English soil, although there have been subsequent battles in Scotland and Ireland as well as twentieth-century air raids on England itself.

Monmouth's followers in the West of England were harshly treated. In a judicial campaign known as the Bloody Assizes, Judge Jeffreys sentenced about 150 men to death and 800 more to slavery in the West Indies.

James's policies hardened in other ways as well. His Catholicism became increasingly evident. He appointed Catholics, including a Jesuit priest, to government posts and military commands, in violation of the Test Act. He attempted to turn one of the Oxford colleges into a Catholic seminary, and he ordered Cambridge to award a degree to a Catholic, in defiance of its statutes. He issued two Declarations of Indulgence, which suspended the penal laws against both Catholic and Protestant nonconformists, and he ordered that the second of these be read publicly at Anglican services. Many people believed that these acts were merely the prelude to the reestablishment of the Catholic church throughout James's realms. They may well have understood the king's intentions correctly.

At this point most Anglican clergy turned against James. Earlier, they had tried to swallow their religious scruples. They found it hard to denounce the ruler, since many of them believed in the divine right of kings and held a high view of the monarchy. But few of them were willing to read the Declaration. A number preached anti-Catholic sermons instead. When seven bishops petitioned James to reconsider the Declaration he had them imprisoned in the Tower, but after hearing the legal argument that all subjects have the right to petition the sovereign, the courts found the bishops innocent of any offense and ordered them freed. It was one of the few instances of a judicial decision that went against the Stuart monarchy and perhaps the only time in the seventeenth century when popular opinion sided with the bishops. There is said to have been dancing in the streets of London in June 1688, when they were released.

Birth of a Catholic Heir

Until 1688 many of those who opposed James II counseled patience. The king appeared to be aging, although he was only fifty-five, and some thought that his reign could not last very much longer. His heirs were Protestant: by his first wife, Clarendon's daughter Anne Hyde, James had fathered two daughters, Mary (who had wed William of Orange) and Anne (who married a Protestant Danish prince). So the religious difficulties should be temporary and might be borne.

After the death of Anne Hyde, James had married an Italian noblewoman, Mary of Modena. Mary was a Catholic, so if she bore children they would be brought up in the Catholic faith, but after fifteen years of marriage there were no living offspring. Then, in June 1688, Mary gave birth to a son. Because males took precedence over females, the infant immediately became the heir apparent and brought with him the prospect of an unending line of

*William of Orange (King William III), copy of
a portrait by Sir Peter Lely.
Reproduced by permission of the National
Portrait Gallery.*

Catholic kings. There were rumors that the baby was a changeling, the child
of other parents introduced into the queen's bed in a warming pan, but it is
not likely that this was true.

Faced with a drastically altered situation, seven men (sometimes known
as the Seven Eminent Persons) gathered together and took it on themselves
to invite William of Orange to invade England and restore Protestant rule.
The "immortal seven" included both Whigs and Tories. Several were noblemen, one was the Anglican bishop of London, and another was Danby, the
half-forgotten Tory minister who now embraced exclusion. At the end of
September William agreed to dethrone his father-in-law and assume the
English crown. His motives were complex. For some years he had regarded
himself as the true heir to the English throne: his mother was a sister of
Charles II and James II, so he could trace his ancestry back to Charles I, and
he thought that the claims of Anne and Mary were dubious, since their
mother had been a commoner. He may have married Mary partly to improve
his chances of gaining the English succession. He was a sincere Protestant,
although not an Anglican, and he probably did feel a responsibility to uphold
the reformed faith in England. It was also his duty to defend the Netherlands
against Louis XIV, and he knew that success would be more likely if

Queen Mary II, copy of a portrait by William Wissing.
Reproduced by permission of the National Portrait Gallery.

he could bring English resources into the conflict with France. By inviting William to take the throne, the English people were actually committing themselves to what was to prove a second Hundred Years' War with the French.

William came to England with a large fleet, in striking contrast to Monmouth. His army numbered fifteen thousand men, some of whom were Englishmen and Scots who had become exiles during James's reign. William's force landed on November 5, Guy Fawkes Day, an ideal time for fanning the flames of anti-Catholic sentiment.

James learned of William's plans but made no serious effort to muster an army. Instead, he sent his wife and son to France, and late in December he fled there himself. On his first attempt to cross the Channel he was apprehended at Faversham, even though he was dressed as a common fisherman, but port authorities were told not to interfere with his escape and a second venture succeeded. As he left London, James threw the Great Seal of England into the River Thames, hoping thus to invalidate the actions of subsequent governments. In fact, it made no difference; any new king would demand a new seal, bearing his own portrait rather than James's.

The Glorious Revolution

The events of 1688, in which the Protestant succession was assured and the throne passed from James to William and Mary, have come to be known as the Glorious Revolution or the Bloodless Revolution. The latter name is apt, for there was no fighting and virtually no blood was spilled—at least in England itself.

Although the Revolution took place with nearly miraculous ease, a constitutional justification had to be provided for it. A Revolution Settlement was needed in 1688, just as the Restoration Settlement had been required in 1660.

Once again a Convention Parliament was summoned—technically a convention because it had not been called together by a king with unquestioned authority to do so. Both Whigs and Tories gathered in January 1689. The Revolution had bipartisan support in England, but attempts to underpin it with political theory produced a party split. The more conservative Tories were reluctant to abandon divine right and hereditary succession. They tried to justify the exclusion of James's son with the "warming-pan theory" (that is, the theory that the child was not James's son), and they toyed with the idea of disposing of James on the grounds that he was senile or insane and needed a regent. These propositions were unconvincing. At best they might have justified the succession of Mary as queen, but William would not hear of becoming merely prince consort. He intended to be king, equal to Mary in theory and dominant in practice, and he expected to continue in place if she predeceased him. No hereditary juggling seemed able to accommodate these demands.

Whig political theory was more radical but more relevant. It now adopted ideas that had been developed by the great philosopher John Locke, perhaps in association with the Whig leader Shaftesbury (now dead). Locke argued that governments were initially formed as the result of a contract or compact among the people to establish a ruler of their choice. In this contract the ruler guaranteed to maintain the life, liberty, and property of his subjects—their natural rights—and the people transferred to him as much of their inherent freedom as was necessary to enable him to do so. Should the ruler violate the natural rights of subjects, the contract was broken, and the people were free to name whatever new ruler they wished, not necessarily one related to the previous monarch.

Borrowing this theory, Parliament voted that James had violated his subjects' natural rights by disregarding the law and by appointing Catholics to

The great philosopher John Locke. This portrait is by Sylvester Brownover. Reproduced by permission of the National Portrait Gallery.

office. The contract was broken, and the throne was vacant. James had also left the country, thus in effect abdicating, though Whig theory did not depend on this action. The Crown was to be vested jointly in William and Mary as long as both lived. Whoever survived longer was to reign independently until he or she died. The throne was to pass to the children of William and Mary, and if they did not have any, to Anne and her heirs. Finally, Parliament declared that it was inconsistent for a Protestant kingdom to be governed by a popish prince. Thus exclusion became part of the Settlement, and Catholics lost the right of succeeding to the throne.

The Revolution Settlement also included a Bill of Rights, which theoretically formed part of the new rulers' contract. This statement, which contained thirteen specific clauses, dealt with various royal abuses that had arisen during the Stuart period. The Bill declared, for instance, that the sovereign could not suspend laws, as both Charles II and James II had tried to do in their Declarations of Indulgence, or collect revenues without parliamentary consent, as Charles I had done. It reiterated that it was lawful for subjects (such as the seven bishops) to petition the monarch. Parliamentary elections were to be free, and freedom of speech was to prevail in parliamentary debate. Controversy about these and some additional related matters was permanently laid to rest.

A final part of the Revolution Settlement was the Toleration Act, passed in May 1689. This allowed most Protestant nonconformists to have their own places of worship, in effect repealing parts of the Clarendon Code. Dissenters were to meet behind unlocked doors, to ensure that they were not plotting against the government, and they were to notify appropriate authorities of the times and places of their gatherings. They were still in theory excluded from public affairs by the Corporation Act and Test Act, but in practice many dissenters were willing to participate in Anglican services often enough to qualify for office. (The practice came to be known as "occasional conformity.") Catholics and Unitarians did not gain similar benefits. In fact, new restrictions were placed on them in 1689, but they were not generally enforced.

An important point about the Settlement is that Parliament deliberately rejected the idea of giving William and Mary adequate ongoing revenues. Even customs duties were granted for the limited period of four years, not for the life of the monarchs. The rulers were also denied the privilege of maintaining a standing army. A later Triennial Act insisted that a new Parliament should meet every three years, but in fact this provision was unnecessary. After 1689, even more than earlier, kings and queens needed regular Parliaments to grant them taxes and the right to raise armies. No year since the Revolution has gone by without a session of Parliament.

In Ireland and Scotland the Revolution was not digested so easily. In March 1689 James II went to Ireland, trusting that he would still be recognized as king there and hoping to use Ireland as a base for operations against England. Although both he and most of the Irish were Catholics, their interests did not entirely coincide, and the Irish forces available to James were undisciplined and ill-equipped. Despite assistance from France, James and his followers were routed at the bloody Battle of the Boyne, 30 miles north of Dublin. James fled; William entered Dublin in triumph.

A Scottish Parliament offered the throne to William and Mary, contingent on their agreeing to eliminate bishops from the Scottish church. Some Catholic Highland clans were not prepared to accept the Protestant succession. They did defeat William's supporters at the Battle of Killiecrankie in July 1689, but their leader (Viscount Dundee) was killed in the fray and no one else could hold the clans together. So the position of William and Mary was secured in Scotland as well as in Ireland.

The Significance of the Glorious Revolution

Historians have held divergent opinions about the significance of the Glorious Revolution. As in the case of the causes of the Civil War, these opinions have varied over time. The so-called Whig historians of the eighteenth and nineteenth centuries idealized the Revolution and regarded it as a historical necessity. For them it represented an essential stage in the coming of liberalism, democracy, and parliamentary government, since it saw the end of divine right hereditary kingship and the clear establishment of a limited monarchy in England.

More recent writers deny the validity of such long-term trends, or at least the inevitability of progress along such predetermined roads. Many view the Revolution as a specific reaction to a unique set of circumstances. Others argue that it was in fact not a revolution at all, for (unlike the later revolutions in France, Russia, and China) it did nothing to alter the social and economic conditions of the time. They see it as little more than a dynastic change, accompanied by a settlement that reiterated policies that were already generally accepted.

It is certainly true that not all divisive matters were settled in 1689, and not all the people who lived in the British Isles were prepared to accept the Glorious Revolution. Subsequent years would witness "Jacobite" rebellions in favor of James's son, who came to be known as the Old Pretender, and his son, "Bonnie Prince Charlie," the Young Pretender. The Anglican church was also to be split for a generation, since some conservative clergy did not feel that they could abandon their belief in hereditary succession and swear an oath of allegiance to the new monarchs. (Because of their refusal to swear, they were called the Non-jurors.) But for most of the British, the revolution deserved to be called glorious. It ushered in a new constitution that resolved most of the problems that had plagued the British Isles since the time of the Tudors, and it prepared the way for the new political systems of the eighteenth century.

Suggested Reading

Barnard, T. C., *Cromwellian Ireland* (Oxford: Oxford University Press, 1975).

Baxter, Stephen, *William III* (New York: Harcourt, Brace and World, 1966).

Bottigheimer, Karl S., *English Money and Irish Land: The "Adventurers" in the Cromwellian Settlement of Ireland* (Oxford: Clarendon Press, 1971).

Feiling, Keith, *A History of the Tory Party, 1641-1714* (Oxford: Clarendon Press, 1924).

Fitzpatrick, Brendan, *Seventeenth-Century Ireland: The War of Religions* (Totowa, N.J.: Barnes & Noble, 1989).

Fraser, Antonia, *Cromwell* (New York: Knopf, 1973).

Fraser, Antonia, *Royal Charles: Charles II and the Restoration* (New York: Knopf, 1979).

Green, I. M., *The Re-establishment of the Church of England* (Oxford: Oxford University Press, 1978).

Hill, Christopher, *God's Englishman: Oliver Cromwell and the English Revolution* (London: Weidenfeld & Nicolson, 1970).

Hutton, Ronald, *The Restoration* (Oxford: Oxford University Press, 1985).

Jenkins, Geraint H., *The Foundations of Modern Wales: Wales 1642-1780* (Oxford: Clarendon Press, 1987).

Jones, J. R., *Charles II: Royal Politician* (London: Allen & Unwin, 1987).

Jones, J. R., *The First Whigs* (Oxford: Oxford University Press, 1961).

Mitchison, Rosalind, *Lordship to Patronage: Scotland 1603-1745* (London: Edward Arnold, 1983).

Ogg, David, *England in the Reign of Charles II*, 2 vols. (Oxford: Clarendon Press, 1934).

Ogg, David, *England in the Reigns of James II and William III* (Oxford: Clarendon Press, 1955).

Pinkham, Lucille, *William III and the Respectable Revolution* (Cambridge, Mass.: Harvard University Press, 1954).

Prall, Stuart, *The Bloodless Revolution* (New York: Anchor Books, 1972).

Seaward, Paul, *The Cavalier Parliament and the Reconstruction of the Old Regime, 1661-1667* (Cambridge: Cambridge University Press, 1989).

Trevelyan, G. M., *The English Revolution, 1688-1689* (London: Butterworth, 1938).

Turner, F. C., *James II* (London: Eyre & Spottiswoode, 1948).

CHAPTER TWELVE

Social and Intellectual History, 1485–1688

The Population

The population of the British Isles grew rapidly during the sixteenth and seventeenth centuries after having remained stable throughout the later Middle Ages. Many of the changes in social history can be traced, in part at least, to the significant changes in demography.

As we have seen, the population of England probably stood between 2.5 and 3 million in 1377; careful demographic studies indicate that it was still about 2.75 million in 1540. It then began to grow, and it increased substantially in the century and a half preceding the Glorious Revolution. There were about 4.1 million people in England at the time of Elizabeth's death in 1603 and 4.9 million in 1689. The population of England probably reached 5 million in 1700. Growth had slowed in the 1630s and 1640s, partly as a result of emigration to the New World, and the total population actually declined in the 1650s, reflecting the casualties and disruptions of the Civil War. Nevertheless, the underlying trend was constantly upward. The population nearly doubled under the Tudors and Stuarts; the increase approximated 1 percent a year.

The population of Wales and Scotland also increased substantially during this period. Wales probably had few more than 200,000 inhabitants in 1485 but had grown to more than 300,000 in 1600 and about 400,000 in 1689. Scotland may have had a population of 500,000 in 1485; 900,000 in 1600; and nearly a million at the time of the Glorious Revolution—it is impossible to be more precise. The pattern in Ireland was different. Far more than any other area, Ireland suffered from violence and warfare. Its population probably doubled between 1500 and 1641, rising from about one million to more than two million, but it fell sharply during the turmoil after the Irish Rebellion and Cromwellian conquest and did not reach two million again until the time of the Glorious Revolution. Even before the Interregnum, much of the island had been devastated; in the early seventeenth century Ulster was described as almost a wilderness and Munster as virtually uninhabited. But a remarkable recovery had taken place by the 1680s.

It is not easy to account for the general increase in population. Improvements in nutrition and housing probably contributed to a decrease in the death rate, especially among children, although infant mortality remained high. The birth rate may have increased as the average age at marriage declined, beginning in the late sixteenth century.

The larger population put severe pressure on the ability of the land to employ and feed the people and thus brought about increased urbanization. The population of towns rose faster than that of the several countries generally, perhaps twice as fast. London, the only true metropolis by international standards, grew from about 60,000 in 1520 to 200,000 in 1603 and had a population of about 575,000 in 1689, nearly a tenfold expansion. Both Elizabeth and the early Stuarts believed that it was growing too rapidly, without adequate supporting services, and they attempted to prohibit new building in the capital. But they were largely unsuccessful; the basic forces causing urbanization were beyond their control.

In 1603 the East Anglian port of Norwich was the second largest city in England, with a population of about fifteen thousand, followed by Bristol and York. It is unlikely that any other urban center in England held as many as ten thousand people. Edinburgh was about the same size as Norwich. Dublin had fallen from about 8,000 in 1540 to about 5,500 in 1600, but it was to grow very rapidly thereafter. By 1689 it was probably the second largest city in the British Isles; half the population of Ireland lived there and in the Pale. In 1600 about 6 percent of the English people lived in towns of ten thousand or more. The number in Scotland was about 3 percent. Both figures doubled during the seventeenth century.

Social Classes

English society remained stratified under the Tudors and Stuarts, as it had been in the Middle Ages. William Harrison, a notable antiquarian who wrote a *Description of England* in 1577, divided English society into four groups: "gentlemen of the greater sort" (these were actually noblemen—dukes, marquesses, earls, viscounts, and barons); "next unto them" the knights, esquires, and gentlemen; the "commonalty" of citizens and burgesses; and "a fourth sort which doe not rule." This last category included the great bulk of the population, identified by Harrison as "day laborers, poor husbandman, some retailers (which have no free land), and all artificers."

Although these groupings remained the same, the early modern period was a time of rapid social change. The topic has fascinated historians and generated a great deal of writing in recent years; unfortunately not all scholars agree in their analyses.

At one time it was common to speak of "the rise of the middle class" during these years. Certainly the number of artisans, yeomen, merchants, and professional people did increase, both in absolute numbers and as a proportion of the population. But this segment of society remained relatively small. A great divide still separated the rich and the poor. Not until the nineteenth century did a middle class, as we normally understand the term, come to dominate British society. Even today the English remain separated by the concept of class more than do residents in the United States and most other countries.

"The rise of the gentry" has also generated much discussion. The gentry, as we have seen, were landowners whose estates brought in sufficient revenue that they did not need to work in the fields themselves—Harrison's knights, esquires, and gentlemen. Most of them were reasonably well educated, and many were interested in politics, at both the county and national levels. As justices of the peace they were the chief local agents of the central government and were kept busy with work for which they were not paid. They made up most of the membership of the House of Commons: they were often elected by boroughs near their estates as well as by the county constituencies. Many of the gentry profited from the dissolution of the monasteries under Henry VIII, for the bulk of the monastic property passed from the monarch into their hands. Not all gentry families enjoyed economic gains under the Tudors and Stuarts. Some were tempted to live beyond their means, erecting lavish country houses in order to impress their neighbors; because of this "conspicuous consumption" they might fall into debt and have to sell lands, thus mortgaging their future. But others, including some who had connections at court, were able to purchase lands as they came on the market. Two basic conclusions seem warranted. First—as is always the case—those who were shrewd and lucky did gain increased wealth and status; those who were not did not. Then, more generally, it appears incontestable that the share of wealth and power held by the gentry as a group increased notably in the two centuries before 1689.

If the gentry probably rose, the nobility probably declined somewhat in influence and aggregate wealth. This shift can be traced in Parliament: although the House of Lords remained a significant force except during the Interregnum, the center of power moved to the Commons. In other areas too there was what has been called a "crisis of the aristocracy." It appears to have been a crisis of confidence as much as one of economics. Noblemen were no longer automatically appointed to the chief positions in government and in the military establishment, as they had been earlier, and some of them came to question just what their role in society was. In the end they succeeded in redefining it; the eighteenth century was to be the greatest age of aristocracy and deference to privilege that England ever knew. But there were strains along the way.

Society in Scotland was even more clearly divided into two groups—the rich and the poor or the landowners and the landless—than in England. There were fewer people of middling status, and the gulf between the two groups was greater. Members of the Highland clans were even poorer than those who lived in the Lowlands. They were more likely to be afflicted by illness, mortality, and chronic seasonal unemployment. The fact that the Scots came to eat more and more oatmeal, less and less meat, can be seen as a sign of deteriorating economic conditions for most people. The situation in Ireland (except for the new English landlords) resembled that in the Scottish Highlands and islands.

The poor "who doe not rule," mainly landless laborers or agricultural workers who had nothing beyond their cottage and small garden, continued to form the great mass of the population throughout the British Isles. They always lived close to the subsistence level, and in the sixteenth and seventeenth centuries they faced several new challenges.

Inflation

Many of the problems experienced by members of all social classes can be attributed to the rapid rise of consumer prices beginning about 1540.

Like the population, prices had generally been stable during the later Middle Ages. Inflation began to be felt in England toward the end of Henry

VIII's reign. At the time of his death the price level was twice what it had
been at his accession. Prices doubled again in the second half of the sixteenth
century, reaching exceptional peaks in the 1590s. They fell slightly in the
early seventeenth century, rose again during the Interregnum, and stabilized
during the Restoration at a level about five times as high as in 1485. In
Scotland severe inflation did not begin until the 1560s, but thereafter the
pattern was similar to that in England.

Economic historians have not found it easy to account for this inflationary
spiral. Some of the specific fluctuations are the result of specific events, like
the bad harvests of the 1590s and the social dislocations of the Civil War and
Interregnum. It may be that the influx of gold and silver from the New World
to Spain was of some importance, for England's economy was tied through
international trade to that of the Continental powers. Henry VIII's extravagance, especially in the military campaigns of his later years, is probably a
more important factor, for Henry chose to pay some of his bills by debasing
the coinage, adding a larger amount of base metals like lead or copper to the
fine silver of which the coinage had previously been made so that a larger
number of coins could be minted at little additional cost. Edward VI and
Mary continued this disastrous policy, although Mary's advisors were attempting to reverse it at the time of her death. Building on their policies, Elizabeth
ordered a return to coins of a high standard early in her reign. All the base
coins were called in and reminted during the great recoinage of 1560. This
slowed the rate of inflation but did not end its advance. Scottish coins were
debased until 1600, and base English coins remained legal tender in Ireland
until the 1650s.

One of Elizabeth's financial advisors was the famous economist Sir
Thomas Gresham. Realizing the damaging effects of debased coinage, he
formulated what came to be known as Gresham's law: "Bad money drives out
good." His point was that those who have fine coins will hoard them, and
only the most debased coinage will circulate. This then causes a rise in prices,
as tradesmen demand more of the debased coins in exchange for their commodities in order to receive a constant value in gold or silver. Gresham's
theory remained valid until the twentieth century, when the introduction of
paper money and a managed currency made the actual value of coins
irrelevant.

Important as these technical causes may have been, it is hard to escape
the conclusion that the inflation in prices was closely linked to the rise in
population. There were simply more people seeking a relatively stable supply
of goods, and their competition drove prices to higher levels.

Most laborers were not able to demand higher wages and so felt the pinch,
as did landowners who had signed leases renting out their properties for long

periods of time at fixed rates. Some clever merchants and professional men, able to take advantage of economic change, profited, and a few of them were able to buy their way into the ranks of the gentry.

The Enclosure Movement

A second important cause of social and economic dislocation was the enclosure movement. This was a revolution in agricultural practice in which the old open fields, where crops had been grown, were enclosed with hedges and fences so that they could be used as pasture, primarily for sheep. Landlords found the change advantageous. Almost every part of a sheep was profitable. Most clothing was made from wool, for cotton and synthetic fabrics were not yet available. Wool continued to form England's most important export, as it had throughout the later Middle Ages. Lamb or mutton could of course be eaten, and sheepskins produced the parchment on which important documents were written. All of these products could be sold in an economy that relied more and more on cash and credit rather than on payment in agricultural commodities. Almost all of the revenue from sheep farming could be retained by the landlord himself, for grazing required a much smaller labor force than did intensive agriculture. One shepherd and his dog might replace several dozen farm workers.

For many agricultural laborers the enclosure movement spelled disaster. Whole villages became deserted as their inhabitants lost their employment. Those who worked in the fields were generally uneducated and unskilled, and they had little hope of finding new jobs. Many drifted to the cities, hoping to obtain charitable relief if not employment.

Social critics tended to blame the enclosure movement for all the ills of Tudor society. The most famous such writer, Sir Thomas More, complained in his *Utopia* that "sheep do eat up men": there was ample land and food for the animals but not for humans. More blamed the covetousness of landlords, indeed the greed of an entire nation. Government leaders too were concerned. A series of statutes and proclamations, beginning in the reign of Henry VII, prohibited enclosures, but it was generally impossible to enforce these measures because they ran counter to the economic interests of the gentry and aristocracy.

Modern historians generally believe that the significance of the enclosure movement has been exaggerated. Not all the land in England was suitable for enclosure, for not all of it had ever been arable open fields. Not all the land that was suitable was actually enclosed, for grain crops were still needed and continued to be produced. Enclosure was mainly limited to the English

Midlands, and even there it occurred over a long period of time, thus soft-
ening its blows. In 1689 about half of England remained unenclosed and was
still farmed on the open-field system. Scotland, Ireland, and Wales were
hardly affected by enclosures at all. Still, it would be a mistake to disregard
the human misery that was caused by enclosing.

Beggars and Vagabonds

Some of those who were displaced by the enclosure movement became
beggars and vagabonds. Even if they were willing to work, they had
little hope of securing employment. Some, out of despair and perhaps
laziness, turned to begging and theft. Almost all left the localities where their
ancestors had lived. They became a large landless group with no firm roots
and no attachment to a "master," who might be responsible for their welfare.
As masterless men they were alienated from society and created social problems that had not been experienced before.

Medieval theology sometimes taught that beggars were holy and thus
idealized poverty. New attitudes were quite different. Although it may be a
mistake to exaggerate the influence of a Protestant "work ethic," it does
appear true that most people came to regard the destitute as indolent, possibly lawless rogues and robbers. At best they were a nuisance; at worst they
presented a serious threat to organized society.

Economic and Social Legislation

The problem of vagrancy forced the Tudors to formulate new policies
for the poor. Parliament and the central government finally acknowledged a responsibility to provide a basic level of poor relief. During
earlier centuries such charitable assistance as existed had been left in the
hands of the church. In the 1530s Henry VIII's great minister Thomas Cromwell proposed a very advanced welfare scheme in which the government itself
would serve as the employer of last resort, setting unemployed men to work
on public projects like dykes, dams, ports, and roads. But the proposal was
ahead of its time; the central government lacked the resources and the administrative machinery for an elaborate welfare system.

The Poor Law actually enacted by the Reformation Parliament made the
parish, not the central government, responsible for relief. (In this sense the
parish was regarded as a secular administrative unit rather than a religious

institution.) Overseers of the poor were to provide relief for those who were aged or infirm (the "impotent beggars") and were to set the able-bodied "sturdy beggars" to work. They were authorized to levy a tax, called the poor rate, but this was not compulsory, and the effectiveness of parish relief varied greatly. In some places, private philanthropy provided the needed revenues, and taxation was unnecessary. Relief was available only in the parish where each person had been born, and beggars could be whipped if they attempted to stay in other places.

During the middle years of the sixteenth century, cities like London and Norwich took the initiative and developed relatively effective mechanisms for dealing with poor persons and vagrants. These arrangements were codified in the famous Elizabethan Poor Law of 1601. The parish remained the administrative unit; the involvement of the central government was minimal.

Able-bodied, transient beggars had to obtain licenses to beg and were sometimes required to wear badges. Those who violated vagrancy laws could be arrested and imprisoned, or at least forced to move on. They might be whipped, or even (under the merciless act of 1572) flogged and subjected to having their ears bored through. The pillory and the ducking stool were common forms of humiliation and punishment. Some vagrants were sentenced to transportation and deported to Newfoundland or the West Indies. Jails or houses of correction, called "bridewells," were established in London and some other places. Originally they were supposed to provide useful work for the poor, but they tended to degenerate into miserable, filthy prisons or workhouses.

After 1660, policies began to change. Vagrants were more and more returned to their place of origin, where they received assistance. Sometimes, especially if they were feeble, they were given "outdoor relief" and allowed to remain in their own homes rather than being transferred to workhouses or other institutions. The arrangements remained in effect until the nineteenth century.

The expenditure on poor relief rose greatly under the Stuarts. It has been estimated that something like £35,000 was spent each year in the reign of James I, increasing to about £200,000 in 1650 and not less than £350,000 at the time of the Glorious Revolution. Vagrancy statutes and Poor Laws were thus a reasonably effective response to a serious social problem and a powerful force in controlling distress and disorder among the needy.

The English Poor Law was supposed to be operative in Wales, but it was much less effective there, and the level of unrelieved poverty remained high. The Scottish Poor Law of 1574 was based on English models. Parishes in Scotland became more effective in providing poor relief during the seventeenth century, especially after the passage of a new Act of Parliament in 1649. Church courts were now able to force landlords to accept responsibility for the poor on their estates. Still, poor relief was less generous than in England, and it was largely limited to the Lowlands; government policy was not easily enforced in the Highlands or off-shore islands. Virtually nothing was done to ameliorate poverty in Ireland, where economic problems were enmeshed with ethnic and religious differences.

Henry VIII's Reformation Parliament passed a variety of additional social measures, including an act that gave local governments the power to undertake urban renewal if buildings or neighborhoods grew derelict. Tudor sumptuary laws attempted to regulate the sorts of clothing that might be worn by men and women of different social ranks: luxury articles such as lace and gold embroidery were reserved for aristocrats. The Statute of Apprentices or Artificers enacted in 1563 gave legal force to the customary seven-year period of apprenticeship for craftsmen, thus demonstrating the continuing importance of the guilds. This act also tried to freeze wages and working conditions as a means of controlling demands by apprentices and journeymen during a period of inflationary pressures, but the restrictive policy did not meet with much success. Wales was included in these pieces of social legislation, but Ireland and Scotland were not.

Industrial Expansion

Small-scale manufacturing activities grew in importance during the sixteenth and seventeenth centuries, so much so that some historians refer to this period as the time of the First Industrial Revolution.

The cloth industry remained most important. The enclosure movement ensured an ample supply of wool, and overseas markets continued to expand until the middle of the sixteenth century. Thereafter the wool trade with Antwerp suffered from the revolt of the Netherlands; the Spanish laid embargoes on English goods when the English went to the aid of the rebels. A new market for lighter-weight woolens was developed in the Mediterranean and partially compensated for declining sales in the North. These "new draperies," as they were called, were woven with techniques brought to England by religious refugees from the Continent. Because they were less expensive than heavier fabrics, they were also purchased by the poor within England. Some of the old cloth towns, like Lincoln and Coventry, were unable to adapt to new conditions and decayed during the Tudor period.

Cottage industries became increasingly common as a way in which hard-pressed agricultural laborers could augment their income. Wool was often spun into yarn by women and then woven into cloth by men, working in their homes. Children might assist them. Other cottage industries included stocking knitting, nail making, leather work, and pottery.

The rural industries of ironworking and glassmaking flourished in Kent, where trees were cut and converted to charcoal to fuel the furnaces. Coal was mined in northern England, Wales, and Scotland. Canons and gunpowder were manufactured to meet military needs during the wars, and paper was produced as printing and bureaucracy required continually expanding supplies.

Exploration, Trade, and Colonization

The roots of English sea power, which eventually led Britannia to rule the waves, and of the trade and colonization that produced the British Empire can be traced to the Tudor period.

The desire for a sea route to China and the "Spice Islands" prompted the earliest voyages of discovery. Because no one knew of the existence of the New World, sailors and geographers believed that one could reach the Far East by sailing west from the British Isles. Some authorities think that English ships actually landed in North America before Columbus did. Certainly the Italian explorer John Cabot, sailing from Bristol under the English flag, reached Nova Scotia in 1497. His son Sebastian also sailed for England, as well as for Spain. More famous are the exploits of the Elizabethan sea dogs John Hawkins and Sir Francis Drake. Hawkins opened up English trade with the Caribbean; Drake circumnavigated the globe between 1577 and 1580.

In order to facilitate trade with territories newly discovered by sea, as well as areas that could be reached by traditional routes, a number of chartered trading companies were established during the second half of the sixteenth century. These are referred to as joint-stock companies because investors agreed to share in the total profit or loss of each enterprise rather than maintaining individual ownership of part of the cargo. The Muscovy Company was granted monopolistic rights on trade with Russia. Commerce with the eastern Mediterranean was allocated to the Levant Company, and the East India Company received trading rights in and around the Indian Ocean.

All of these companies brought luxury articles, including sugar, silks, and spices, to Britain, and they created export markets for timber, fish, and cattle as well as woolen cloth.

Some colonization was undertaken by chartered companies as well. The earliest attempts to send English settlers to Virginia (named for Elizabeth, the Virgin Queen) ended in failure when the Roanoke colony disappeared mysteriously in 1586, but Virginia was successfully colonized under royal charter in 1607. Jamestown was founded under James I, Charlestown under Charles II, and Williamsburg under William and Mary. Additional colonies along the southeast coast of North America were established in the later seventeenth century. Like Virginia they were founded primarily for commercial purposes.

Colonization in New England had different motives. Here the settlers banded together for religious reasons; they left England because they dissented from the official religion of the state church and were determined to live where they could follow the dictates of their own conscience. Plymouth was founded by the so-called Pilgrims, sailing in the Mayflower, in 1620. The Massachusetts Bay Colony, financed by a group of Puritan businessmen, was settled in 1628. More radical Puritan groups were established in Rhode Island and Connecticut during the 1630s (the personal rule of Charles I). British control of virtually the entire North American coast, as far south as Florida, was gained during the Restoration, when England received New York and New Jersey from the Netherlands in the treaty ending the Second Dutch War. The population of the American colonies was still small at the time of the Glorious Revolution, however, and (except for the export of tobacco from Virginia, beginning in the seventeenth century) they did not contribute significantly to the British economy.

Family Structure

A topic that has particularly interested historians in recent years is the study of family structure. Their investigations, which have largely been limited to England, reveal interesting patterns that are in some ways quite different from those we know today.

Two special characteristics of Elizabethan and Stuart society were the late age at which many people married and the large number of those who never married at all. The average age of marriage was about twenty-six for women, about twenty-eight for men. Between 10 percent and 20 percent of the population remained unmarried. About a quarter of the children born in

England died before reaching their tenth birthday. The late age of marriage, together with the frequency of early death, meant that few couples could expect their marriages to last more than a decade or two. It was uncommon to know one's grandchildren.

Marriage was usually postponed until a suitable home could be provided, either through inheritance of land or by attainment of fixed employment. Prosperous periods, with exceptionally good harvests, could produce a "boom" in marriages. A trend toward younger marriage seems to have begun in the late sixteenth century, perhaps reflecting improved economic conditions that made it easier to set up a household. But not everyone approved of the development. One of Lord Burghley's friends wrote him complaining that young persons were marrying with "no regard how to live nor where to dwell."

Among the nobility and gentry, marriages were usually arranged by parents, often as a means of advancing the wealth and social rank of the family. Such marriages might occur while the partners were still young, and they were often contracted for even earlier. The young men and women involved were at most given the opportunity to veto their parents' plans. Lower-class marriages were generally based on the wishes of the husband and wife themselves, although it was usual to seek the blessing of parents as a formality.

It was not uncommon for lower-class women to be pregnant at the time of their marriage. The rate of illegitimate birth was relatively low, generally about 3 percent. The social stigma associated with bastardy was partly based on the fear that parishes might have to provide funds for the upbringing of fatherless children; the practice of hounding unmarried pregnant women out of villages to prevent their babies from being born there is one of the cruelest customs of the age. Because the church, both before and after the Reformation, regarded marriage as a lifelong sacramental relationship, divorce was difficult. Church courts, influenced by Puritanism, were if anything more rigid about sexual matters after the Reformation than they had been earlier. But when one partner died before the other, remarriage was common.

Women in Early Modern Society

One writer has described early modern England as a veritable "paradise for women," since they enjoyed stronger legal rights and a more independent place in society there than in other parts of Europe. The comparative judgment may be sound, but many women who lived in Britain during the sixteenth and seventeenth centuries would have had a less optimistic outlook on their situation. Far from possessing equal rights, they were subordinate to men. A fortunate few lived lives of leisured boredom, but the vast majority experienced unremitting toil and hardship.

Because most women married, their principal role in society appeared to be that of wife and mother. Marital relationships were therefore of overriding importance to them.

Some historians detect a trend toward a warmer, more affectionate spousal relationship beginning in the later seventeenth century. Others argue that marriages (at least in England) were always companionable, that husbands and wives were usually the best of friends. It may help to note the difference between theory and practice. The subordination of women remained the theoretical ideal. St. Paul had told wives to obey their husbands, and contemporary writers often described the supreme authority of the husband as being both natural and divinely ordained. In reality many women demonstrated that they had minds of their own, either by arguing with their spouses (diaries provide numerous instances of such quarrels) or by simply assuming responsibilities and fulfilling them well.

There were also class differences. Aristocratic ladies were usually kept in the background while their husbands dealt with economic and political matters. Some of these wives complained of the loneliness, frustration, and lack of useful employment that accompanied their position. The isolation of life in a country house could be deadly: one countess said that the marble pillars of her great mansion formed for her only a "gay arbor of anguish." But some noblewomen found satisfaction in managing servants, bringing up children, entertaining guests, and perhaps producing needlework or making music on virginals and spinets.

The female servants in aristocratic establishments certainly outnumbered their mistresses, but—rather surprisingly—far more men than women were employed in the country houses. Even cooks and cleaners, during the period before the eighteenth century, were usually men. Lower-class women were more likely to work alongside their husbands in the fields or to do spinning or run alehouses. Unlike their social superiors, they were fully and usefully employed. The "mutuality" of marriage relationships, as described by some historians, does not seem to differ much from the "partnership" found in marriages of the later Middle Ages.

Queen Elizabeth's success in governing England demonstrated once and for all that women could be effective rulers. Ladies in waiting at her court were accorded ceremonial roles that had been filled by men when there was a king. It is notable, however, that all of Elizabeth's ministers and advisors were men. She did not introduce any basic change in the structure of government or court society but rather demonstrated that an exceptional woman like herself could survive in a masculine ethos.

Some aspects of the Reformation affected women in important ways. The dissolution of the monastic houses meant that nunneries could no longer serve as communities for single women. Earlier they had housed nearly two thousand nuns. Conversely, the end of clerical celibacy meant that priests were available as marriage partners. Some of the wives of Elizabethan bishops were very able women, even though they were socially and legally disadvantaged because of the queen's distaste for clerical marriage. We have little direct evidence about the role of those who married parish priests, but it seems certain that many of the clergy found their lives and ministries enriched by the companionship of wives and children.

A number of women held strong views about religion. One writer has attributed this to their frustration at having other intellectual matters closed to them. Some women died for their beliefs. The execution of Elizabeth Barton, the Maid of Kent, for criticizing Henry VIII's divorce has already been noted. Another Henrician martyr was Anne Askew, a gentlewoman from Lincolnshire, who was condemned as a heretic because she did not hold orthodox beliefs about the Eucharist. Only one woman was burned during the reign of Edward VI: Joan Bocher, an Anabaptist who rejected infant baptism, held views that were too advanced for even the Edwardian reformers.

Foxe's *Book of Martyrs* identified 275 persons executed under Bloody Mary, of whom fifty-five were female. Foxe referred to the "weak imbecility" of these "silly poor women," arguing that they should have been pitied because they were generally unlearned and drawn from the lower ranks of society. Ten were widows and twenty-eight were married women, of whom eight had seen their husbands executed before they were killed themselves. The rest were servants or children whose status was not defined. At least 125 of the 788 known Marian exiles (excluding servants and children) were women. Katherine Willoughby, the dowager duchess of Suffolk, was the most notable member of this group. Although Katherine's mother was a Spanish lady who had come to England in the train of Catherine of Aragon, Katherine herself had become a staunch Protestant, responsible for removing images from her chapel during the reign of Edward VI. She and her husband took a household of thirteen (including a jester) to the Continent with them. Only three women were executed for the sake of religion under Elizabeth. All of them have now been canonized by the Roman Catholic church.

The aristocracy of Elizabethan England could count some very learned women. Two of the most distinguished were sisters, Mildred and Anne Cooke. Both married leaders in Elizabeth's government: Mildred became the second wife of Sir William Cecil, Lord Burghley (he had earlier been married to Mary Cheke, the sister of Edward VI's tutor), and Anne was wed to

Nicholas Bacon, the keeper of the Great Seal. Both were active as translators. Anne's version of the *Apology for the Anglican Church,* written by Bishop John Jewel to justify the independence of the Church of England, was published and widely read. None of Mildred's translations was printed, but contemporaries were aware of her expertise in dealing with Greek writers, especially the church fathers. Mildred's daughter Anne Cecil married Edward de Vere, earl of Oxford, a poet and patron of the theater. (Those who think Shakespeare did not actually write Shakespeare's plays sometimes argue that the earl of Oxford was their author.) Sir Philip Sidney's sister Mary, who became the countess of Pembroke, was a fine poet in her own right and was active in publishing her brother's writings after his death at the Battle of Zutphen.

Perhaps the most learned woman of the mid-seventeenth century was Margaret Cavendish, duchess of Newcastle. Rather unconventionally, she was interested in science. She wrote on experimental philosophy and on microscopic observations and once dressed in men's clothes to attend a meeting of the Royal Society. A second remarkable woman was Mary Rich, countess of Warwick, who wrote a diary and autobiography covering the period from 1666 to her death in 1678. They are exceptional documents, describing in intimate detail Mary's religious conversion and her anguish at the death of her son and her husband. Another writer of the later Stuart period, Aphra Benn, left behind a great quantity of poems, novels, histories, and plays. Unique in various ways, she was perhaps the first woman to make a living as a professional writer, although her works were not of high quality and are largely forgotten today.

Such literate women formed a small minority of the population. Most women could not read and write; the universities, and to a great extent the secondary schools, were closed to them. Women's opportunities may have been increasing, but they were still very limited.

The Witchcraft Craze

In both England and Scotland, women were more likely than men to be prosecuted as witches. The craze had long roots in popular belief, and an act of the English Parliament in 1542 made witchcraft a legal felony. Causing death by witchcraft became a capital offense, punishable by execution, in 1563. James I, so enlightened in other areas, was a firm believer in witches, and witch-hunts became more common during his reign, reaching a peak in the 1640s.

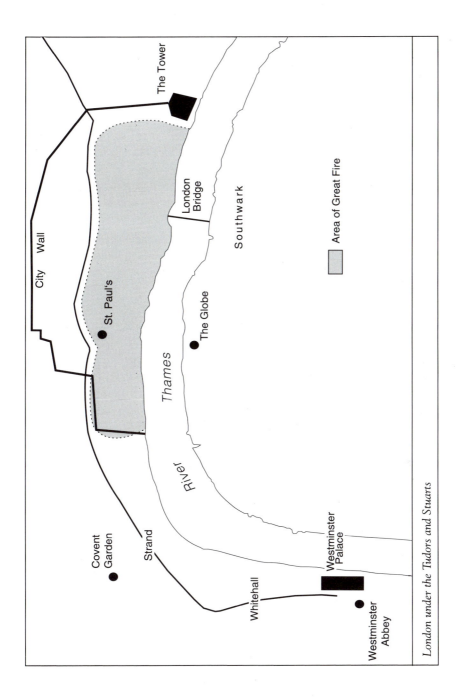

The Tower

City Wall

St. Paul's

London Bridge

Southwark

The Globe

Thames

River

Covent Garden

Strand

Whitehall

Westminster Palace

Westminster Abbey

Area of Great Fire

London under the Tudors and Stuarts

Persons accused of witchcraft were generally older women, often widows, who did not fit easily into society and were suspected by their neighbors of causing trouble, especially the illness of human beings or farm animals. A higher proportion of Scottish witches were men, and here persecutions continued longer than in England. As late as 1697 there was a severe episode centered in Paisley. The Highlands, islands, and Ireland seem to have been relatively immune to these troubles, perhaps because the survival of pagan ideas made supernatural activities more acceptable there. By the time of the Glorious Revolution, belief in witches was dying out. The last trial for witchcraft in England was held in 1712, and the last execution in Scotland took place in 1722.

Housing and Architecture

The Tudor period ushered in the Age of the English Country House. Just as cathedrals may be thought of as the buildings that typify the medieval period—the Age of Faith—and high-rise office towers serve as symbols of the twentieth century, so the great country houses erected by members of the aristocracy and gentry are the most important examples of English architecture in the sixteenth, seventeenth, and eighteenth centuries.

English aristocrats have always preferred to live in the country, surrounded by their own agricultural estates, rather than in cities. During the Middle Ages many of them had castles, moated, crenellated, and walled to prevent attack by enemies. The more settled conditions that prevailed after 1485 meant that defense was a less important consideration; dwellings could concentrate on luxury, convenience, elegance, and ostentatious display. A large country house came to be a social necessity, for squires and noblemen were expected to live grandly and to entertain their friends, tenants, and even members of the royal family who might come to visit during their summer progresses through the realm.

Although not a typical country house, Hampton Court Palace is the finest example of an early Tudor building. Originally erected by Cardinal Wolsey on the River Thames, a few miles upstream from Westminster, it was taken over by Henry VIII at the time of Wolsey's fall and continued to be a favorite royal residence until the middle of the eighteenth century. It is built of red brick with stone dressings and ornaments. The grandest rooms are the great

Hampton Court Palace, the finest example of an early Tudor building. The clock court was erected by Cardinal Wolsey about 1520. The round medallions display busts of Roman emperors. Reproduced by permission of the Royal Commission on the Historical Monuments of England.

hall and chapel; both have large Perpendicular style windows and elaborate wood roofs similar to those found in late Gothic churches. A series of internal courtyards makes it possible for every room to have light and air, and large numbers of brick chimneys serve the fireplaces that provided heat. Formal gardens ran down to the river. Henry VIII added an indoor tennis court. According to his contemporary biographer, Wolsey had as many as five hundred servants, and Hampton Court contains enormous kitchens capable of preparing food for vast throngs of courtiers, dignitaries, and retainers.

"Prodigy Houses"

The great private homes dating from Elizabeth's reign are sometimes called Elizabethan Prodigy Houses. Certainly they are prodigiously large and elegant, and they cost prodigious sums of money. Among the finest, many of which survive and are open to the public, are Longleat and Hardwick. Longleat, built in a beautiful valley near Bath, was erected by Sir John Thynne, who had been Protector Somerset's chief assistant during the reign of Edward VI, and is still owned by his descendants. Hardwick Hall in Derbyshire was the last of several houses put up by an amazing woman, Elizabeth, countess of Shrewsbury, better known simply as Bess of Hardwick. Bess outlived several husbands, each richer than the one before, and whenever she inherited an estate she built a new house. Hardwick is a particularly elegant piece of architecture, partly designed by Bess herself. Its enormous windows flood the principal rooms with light; tapestries and family portraits line the walls of its long gallery. As a widow, Bess had total control of activities at Hardwick. Earlier she had quarreled with her successive husbands, sometimes because she was trying to divert to her own use estates that would normally have been inherited by sons born to previous wives. Marital difficulties also dominated the marriage between Sir Francis Willoughby, the

Longleat, one of the great Elizabethan Prodigy Houses. The view from the southwest shows the symmetry of the façades.
Reproduced by permission of the Royal Commission on the Historical Monuments of England.

Hardwick Hall, a Prodigy House in Derbyshire, was built by Bess of Hardwick late in the reign of Elizabeth I.
Reproduced by permission of the Royal Commission on the Historical Monuments of England.

Hatfield House, near London, was built for Sir Robert Cecil, Lord Salisbury, about 1610.
Reproduced by permission of the Royal Commission on the Historical Monuments of England.

*The Banqueting House in Whitehall, designed by Inigo Jones for James I.
Reproduced by permission of the Royal Commission on the Historical Monuments
of England.*

*The Queen's House at Greenwich, designed by Inigo Jones. The buildings in the
background, fronting on the River Thames, were designed by Sir Christopher Wren
and John Webb for the Royal Naval Hospital.
Reproduced by permission of the Royal Commission on the Historical Monuments
of England.*

Sir Christopher Wren. This portrait is by Sir Godfrey Kneller. Wren is shown with a floor plan of St. Paul's Cathedral, his greatest achievement.
Reproduced by permission of the National Portrait Gallery.

builder of another Prodigy House, Wollaton Hall, and his wife Elizabeth. Neither of these strong-minded ladies was content to remain in the background as an ornamental hostess at a great mansion.

The accession of the Stuarts made little difference to building style, and Prodigy Houses continued to be erected under James I. The best of these, Hatfield House, was built only a few miles north of London by Sir Robert Cecil, the first earl of Salisbury, and remains in the hands of his descendants. A revolution in design did arrive in the 1620s, when Inigo Jones, one of England's greatest architects, introduced pure Classicism, based on the style of the ancient Greeks and Romans as interpreted by the architects of Renaissance Italy. Inigo's Banqueting House in Whitehall, part of the royal residence in London, and his Queen's House at Greenwich, built for the wife of James I, demonstrate the sophisticated taste of the early Stuarts. Had there been more money there would have been more construction. Inigo Jones produced plans for the complete replacement of the court buildings, but James and Charles were never able to implement them.

The work of Sir Christopher Wren dominated architecture in the late seventeenth century. Originally a professor of mathematics and astronomy at

St. Paul's Cathedral. Top: view from the southeast. Bottom left: west façade.
Bottom right: the interior from the west, looking toward the high altar.
Reproduced by permission of the Royal Commission on the Historical Monuments
of England.

Hampton Court Palace, the fountain court.
Wren built this for William and Mary.
Reproduced by permission of the Royal
Commission on the Historical Monuments of
England.

Oxford, Wren made his name when he was placed in charge of rebuilding the city of London following the Great Fire of 1666. His designs introduced the Baroque style to England. Although based on Classicism, his forms are freer and are calculated to produce maximum visual impact. St. Paul's Cathedral is his greatest achievement and one of the world's greatest buildings; its dome dominated the London skyline until modern office blocks began to offer competition. Wren also rebuilt dozens of churches and some other public buildings. Following the Great Fire, building codes forbade construction in flammable materials, so a city made of brick and stone replaced one dominated by wooden houses with thatched roofs. Wren did relatively little work on country houses, but he was called in by William and Mary to enlarge

Panorama of London, showing the skyline as it appeared following the great rebuilding. Note the prominence of Wren's great dome and church towers. This engraving is by the Buck Brothers, 1749.

Hampton Court, where the most elegant interiors date from the years immediately after the Glorious Revolution. He also built the Royal Hospital in Chelsea, a home for retired members of the army, and drew plans for the Royal Naval Hospital in Greenwich.

The Great Rebuilding

To accommodate urban merchants and agricultural workers, more ordinary houses were also constructed in large numbers, partly to meet the needs of an increasing population. Indeed, there was so much construction that the Tudor-Stuart period is occasionally referred to as the Age of the Great Rebuilding. The new houses were larger and more comfortable than earlier dwellings; they contained more private rooms, they were better lit by large glass windows, and they were warmed by fireplaces rather than by smoking open fires. Stone was often used for village houses in the Cotswolds and in other areas where it was plentiful. Elsewhere red brick was common, and "half-timbered" buildings of wood and plaster continued to be built in the Northwest.

Houses of the wealthy in Wales, Ireland, and Scotland were not greatly different from those in England but were generally smaller and less advanced in architectural style. The older sections of Edinburgh, including Holyrood House and the "royal mile," still convey a good idea of what a prosperous part of that city would have looked like under the Stuart monarchs. The difference in wealth between England and the Celtic countries was seen most clearly in the homes of the laboring poor. Even at the end of the seventeenth century, agricultural tenants and laborers in Wales, Scotland, and Ireland lived in small huts made of stone or wattle and daub, with no floors, windows, or fireplaces.

Intellectual History and Literature

The early Tudor period witnessed an intellectual revolution as well as dramatic changes in religion and society. The era is known as the English Renaissance, and the "new learning" is called humanism. All of these terms refer to the influence of the Italian Renaissance and to the attempt to recover the intellectual heritage of classical antiquity.

Beginning about 1500, a number of English scholars were eager to read the works of the great writers of ancient Greece and Rome, and they undertook the study of the ancient languages so that they could do so. Greek was virtually unknown in medieval England, and the first humanistic scholars had to travel to Italy in order to study it, but by the reign of Henry VIII it was taught regularly at both Oxford and Cambridge. Latin had always been used as the international language of learning and the church, but medieval Latin had grown corrupt, and the sixteenth century witnessed an important movement to purify it and to provide dictionaries of classical vocabulary. Classical writings came to form the basic fare of instruction, both in the grammar schools and in the universities. Some ancient works were translated into English, and others were popularized for general readers by such Englishmen as Sir Thomas Elyot and Roger Ascham. Classical ideas increasingly affected such fields as literature and medicine, and, as we have seen, architects also adopted ancient styles.

Sir Thomas More is the best known of the early Tudor humanists. His *Utopia*, first published in 1516, continues to challenge readers because of More's provocative discussion of perennially troubling topics like social organization, greed and private property, and the role of the intellectual in government. In form, *Utopia* is a dialogue, much like the dialogues of the ancient Greek philosophers, and some of its ideas can be traced to Plato's *Republic*. More was the leading intellectual in early sixteenth-century England, and his home attracted many learned men and artists, including the European scholar Erasmus and the German painter Hans Holbein, who later found employment at the court of Henry VIII. More himself saw to the

Sir Thomas More, the best-known early Tudor humanist. More is wearing the chancellor's "collar of S's." This portrait is by Hans Holbein the Younger.
Copyright The Frick Collection, New York City.

education of his daughter, Margaret Roper, who probably knew more Latin and Greek than any other woman of her day. (Margaret's own daughter, Mary Bassett, was also a scholar and translator.) In later life much of More's time was taken up by government service and by polemical religious writing, in which he attempted to refute the Protestant ideas of Martin Luther and his followers. His execution robbed England of its finest mind.

Elizabeth's reign was the golden age of English literature. Shakespeare's plays and sonnets, the poetry of Edmund Spenser and Sir Philip Sidney, and the dramas of Christopher Marlowe have never been surpassed. All of these were rooted in humanistic learning, though all display the individual genius of their authors. The early seventeenth century produced the mysteriously beautiful "metaphysical" poetry of John Donne and George Herbert, both devout Anglicans, as well as the towering epics of the Puritan writer John Milton. By contrast, the poetry and drama of the Restoration era seem flippant and superficial, but they still display literary sophistication and elegance of style.

A literary form peculiar to the early Stuart period was the masque. Essentially entertainments for the royal court, masques combined visual, dramatic, and musical elements. They were generally based on historical or mythological episodes, treated allegorically. Members of the royal family themselves often took part. The greatest masques were the product of collaboration between Ben Jonson (who wrote the words) and Inigo Jones (who produced fantastic scenery and costumes). Glamour and sophistication characterized these spectacles, though they were often the occasion for drunkenness and debauchery. They tended to demonstrate the increasing isolation of the court from real life and the concerns of ordinary people.

Printing and Literacy

The importance of printing in British intellectual development can hardly be exaggerated. The first English printer was William Caxton. He learned the craft on the Continent, probably in Germany, and set up a press in London in 1476. By the time of his death in 1491, he had published nearly eighty separate books, including humanistic works as well as his own translations of French romances. Other presses followed rapidly. Scholarly publishing at Oxford and Cambridge can be traced back to the reign of Henry VIII. The first printing press in Scotland was set up in 1507. More than twenty thousand works were printed by English publishers between 1476 and 1640.

The availability of relatively inexpensive printed books, instead of laboriously copied manuscripts, helped promote a great increase in literacy. It has been estimated that only 10 percent of the adult males in England could read and write in 1500, but more than a quarter of the men were literate by 1600 and about half the male populace by 1700. Fewer women learned to read and write. Perhaps only 2 percent were literate in 1500, about 10 percent in 1600, and 25 percent in 1700. Protestant culture, in which Bible reading assumed great importance, doubtless helped motivate the growth of a literate populace. Literacy rates in Scotland and Ireland, predictably, were lower than in England, especially for women.

The Scientific Revolution and the Royal Society

The humanists of the sixteenth century were content to draw their ideas about science and medicine from the ancients, particularly Aristotle and (in medicine) Galen. Thomas Linacre, the founder of the Royal College of Physicians, was responsible for translating some of the most important ancient medical writings from Greek into Latin, so that they could be studied by British doctors. Sir Thomas Elyot popularized classical theories in his English-language compendium *The Castle of Health.* The basis of humanistic medicine was the ancient belief that the world was formed of four elements (earth, air, fire, and water) and the human body of four "humors" (blood, phlegm, choler, and melancholy or black bile). The dominance of a given humor was thought to determine both health and personality. The humanists did not really understand anatomy or physics, and they did not perform experiments to advance knowledge.

Modern experimental science began in the seventeenth century with what is often called the Scientific Revolution. One of the earliest figures in this movement was William Harvey, who discovered the circulation of the blood in 1616. A graduate of Cambridge, he was physician to James I and served at St. Bartholomew's Hospital in London, where he was able to conduct anatomical studies. Sir Francis Bacon, too, advocated empirical study and propounded inductive theories of knowledge, mainly in his famous work the *Novum Organum.* He contracted the illness that led to his death while he was examining the effect of cold in preserving food.

The greatest scientist of this era was Sir Isaac Newton (1642–1727). An unrivaled genius at mathematics, he conceived his theory of universal gravitation, as well as the binomial theorem and differential calculus, while still a university student but during a period when he had fled Cambridge because of the plague. (The story that he was inspired by watching an apple fall dates from a later period and is probably untrue.) After the study of optics convinced him that refracting telescopes could never be perfected, he helped develop the reflecting telescope. Next he studied prisms and color. His later researches primarily involved the physics of motion. A professor at Cambridge University, he represented the university in Parliament at the time of the Glorious Revolution. His most important treatise, called *Principia,* was first published in 1687. A statue of Newton dominates the entrance to the chapel of Trinity College, Cambridge, and guides have been known to quip that this reflects the college's greater interest in rational science than in religion.

The progress of the Scientific Revolution was marked by the founding of the Royal Society. This grew out of meetings of philosophers and scientists held in London as early as 1645 and more particularly out of James Harington's "Rota" club, which was active late in the Interregnum. With the restoration of the monarchy in 1660, a group of twelve men, including Christopher Wren and Robert Boyle, the father of modern chemistry, began to meet regularly. Their organization received the support of Charles II and was incorporated as the Royal Society in 1662. The Royal Society was dedicated to advancing experimental science and to promoting public acceptance for it. A number of men prominent in public life, as well as practicing scientists, became fellows. Very vigorous and influential in its early years, the Royal Society remained strong in the 1680s, when Samuel Pepys served as president. Thereafter it declined, but it was reinvigorated by Newton, who became president in 1703. Under Newton the Royal Society sponsored experimental research and served as a vehicle for contact with scientists from the Continent, a number of whom were brought to England for scholarly visits. The distinction of being designated a Fellow of the Royal Society is still the most coveted honor for British scientists.

Political Theory

The later Stuart period was also an exceptionally important period in the development of English political thought. Experimentation with different forms of government during the Interregnum made it clear that the old monarchy was not fixed and immutable, and dissatisfaction with each successive model led some writers to consider what an ideal constitution might be. One of the most interesting works of the Interregnum is James Harrington's *Oceana,* published in 1656. It has fascinated some modern historians because Harrington advances the theory that any government, to be stable, must reflect the economic basis of society: power must be based on wealth. The English Civil War, in Harrington's view, was caused by the fact that the king and aristocracy had declined in wealth but had not relinquished political control, and groups like the gentry and merchants had not acquired the power that their increasing share of the national income justified. In this respect Harrington's philosophy foreshadows the economic determinism of Karl Marx.

The deductive procedures of the Scientific Revolution were also influential in the area of political theory. Thomas Hobbes, one of the most brilliant men of the seventeenth century, attempted to analyze both the psychology of individual men and women and the corporate society of the state by using the same logical procedures he had earlier applied to mathematics and optics. He was one of the earliest truly secular political thinkers—earlier writers, like James I, had based their arguments on religion and the necessity for humans to serve God. The treatises of John Locke, which as we have seen were of enormous influence following the Glorious Revolution, disagree with Hobbes's formulations in detail but demonstrate the same urge to base government on principles that are secular, logical, and universal in application.

"Young Man Among the Roses," a miniature by Nicholas Hilliard. The figure is sometimes thought to be the earl of Essex, who was executed in 1601.
Reproduced by permission of the Victoria and Albert Museum.

The Arts

The arts of painting and music flourished under the Tudors and Stuarts. Most of the finest painters held appointments at court, and, curiously, most of them were foreigners, who brought to England the most advanced styles of Italy and northern Europe. Our picture of Henry VIII's court derives largely from the work of Hans Holbein, a German artist who was associated with the English humanists and left wonderfully penetrating portraits of More, Erasmus, Warham, and Cromwell, as well as the

"Charles I on Horseback" by Sir Anthony Van Dyke. This is one of the famous paintings that established a mystique of royalty during the early Stuart period. Reproduced by permission of the National Gallery, London.

king and several of his wives. During Elizabeth's reign, miniature portraits were very popular. Many were painted with exceptional skill by Nicholas Hilliard, an Englishman who had begun his career as a goldsmith. Many country houses had paintings of the queen as well as portraits of family members, but most of the Elizabethan artists remain anonymous, and their works are less distinguished than Holbein's. The great Dutch painter Anthony Van Dyke was employed by Charles I. He had a large studio, grew rich, and had his social status recognized by a knighthood. Another Dutchman, Sir Peter Lely, produced portraits of the women at the court of Charles II. Sir Godfrey Kneller, a German, was active at the time of the Glorious Revolution. It is interesting to note that there was virtually no demand for paintings other than portraits. Religious pictures were not popular after the Reformation, and still lifes or landscapes did not come into favor until the eighteenth century.

Much of the great music of the era was written for the church. The greatest of the Tudor composers were Thomas Tallis and William Byrd. Tallis had been a monk before the Reformation, but he accepted the break with Rome and produced settings of the English services from the Book of Common Prayer. For a time he and Byrd jointly directed the music at the Chapel Royal, and they also shared a monopoly on the printing of music in England. Although Byrd composed large numbers of anthems and canticles for the Anglican church, he himself remained a Roman Catholic, and his most sublime works—his masses—could not legally have been given public performances during his lifetime. The finest composer of the early seventeenth century was Orlando Gibbons, and the greatest musician of the Restoration era was Henry Purcell, who produced quantities of music for the stage as well as for the church before his early death in 1695. Madrigals, airs, secular songs, and instrumental dance music, written by such composers as John Morley and John Dowland, were popular, as were carols (not just for Christmas).

Education

The sixteenth century witnessed major changes in the English educational system. Not only was a humanistic curriculum introduced but also the entire structure of elementary and secondary education was renewed and secularized.

Prior to the Reformation most organized education remained in the hands of the church. In many villages and towns chantry priests served as schoolmasters. They drew their livelihood from endowments providing masses and prayers for the dead, but after these services were completed they spent their time teaching groups of boys. With the dissolution of the chantries in 1547, these schools ceased to exist. In some cases Edward VI's government allowed local authorities to retain endowments so that schools could continue. It was more common, however, for new grammar schools to be founded and endowed with fresh gifts from merchants and neighboring gentlemen. The new schools were no longer operated under the aegis of the church, and the teachers no longer had to be clergymen. In many places, including Stratford-on-Avon, a "King Edward VI Grammar School" still exists. The name is sometimes taken to imply that the young king founded or funded the school, but in fact the initiative was local and the title merely indicates the date of foundation. It used to be common for historians to deplore the way in which governmental greed wrecked the educational system, but newer interpretations argue that the chantry schools were of poor quality, whereas the secular institutions that took their place provided far better instruction, along the lines recommended by humanists like More and Ascham.

Oxford and Cambridge remained the only universities in England. Both experienced declining enrollments and other difficulties in the middle of the sixteenth century. In the Middle Ages their role had been primarily the training of priests for the church, but with the unsettled state of religion, especially under Edward VI and Mary, fewer young men felt drawn into the ministry. Eventually the universities too accommodated themselves to a more secular society. Increasingly large numbers of men destined for careers in government or as country gentlemen sought higher education. A number of new colleges at both universities were founded during the Tudor period. Henry VII's mother, Lady Margaret Beaufort, endowed both St. John's and Christ's College, Cambridge. Henry VIII consolidated several existing halls into Trinity College, the largest of the colleges at Cambridge. Cardinal Wolsey set up the largest college at Oxford, originally known as Cardinal's College but renamed Christ Church after his fall. At Cambridge several new foundations were established specifically for the training of Puritan ministers. One of these, Emmanuel College, was erected by Sir Walter Mildmay, Queen Elizabeth's chancellor of the Exchequer. Oliver Cromwell attended another, Sidney Sussex College.

Tudor-Stuart buildings abound at both Oxford and Cambridge. These include living accommodation for students and teachers (faculty members were not allowed to marry until the nineteenth century, and most lived in their colleges) as well as dining halls, libraries, and chapels. The marvelous chapel of King's College, Cambridge, was completed by Henry VIII, whose gifts paid for the fan vault, Flemish glass windows, and carved wood screen and stalls. Henry VIII is also largely responsible for the Great Court of Trinity College, Cambridge. Sir Christopher Wren built a new library for Trinity and chapels for Pembroke and Emmanuel Colleges at Cambridge as well as the Sheldonian Theatre at Oxford, used for the granting of degrees and other ceremonial occasions.

The Inns of Court, where lawyers practiced their profession and law was taught to aspiring students, continued to serve London as something like a third university. The Inns actually had more students than Oxford and Cambridge combined, and those who attended were likely to be from richer families. Under the Tudors and Stuarts they were important as social centers

The Great Court of Trinity College, Cambridge.
Reproduced by permission of the Royal Commission on the Historical Monuments
of England.

and patrons of drama. Several Elizabethan plays received their initial performances in the halls of the Inns.

The new learning and the need to educate Protestant ministers affected
the Scottish universities as well as the English ones. The sons of gentry (the
Scottish "lairds") and merchants began to attend the universities at St.
Andrew's, Glasgow, and Aberdeen. The desire for higher education was also
felt at Edinburgh, where a college was planned in 1558 and opened in 1583.
Trinity College, Dublin, the only institution of higher learning in Ireland,
was also established during Elizabeth's reign and was endowed with some
properties that had earlier belonged to Irish monasteries. It taught humanism
and Protestantism and served mainly the Anglo-Irish. The Scottish and Irish
universities were considerably smaller than their English counterparts. Wales
had no university, but a number of young men from Wales studied at Oxford,
and some Welsh scholars taught there.

In almost every area of human activity—agriculture and industry, trade,
social change, building and architecture, literature and the arts, science,

Dining hall of the Middle Temple, one of the Inns of
Court.
Reproduced by permission of the Royal Commission
on the Historical Monuments of England.

political theory, and the advancement of learning—the peoples of the British
Isles had made giant strides under the rule of the Tudor and Stuart dynasties.
Such periods of rapid change are often times of special stress in society. In
part the Civil War and the Glorious Revolution were responses to these
challenges. Once the Revolution was digested, society throughout the British
Isles was ready to enter a period of greater self-confidence and stability.

Suggested Reading

Beier, A. L., *Masterless Men: The Vagrancy Problem in England, 1560–1640* (London: Methuen, 1985).

Clark, Peter, and Paul Slack, *English Towns in Transition, 1500–1700* (Oxford: Oxford University Press, 1976).

Clay, Christopher, *Economic Expansion and Social Change* (New York: Cambridge University Press, 1984).

Cressy, David, *Literacy and the Social Order: Reading and Writing in Tudor and Stuart England* (Cambridge: Cambridge University Press, 1980).

Hogrefe, Pearl, *Women of Action in Tudor England* (Ames: Iowa State University Press, 1977).

Hoskins, W. G., *The Age of Plunder: The England of Henry VIII, 1500–1547* (London: Longman, 1976).

Houlbrooke, Ralph A., *The English Family, 1450–1700* (London: Longman, 1984).

Houston, R. A., and I. D. Whyte, eds., *Scottish Society 1500–1800* (Cambridge: Cambridge University Press, 1989).

Macfarlane, Alan, *Marriage and Love in England: Modes of Reproduction, 1300–1840* (Oxford: Basil Blackwell, 1986).

Mendelson, Sara Heller, *The Mental World of Stuart Women* (Amherst: University of Massachusetts Press, 1987).

Palliser, D. M., *The Age of Elizabeth: England Under the Later Tudors, 1547–1603* (London: Longman, 1983).

Pound, John, *Poverty and Vagrancy in Tudor England*, 2nd ed. (London: Longman, 1986).

Prior, Mary, ed., *Women in English Society, 1500–1800* (London: Methuen, 1985).

Stone, Lawrence, *The Crisis of the Aristocracy, 1558–1641* (Oxford: Clarendon Press, 1965).

Stone, Lawrence, *The Family, Sex and Marriage in England, 1500–1800* (London: Weidenfeld & Nicolson, 1977).

Thomas, Keith, *Religion and the Decline of Magic* (London: Weidenfeld & Nicolson, 1971).

Underdown, David, *Revel, Riot and Rebellion: Popular Politics and Culture in England, 1603–1660* (Oxford: Oxford University Press, 1985).

Warnicke, Retha M., *Women of the English Renaissance and Reformation* (Westport, Conn.: Greenwood Press, 1983).

Wrightson, Keith, *English Society, 1580–1680* (London: Hutchinson, 1982).

Wrigley, E. A., and R. S. Schofield, *The Population History of England, 1541–1871* (Cambridge, Mass.: Harvard University Press, 1981).

Youings, Joyce, *Sixteenth-Century England* (Harmondsworth, Middlesex: Penguin Books, 1984).

The British Isles in 1688

Although several dates mark major turning points in the history of the British Isles, 1688 is in some ways the most significant. It is useful to take stock of the situation at the end of the Glorious Revolution.

The Revolution capped a series of important developments in government and politics. By 1688, political parties had established themselves. The two-party system, eventually to be exported to the United States and other English-speaking countries, was in place. Party leaders, if not yet true prime ministers, had achieved positions of power and influence. The nature of the monarchy had changed, partly because Locke's political theory supplanted the notion of divine right and partly because control of the government passed more and more from the sovereign into the hands of Parliament and politicians. A number of ambiguous and divisive issues were finally settled by the Bill of Rights, leaving England free to concentrate its energy on new matters.

By 1688 Wales had been integrated into the English system of government for more than a century, while retaining its own ethnic and cultural identity. Ireland had been affected profoundly by English colonization. Its continuing problems, if not the answers to them, were in place. Scotland and England had shared a single king for nearly a century, and they were soon to be brought into a still closer relationship by the Act of Union passed in 1707. Yet society in Ireland and Scotland retained unique characteristics and would continue to do so.

In the final years of the seventeenth century, British society stabilized after undergoing a series of upheavals. Most of the sixteenth century had been devoted to implementing the Reformation and reacting to the policies of the state church. The Civil War had resulted in part from the bitter religious divisions that resulted. Although these remained, they were to be less important after 1688, for the Toleration Act at last gave Protestants who dissented from the Church of England the right of worshiping as they wished.

Especially after the Restoration in 1660, society was more secular in orientation than it had been earlier. Education and poor relief were among the matters handled primarily by civil authorities rather than by the church. The basic outlook of humanism, with its admiration for the secular cultures of Greece and Rome, permeated the upper levels of British society. The Scientific Revolution made possible great advances in physics, chemistry, mathematics, and anatomy. Class patterns settled into place after 1688 and were to survive virtually unchanged for another century. Economic conditions also stabilized. Colonies were firmly planted in the New World. Many of the finest buildings of England and Scotland, country houses and castles as well as churches and cathedrals, were already in existence. Literature, music, and the arts flourished.

The achievements of those who lived on two small islands with limited resources were extraordinary. Throughout the Middle Ages, England had generally been regarded as a realm of secondary importance among the nations of Europe, and Scotland, Ireland, and Wales were of even less prominence. Wealth, prestige, and sophistication had increased under the Tudors and Stuarts, and a sort of integration, if not a unified system of government, had been achieved as well. By the end of the Glorious Revolution the British peoples were poised to assume their role as one of the great powers of the modern world.

APPENDIX

Genealogical Tables

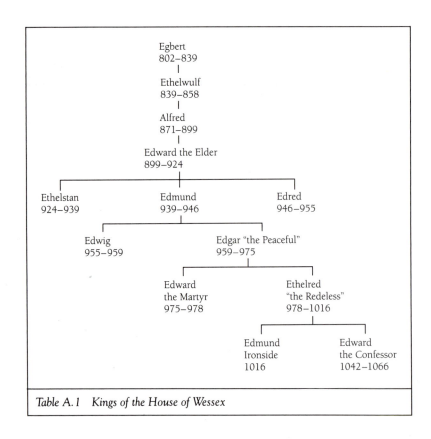

Egbert
802–839
|
Ethelwulf
839–858
|
Alfred
871–899
|
Edward the Elder
899–924

Ethelstan
924–939

Edmund
939–946

Edred
946–955

Edwig
955–959

Edgar "the Peaceful"
959–975

Edward
the Martyr
975–978

Ethelred
"the Redeless"
978–1016

Edmund
Ironside
1016

Edward
the Confessor
1042–1066

Table A.1   *Kings of the House of Wessex*

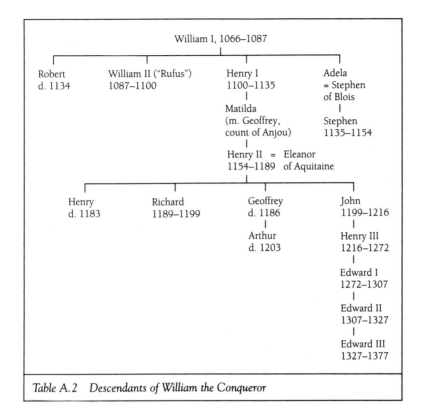

Table A.2   Descendants of William the Conqueror

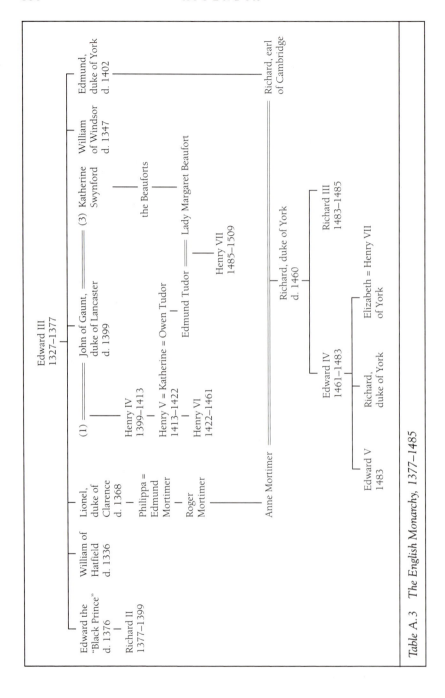

Table A.3   The English Monarchy, 1377–1485

```
            (1)  =  Robert I      = (2)
                 |  1306–1329  |

            Marjorie      David II
                 |        1329–1371
            Robert II
            1371–1390
                 |
            Robert III
            1390–1406
                 |
            James I
            1406–1437
                 |
            James II
            1437–1460
                 |
            James III
            1460–1488
                 |
            James IV = Margaret Tudor
            1488–1513
                 |
            James V      = Mary of Guise
            1513–1542  |  d. 1560

Francis II (1) = Mary, queen of Scots  = (2) Lord Darnley
of France        1542–1567          |  (3) Earl of Bothwell
                                    |

                         James VI, 1567–1625
                         (James I of England, 1603–1625)
```

Table A.4   The Scottish Monarchy, 1306–1625

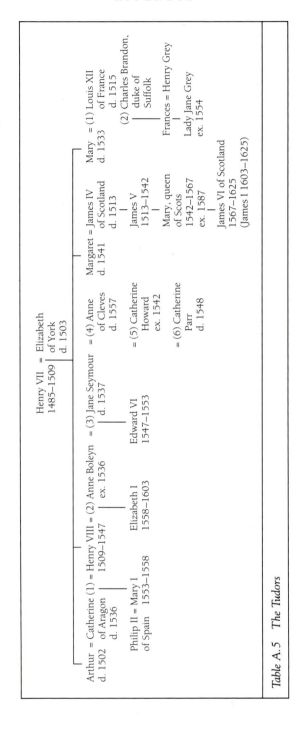

Table A.5　The Tudors

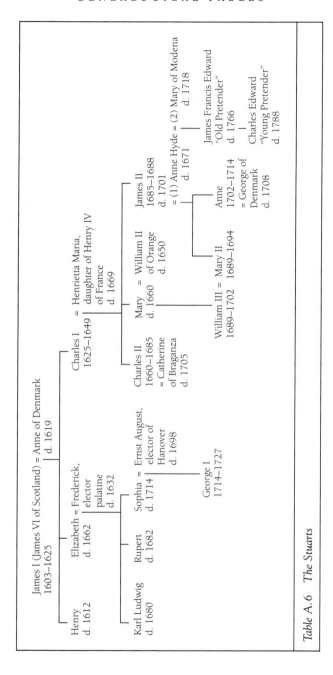

Table A.6   The Stuarts

Index